Counterrealism and Indo-Anglian Fiction

Counterrealism and Indo-Anglian Fiction

Chelva Kanaganayakam

Wilfrid Laurier University Press
WLU

This book has been published with the help of a grant from the Humanities and Social Sciences Federation of Canada, using funds provided by the Social Sciences and Humanities Research Council of Canada. We acknowledge the financial support of the Government of Canada through the Book Publishing Industry Development Program for our publishing activities.

Library and Archives Canada Cataloguing in Publication

Kanaganayakam, C. (Chelvanayakam), 1952–
    Counterrealism and Indo-Anglian fiction

Includes bibliographical references and index.
ISBN 978-1-55458-062-0

1. Indic fiction (English)–History and criticism. 2. English fiction–20th century–History and criticism. I. Title

PR9480.1.K35 2002   823   C2002-900016-5

© 2002 Wilfrid Laurier University Press
Waterloo, Ontario   N2L 3C5
www.wlupress.wlu.ca

Cover design by Leslie Macredie.

Every reasonable effort has been made to acquire permission for copyright material used in this text, and to acknowledge all such indebtedness accurately. Any errors or omissions called to the publisher's attention will be corrected in future printings.

This book is printed on Ancient Forest Friendly paper
(100% post-consumer recycled).

Printed in Canada

For Professor K. Sivathamby, an extraordinary scholar, whose
vision showed me how to inhabit many worlds.

Contents

Acknowledgments

A former version of the first chapter appeared in the *University of Toronto Quarterly* (2000), and a short essay on "Midnight's Grandchildren" was published in *Sharing a Commonwealth* (2001). The staff at Wilfrid Laurier Press have been very helpful, supportive, and knowledgeable. My thanks to Brian Henderson, Elin Edwards, Jacqueline Larson, and Leslie Macredie. I am also grateful to the anonymous readers who offered valuable suggestions. My sincere thanks to S.S. Sharma and Linda Hutcheon for reading the manuscript at very short notice, and for their insightful comments.

CHAPTER 1

Counterrealism as Alternative Literary History

This book is at least partially a belated response to a significant, polemical, and neglected monograph entitled *Indian Writing in English: Is There Any Worth in It?* written by Subha Rao and published in 1976. The monograph is a re-working and elaboration of a paper presented, appropriately, at the University of Mysore, then the centre of Indo-Anglian and postcolonial studies in India. Had this trenchant critique of Indo-Anglian writing been written from the perspective of what has been dubbed the "colonial cringe," namely, an uncritical defence of a canonical, largely British, tradition, a response would be an unprofitable exercise since it would seek to resolve on a literary plane what is clearly an expression of cultural bias. Rao's work, admittedly, does include references to British literature—in fact, *Middlemarch* is used to judge the only Indo-Anglian text the author refers to, namely, Balachandra Rajan's *The Dark Dancer*. But the core of the argument is derived from socio-cultural premises that have a specific and local significance for India, and by extension for countries and regions where alternative linguistic traditions have been revived and foregrounded as an auxiliary to decolonization and nationalism. The failure of Indian writing in English, according to this view, is a consequence of factors more complex than that of a duality based on authenticity versus imitation.

Subha Rao is not merely dismissive of certain authors or texts: rather, he questions the entire corpus of Indo-Anglian writing for its relevance to an Indian audience, importance in relation to social realities, and absence of formal sophistication. He identifies the project of writing in the English language as the cultural voice of a particular class, its power in postcolonial India, and its capitulation to the hegemonic effects of colonialism in the country. Says Rao: "Our writing in English is 'the language' of the urban rich and the educated classes, in association with a kind of life I call the unindian life, to which all of us aspire by the nature of our present ambitions and hopes" (12). English writing, from this perspective, reflects the voice of the colonizer, the vision of Prospero masquerading as the story of Caliban.

The problematic status of the English language in relation to the vernacular languages, its valorization by the postcolonial elite, the associations that underlie the use of the language, the audience for whom the texts are intended, the distance that the works demonstrate from a vital indigenous culture, the temptation for authors to exoticize and present the local in a flattering or self-deprecating manner—all these form part of the critique: "When the mind fails in the language in which it is counted a great value to be successful, we will have false standards of success—and also false standards of mental development—because it is not our language, in which we may never be successful" (Rao 14).

The hegemonic status of the language, its historical role in the process of colonization, and its declining popularity as a language of everyday speech are thus crucial factors in his evaluation.[1] Rao argues that unlike the ambiguity associated with English, indigenous languages, in addition to having a rich and continuous tradition, have evolved with the growth of nationalism; their role has been more significant than that of English. Both at national and regional levels, the socio-cultural forces unleashed concurrently with decolonization found in Indian fiction and poetry a powerful medium of dissemination. Literature altered, questioned, reflected, and was in turn nourished by centrifugal tendencies in the national imaginary.

Rao's argument is cogent, and it is certainly possible to compile a comprehensive roster of texts that would substantiate his claim. However, his thesis finally rests on a simple binary system: namely, the preservation and celebration of an indigenous, authentic culture in a vernacular language versus mimicry, complicity, and subservience to an alien culture through a continued use of English. In this essentialist scheme, the mindset that goes with English writing "stands opposed to the value of our languages, of our religion, our metaphysics, our great rituals, our music, and our folk-spirit. In short, our life" (Rao 13). Rao's argument is not entirely new, but its force lies in the way it combines the literary and aesthetic with the social and cultural to advance a critique that, if it's valid, would have far-reaching implications for the literary scene.

While Rao's stance is particularly uncompromising, the issues he raises have been addressed, in varying degrees, by comparatists, "nativist" critics, and even authors of literary histories in English. For those who have advocated the notion of a pan-Indian poetics and sought its expression in vernacular languages, the practice has often been one of excluding English writing altogether or acknowledging it in perfunctory fashion. Thus works such as *The Novel in India: Its Birth and Development* or *Four Decades of Indian Literature: A Critical Evaluation* implicitly deny legitimacy to English writing. The former confines itself to fiction written in Marathi, Urdu, Hindi, and Tamil, while the latter makes the clear assertion that "[English], as wielded by Indians, has made a thin contribution to the mainstream of Indian creative writing" (19). Even a recent work such as *Vibhava: Modernism in Indian Writing*, which adopts a comparative and teleological approach to offer a theoretical matrix for evaluating modern writing, chooses to focus on Bengali, Hindi, Kannada, and Malayalam, paying no attention to English writing. The omission is deliberate, and suggests both resistance and subversion.

One of the obvious ironies of such works is their acknowledgment that modern Indian writing is, for the most part, a consequence of British colonialism, the interest of orientalists and Indologists in rediscovering Indian, mainly Sanskrit, classics, and the colonial policy of implementing a system of English education. What the editors of *Vibhava* refer to as an act of patricide (namely, the process by which a literature freed itself from the conventions of the past to experiment with new forms), was a direct result of the influx of Western literature through schools, journals, newspapers, and the like. The possibility of comparing fiction in Tamil with its counterpart in Bengali, for example, is the result of both the introduction of new (read Western) forms of expression and their dominant mode of realism. While the West is thus acknowledged without any reservation as a constitutive factor in the genesis of modern Indian writing, writing in English is seen as both irrelevant and impoverished.

An extension of such an engagement with poetics would be the work of "nativist" critics who are less concerned with Western systems than with the diverse traditions that predated the arrival of the British. For example, Indra Nath Choudhuri's *Comparative Indian Literature: Some Perspectives* establishes a framework for comparative studies on the basis of Sanskrit poetics, the Bhakti movement, and the conventions that governed vernacular languages. In this scheme, the influence of the West is given very little attention. Perhaps the best known exponent of the nativist aesthetic is G.N. Devy whose *After Amnesia: Tradition and Change in Indian Literary Criticism* is a staunch defence of the "bhasa" tradition which, in one form or another, continues to inform modern writing. Against the classical Sanskrit tradition, *bhasa* denotes all modern Indian languages that have, over a period of several centuries, evolved their own poetics. In short, Devy's argument is based on the premise that a literary historiography that locates its origins in the work of orientalists would claim that "classical India [is] 'glorious' and British India [is] 'progressive', but the intervening centuries [are], culturally, a period of continuous vulgarization" (5). His project, then, is to recuperate the validity of this middle period by redis-covering local or "bhasa" traditions.

Working with a broad pan-Indian perspective, Meenakshi Mukherjee, in her *Realism and Reality* attempts a more inclusive approach that goes beyond asserting that the Indian novel was a direct descendent of British fiction. Instead of evaluating the strengths of vernacular writing against the achievement of Indo-Anglian literature, she looks at the diverse strands, particularly indigenous ones, that shaped the Indian novel. "Without attempt-ing to arrive at any definition of the Indian novel" says Mukherjee, "it will be our purpose to examine the synthesis of a borrowed lit-erary form and indigenous aesthetic–as well as cultural expecta-tions–in order to determine the extent to which the form has undergone mutation in the process" (18).

Equally important in this respect is the work of Makarand Paranjape who refuses to endorse the uncritical adulation of Indo-Anglian writing, particularly in the West. His recent work, *Towards a Poetics of the Indian English Novel,* is a sustained critique, from a very different perspective, of the fundamental assumptions that account for the valorization of this body of writing and its failure to live up to the expectations it has generated. Unlike Subha Rao, Paranjape moves from one critical position to another to test the validity of his hypothesis. Regardless of their theoretical stance, Indo-Anglian writers, in his appraisal, achieve very little and bask in undeserved praise. For example, in an article that appeared in 1997, Paranjape demonstrates the limitations of Anita Desai's novel *Journey to Ithaca* and then makes a logical transition to the whole corpus of Indian writing. He concludes by saying: "I shudder when I have to read these texts. Such interminable narcissism! Such stylish hypertrophy! Such garrulous gimmicry! Yet not a single great book" (410).

The proliferation of such theoretical works in the last three decades or so–all of which establish a range of positions–has to be seen in the context of cultural nationalism, the resurgence of national literatures, and the more general process of decoloniza-tion. The role of vernacular writing in relation to nationalist assertions can hardly be underestimated, and even a study like *The Empire Writes Back*, whose theoretical premise is one of totalization, of providing a rationale for oneness in postcolonial literature, wonders about the future of Indian writing in English. Despite the distinctiveness of this body of literature–suggested by what the authors call "english" writing–its survival remains uncertain:

> Since writing in english in India is now more than a century and a half old it is to be hoped that even if the future decrees that it will be replaced entirely by writing in Indian vernacular languages (and this is far from certain, or even likely) that the work already writtenwill justify the continued study and criticism of this corpus. (Ashcroft et al., 123)

If the anticipated process is one of gradual attrition, that would give greater force to V.S. Naipaul's comment about the "aimlessness of Indian writing." Speaking of R.K. Narayan in particular and Indian writing in general, Naipaul mentions the "profound doubt about the purpose and value of fiction" that denies the Indian writer any depth and causes the works to become "documents of Indian confusion" (216). That Naipaul considers only Ruth Prawer Jhabvala free of this taint blunts the force of his argument and raises questions about his norms and prejudices, but his overall critique of the dichotomy between form and attitude merits attention. Does the stigma of pretentiousness and fear of writing without a clear sense of audience explain why, while several Indo-Anglian writers have felt the need, at some stage, to defend their use of English, no one writing in, say, Bengali, Hindi, or Tamil has felt the need to justify their use of a particular language? Would this also account for, say, Anita Desai's (somewhat defensive) comments about the language having chosen her or Kamala Das's angry assertion of her commitment to the English language in her well-known poem entitled "An Introduction"? Would it also explain Raja Rao's foreword to the novel *Kanthapura* in which he speaks of the need to refashion the English language, and R. Partha-sarathy's more recent decision to abandon writing in English and return to the Tamil language?[2] One could think of parallel situations in other postcolonial countries, the most obvious of which is Ngugi wa Thiong'o's resolve to write in Gikuyu and his comment that "[the English] language was the means of…spiritual subjugation" (9). In each instance, the perception is that the English language is resistant to the expression of certain realities.

The decision to write in English immediately places an author in an awkward situation. To write about a people in a language that is, for the most part, alien to them is to incur the charge of appropriation. As Paranjape puts it so astutely: "These writers live abroad but write about India regularly and compulsively. In effect a new type of orientalism is being fostered by them, aided by the power and might of Euro-American media and publishing conglomerates" (*Towards* 94). The charge has some validity, for writers have, often unconsciously, slipped into essentialisms that distort the reality of the ethos they depict. Particularly for Indian writing in English, the two forces, one following the other, that allowed its survival and empowerment, are colonialism and globalization. Colonialism ensured its popularity for almost a century, starting in the second half of the nineteenth century, and globalization gave it a new lease on life, starting in the early 1980s. The response to this impasse is not to abandon writing in English altogether, but to write in a manner that acknowledges its own artifice, and in the process turn the limitations imposed by language into strengths. Quite often, novels that parade the constructedness of the worlds they create fare better than works that strive for the transparency of mimesis. Mimetic writing is not necessarily doomed to mediocrity or irrelevance—the objective of this study is not to denigrate mimesis and celebrate experiment. (The large circulation of English newspapers and magazines in India is a testimony to the existence of a group—and a class—whose daily language is English and whose world view is substantially Western.) But literature that works with artifice as a central organizing principle does in fact sidestep the troubling questions raised by the implied transparency of realism. Such a counterrealistic tradition has not been acknowledged adequately in literary histories, with the consequence that for comparatists and purists alike, Indian writing in English has come to symbolize a doffing of the cap by neo-colonialists to former imperialists.

In a different but related context, Ananda K. Coomaraswamy, the well-known cultural critic and historian, in his seminal work on Indian culture and aesthetics, *The Dance of Siva*, expresses a similar skepticism about hybrid forms of cultural expression in relation to the paintings of Ravi Varma. While lamenting the syncretism of the Gandhara sculptures, he claims: "We have the parallel modern example of the late Raja Ravi Varma, who, despite the nominally Indian subject matter of his paintings, entirely fails to reflect the Indian spirit" (52-53). To anyone familiar with the paintings of Ravi Varma, the comment would seem surprising because the famous nineteenth-century painter depicts a profound apprehension of beauty, a vision that combines the grandeur of Indian myth with the attention to quotidian detail characteristic of a more secular age. The comment is also intriguing, considering that Coomaraswamy is decidedly anti-puritanical in his views and his discussion of Indian aesthetics accommodates the sensuous and the erotic. But the distinction he implies is crucial, for the juxtaposition of the religious and the secular that he perceives in ancient Indian culture is part of a *Weltanschauung*, a totality he perceives to be enshrined in the *Vedas*. His view of what constitutes the essence of Indianness, not surprisingly, hardly acknowledges the subaltern, the marginalized or the ex-centric. "Indian philosophy," he claims, "is essentially the creation of the two upper classes of society, the Brahmans and the Kshattriyas. To the latter are due most of its forward movements; to the former its elaboration, systematization, mythical representation, and application" (4). The painting of Ravi Varma, then, must fall outside this frame in its inclination to combine the indigenous and the acquired in a manner not sanctioned by tradition. It fails, presumably, because it is in some ways an expression of individualism, a desire to alter, to experiment, and refashion in a manner that foregrounds the private over the collective, the syncretic over the authentic. In short, the multiplicity of traditional Indian art is circumscribed by the *Vedas* and any work that destabilizes this paradigm fails to meet his aesthetic requirements.

For Coomaraswamy the British period was one of decline and the project of colonialism a total failure: "it should not have been regarded as the highest ideal of Empire 'to give to all men an English mind'" (131). While he is pragmatic enough to recognize the impossibility of returning to the past, he is equally insistent about the need to cherish what has been lost: "to understand, to endorse with passionate conviction, and to love what we have left behind us is the only possible foundation for power" (132). His approach is decidedly nostalgic with all its ideological complexities.

The ideal of art, for him, is the creation of *Rasa*, which he defines as aesthetic emotion. *Rasa*, along with its subordinate features, namely, *vibhava*, *anubhava*, *bhava,* and *sattvabhava* become the constitutive features of Indian aesthetics. The vision, framed by religion, sanctioned by theory, and justified by classical art, is essentially holistic and monistic. As he mentions, "the theory of *rasa* set forth according to Visvanatha and other aestheticians, belongs to totalistic monism; it marches with the Vedanta. In a country like India, where thought is typically consistent with itself, this is no more than we had a right to expect" (37). According to the paradigm he formulates, Indian art, and, by extension, Indian literature must stand or fall on its capacity to conform to traditional Indian aesthetic standards.

Both Rao and Coomaraswamy either celebrate or endorse an indigenous system whose values remain a touchstone against which any deviation seems a contamination. Thus the very act of writing in English is, for them, a self-defeating enterprise. The rationale for such a formulation is reinforced by an East-West binarism which preserves an unchanging homogeneity by adopting a rigid linear process of perceiving history. Interestingly, the atemporal and the static, which are so carefully described in Coomaraswamy's commentary on the dance of Shiva, are then underscored by a methodology that posits linear temporality. But the force of the argument is not lost, particularly in a country of such physical magnitude where the use of English has declined noticeably and where the majority of people about whom literature may be written can neither speak nor understand English. For Coomaraswamy, a holistic view of art pre-empts any form of hybridity. For Subha Rao, language as the repository of values effectively prevents any literature written in the English language from access to authentic India. The binary system which serves the theories of both Coomaraswamy and Rao is itself a product of colonialist and orientalist discourse. If, for one, the realm of art has no referential function and thus no links with historical realities, for the other the presence or absence of a readership becomes a determining factor.

Nationalist discourse in India was, in practice, essentially ambivalent and pluralistic, although in principle it assumed, inevitably, a binary configuration that maintained a neat division between East and West. Establishing the right to self-determination involved mirroring the colonizer, and in fact demonstrating that the civilizing mission had run its course and fulfilled its function of educating the native, despite enemy camps refusing to acknowledge common ground. (Syncretism and ambivalence can hardly be counted as strategic points to install defences, although not even the most ardent nationalist who renounced anything that belonged to the West could in practice achieve that separation.) Hence Benedict Anderson's point that "nationalism has to be understood by aligning it, not with self-consciously held political ideologies, but with large cultural systems that preceded it, out of which—as well as against which—it came into being" (19).

Thus the processes of nationalism and postcolonialism are ambivalent and highly complex; the lines of demarcation are far from clear. As Partha Chatterjee states:

> Nationalism denied the alleged inferiority of the colo-
> nized people; it also asserted that a backward nation
> could "modernize" itself while retaining its cultural
> identity. It thus produced a discourse in which, even as
> it challenged the colonial claim to political domination,
> it also accepted the very intellectual premises of "moder-
> nity" on which colonial domination was based. (*Nationalist
> Thought* 30)

To some extent this assimilation is true of any process of conquest
and liberation, although in India, again paradoxically, the effect of
Mughal rule was arguably different. The Mughals came to conquer
and to stay, but in cultural terms the effect of Mughal rule was to
spread Islam and win converts while leaving the ontology of the
Hindu world relatively untouched. Syncretic forms did emerge, as
is evident, for instance, in music and architecture, but Hinduism
remained intact. But British rule, as Gauri Viswanathan and several
others have pointed out, was curious in that it was always seen as
temporary although its process of subjugation meant to ensure its
permanence.[3] Its practice as a colonial power so problematized the
process of defining the nation, that as Homi Bhabha rightly says
"the liminal figure of the nation-space would ensure that no political ideologies could claim transcendent or metaphysical authority
for themselves" (299). In that sense, dichotomies are suspect and
Ashis Nandy's point about the futility of insisting on dualities is
valid. As Nandy observes, "the two Indias which the ideologies
project are both products of Western intrusion and both are
attempts to reconstruct Indian culture according to categories consistent to the modern Western mind" (82).

Indo-Anglian literature is, then, inevitably Western in many of its
preoccupations. If, as Anita Desai puts it, the English language
"shed the unsuitable costumes of the stiff and unbending
Englishman in the tropics, and gradually unbent so far as to take to
the handspun native costume, sit crosslegged on the floor and eat
chillies" ("On the English Language" 2), its adaptability was part of

a larger process of establishing a niche that ensured its survival and significance. Indian writing has never been able to shake off its "foreignness" in ways that other remnants of colonialism, such as cricket, have succeeded in doing. Sachin Tendulkar, the talented captain of the Indian cricket team, is a national hero, but the Indo-Anglian author remains a neo-colonialist, standing outside the general framework of Indian literature. And literary histories, working with monolithic models, have not been able to overcome this pervasive bias.

For literary historians the tendency has been, given the relatively short history of Indian writing in English, to establish teleological patterns in the broadest possible terms to encapsulate a diverse body of material. William Walsh's *Indian Writing in English* chooses to begin its discussion with religious and autobiographical writing, not without some justification, since works by Aurobindo and Nehru, for instance, are substantial achievements in their own right. At the other end of the spectrum are critics such as C.D. Narasimhaiah whose notable *The Swan and the Eagle: Essays on Indian English Literature*, after a brief introduction, moves to a study of R.K. Narayan, Raja Rao, and Mulk Raj Anand. Among those who have tried to be totally comprehensive, the major critic is K.R. Srinivasa Iyengar whose *Indian Writing in English* is clearly a substantial achievement, although its methodology conventionally establishes a very broad periodization on the basis of literary and political watersheds. A more sustained attempt to narrow the scope of literary history is made by Meenakshi Mukherjee whose well-known *The Twice-Born Fiction* is based on the premise of thematic emphasis as she argues in favour of a two-part approach to literary history. She, together with M.E. Derrett (*The Modern Indian Novel in English: A Comparative Approach*) have made some attempt to locate Indo-Anglian literature within a larger national framework, but they too discuss Indo-Anglian writing in relation to a single stream.

There has also been some acknowledgment of the inherent difficulties associated with attempting literary histories. Writing in 1977, Syd Harrex in his two-volume work *The Fire and the Offering:*

The English Language Novel of India suggests the possibility of two traditions, one social and public and the other private and psychological, to encapsulate this diverse body of writing. But he goes on to admit that R.K. Narayan, Raja Rao, and Mulk Raj Anand "can hardly be said to resemble or to have influenced each other in any significant sense" (118) before he settles on an in-depth study of individual authors.

Other groupings are, of course, possible. Fawzia Afzal-Khan has demonstrated one such in *Cultural Imperialism and the Indo-English Novel* where she uses the motif of myth to deal with four authors, namely, R.K. Narayan, Kamala Markandaya, Anita Desai, and Salman Rushdie. By the same token, one could attempt classifications on the basis of thematic preoccupations in ways that would make interesting connections. Thus works such as Shoshee Chunder Dutt's *The Young Zemindar*, with its emphasis on historical material, would find a parallel in, say, the work of Ahmad Ali, Manohar Malgonkar, or Khushwant Singh. The political preoccupations of the early novels by K.S. Venkataramani would be carried on in the work of Chaman Nahal and Nayantara Sahgal. The social realism of Kamala Markandaya would emerge again in Bhabani Bhattacharya or in some works by Vikram Chandra. Such classifications based on connections in subject matter are perfectly valid, and have been attempted on occasion, but they are based largely on thematic parallels rather than a pattern of evolution. For the most part, there was no real sense of a "literary school" nourished by societies, journals, or a tradition of criticism that would provide a strong basis for literary continuity and evolution.

Particularly in the study of fiction, the focus has been on common themes or certain responses to social realities, but hardly any attention has been paid to formal innovation as a recurring pattern, or as a basis for typology. Much of the criticism in the West, particularly in the post-Rushdie period, has focused on formal innovation. Postmodernists, structuralists, feminists, and Marxists have all published a number of articles on a limited number of authors and texts. Their objective has been, for the most part, to unpack the novels by establishing linkages with Western and Latin American narrative modes. Their attempt has not been to interrogate a whole literary tradition or engage with the different viewpoints about the corpus in general. The strategy of looking at Indian fiction from the twin perspectives of realism and experiment has the advantage of setting up a manageable framework for understanding both the strengths and weaknesses of this body of writing. While common features do link the two traditions, significant differences exist between the two, and establishing such a paradigm is one possible way to deal with the multiple issues that surround Indian writing in English.

To establish a taxonomy on the basis of form rather than subject and to move away from a monolithic literary history is not necessarily to establish a privileged niche for innovative writing. The realism of Vikram Seth, as seen in his ambitious novel *A Suitable Boy*, was overwhelmingly successful (if one is to judge by its reception in both India and the West). Equally popular is Rohinton Mistry's recent novel, *A Fine Balance*. Realism has its strong defenders, including Georg Lukács who mentions dismissively that "formal novelty, and an affected originality, often conceals a subjectivist dogmatism" (50) and goes on to establish the conditions that ensure the success of realism. The distinction, then, is not necessarily to salvage one tradition by jettisoning the other. Rather, it serves the purpose of establishing the norms by which each tradition needs to be judged. The referential novel works within a certain framework of expectations that is quite unlike the rationale that underscores experimental fiction.

To claim two distinctive traditions is not to endorse the notion that writers always belonged to one or the other, or that these two were mutually exclusive. Writers such as Raja Rao and Vikram Chandra sometimes moved from one to the other and in works such as Arundhati Roy's *The God of Small Things*, the dividing line between realism and experiment is often thin. However, despite any overlap, the fundamental impulse behind these two traditions is decidedly different. Realism implies transparency; it claims implicitly that the world of fiction reflects the "real" world outside (despite the obvious problems of that assertion). Experiment acknowledges its artifice and its hybridity and works on the assumption that there is a hiatus between the real world and the fictive universe. In an essay that formulates itself as quasi-fiction, J.M. Coetzee makes the observation that "realism has never been comfortable with ideas: realism is premised on the idea that ideas have no separate existence, can exist only in things. So when it needs to debate ideas, as here, it is driven to invent situations—walks in the countryside, conversations—which give voice to contending ideas and thereby in a sense embody them" (65). Even if one could not agree that "ideas" and "realism" occupy mutually exclusive spaces, one would endorse the notion that realism requires a socio-cultural "frame" that shapes and often determines its vision.

When Indo-Anglian literature masked its hybridity in mimetic writing, it ran the risk of working with a paradoxical situation. Realistic writing in English ignores the crucial gap between content and audience, thereby problematizing its own project. The mimesis of K.S. Venkataramani's *Murugan the Tiller* (1927) and Mulk Raj Anand's *Untouchable* (1935), is, for instance, inherently self-defeating since the novels deal with issues that hardly affect their upper-middle-class, Westernized readers. The concerns are relevant, but the predicament of the farmer and the harijan do not mirror their own. As Paranjape remarks "India for the bourgeois novelist is a pretty secure and comforting place" (*Towards* 44). Although the class that gets represented in the fiction does not speak English or have access to these texts, in the West these works take on a metonymic—and often essentialist—dimension. Vernacular literature, similar in its preoccupations and equally mimetic, comes across as more nuanced, direct, and forceful. A referential work in Tamil, whether it is first serialized in a popular magazine or published as a book, works with a potential readership of sixty million who would judge the work on the basis of its authenticity. To make this point is not to invoke an essentialist scheme in which the "real" India lies outside the authors who write in English and their readers—contemporary India is, to some extent, a Western invention. But for the Indo-Anglian author, the hiatus between language and reality is always problematic; while realists pretend that the gap does not exist, counterrealists use it to their advantage.

It is important to recognize that vernacular literatures in India were hardly untouched by British influence. In fact, non-English writers have been profound admirers of Western writers and have openly used acquired forms to reshape and rejuvenate dated and atrophied modes of expression. Fiction is largely a consequence of Western influence, as are various forms of lyric poetry. And yet regional literatures have been perceived to be more authentic and relevant than Indo-Anglian writing. The role of the writer as spokesperson and conscience was reserved for the vernacular writer. Charges of elitism, opportunism, and essentialism are levelled at authors writing in English and hardly ever at those writing in regional languages. Issues of class, audience, and colonialism relate to this dichotomy, but it remains a paradox that while English and vernacular writing traversed the same ground most of the time, English served a function that was beyond the reach of the vernacular. Realism was a common factor in both English and vernacular literatures, but while it led to "novels of consolidation" (Wilson Harris's admirable term for a particular kind of realistic novel in the West Indies) in Indo-Anglian writing, it created works of resistance and reform in the vernacular literature. Wilson Harris points out that "one of the ironic things about West Indians of [his] generation is that they may conceive of themselves in the most radical light but their approach to art and literature is one which consolidates the most conventional and documentary techniques in the novel" (*Tradition* 45). In Harris's view, what the Caribbean novel needed to project, given the historical vicissitudes of the country, was *fulfillment* rather than *consolidation*. Indian authors writing in English, for the most part, moved towards consolidation, while vernacular writers who worked with the expectations of a very different readership, exploited the potential of realism.[4]

Indo-Anglian works are not often translated into regional languages. Even if a writer like Narayan, whose reputation in the West is largely dependent on his capacity for realistic portrayal, were to be translated widely in vernacular languages, the response of the audience is likely to be lukewarm. This is not to imply that Narayan is less significant so much as to assert that vernacular literatures are different, partly because they address a different audience, and partly because they work with a different agenda. Mulk Raj Anand's treatment of caste evokes pathos and disbelief, but it falls short of the indignation and anger inspired by a work such as *Samskara* by U.R. Anantha Murthy. In some respects, the classic realist text in English, when it percolates to the vernacular through the system of education, adapts itself much more readily to local surroundings than Indo-Anglian writing where realism works with essentialisms and often performs a quasi-documentary and tendentious role. Not surprisingly, Anglo-Indian novels which were most admired worked with similar objectives.

Meenakshi Mukherjee has rightly pointed out, in her work entitled *The Twice-Born Fiction*, that Forster has been a dominant presence in most of Indo-Anglian writing. Among works that deal with cultural conflict, interaction between the British and Indians, and the incomprehensibility of spiritual India, *A Passage to India* remains a major work. If one were to explore further, one would find considerable overlap between Anglo-Indian writing and early Indo-Anglian literature. Encouraged and sustained by a system of education, the process was one of osmosis. And it is hardly surprising that the mantle of Anglo-Indian writing fell on Indian writing in English. The crucial difference, however, is that the Anglo-Indian novel, for the most part, uses Indian subject matter, but is written by Western authors for the West. The Indo-Anglian work, particularly the referential novel, is written by Indians, using Indian subject matter, but transformed in order to suit a Western or Westernized audience.

The average Indo-Anglian novel is thus shaped by the conventions of expressive realism since it developed in the shadow of

Victorian fiction. In fact, the uncritical emulation of this alien form
has led to what many see as conspicuous weaknesses in Indo-
Anglian writing. The fundamental premises of realism—its assumptions about people, property, and religion, its faith in liberal humanism and its need for consolidation—were specific to a particular
historical phase. Its transplantation to India was bound to be problematic, particularly because of noticeably different conditions in
India. Realistic fiction in the vernacular adapted itself more readily,
partly as a result of the rapid changes in social, political, and literary conditions, but also because it drew heavily on local material
(including myth, oral literature, classical texts, etc.) in order to
reshape an alien form to suit local needs. For the novel in English,
which had a specific audience in mind, much of this was unavail-
able. Compounding this problem was the issue of style, which
required the authors to "pretend" that their characters spoke
English, in order to preserve the conventions of realism. The tendency to rely heavily on "telling" rather than "showing" among referential novels is at least in part a result of this peculiar conundrum.[5]

Given the complexity of the political, social, as well as cultural
situation, it's hardly surprising that even the more successful works
were tempted to slip into stereotypes. A case in point is Raja Rao's
Kanthapura which provides this description of a "typical" house-
hold:

> One day, when Bhatta was returning from the river after
> his evening ablutions, he did not turn at the Mari-tem-
> ple corner, but went straight along the Lantana lane and
> hurried up the steps of the Kannayya house. Old Rama-
> krishnayya was sitting on the verandah, his hand upon
> his nose, deep-breathful in meditation. Satamma was
> lying by the door, her head upon her arms, resting. And
> from the byre came the sound of milking—Rangamma
> was there. (25)

What is given here purports to be mimetic, even to the point of a linguistic innovation with "deep-breathful," when in fact it is a projection of an essentialist vision. To rely entirely on acquired standards of writing and on external focalizations and representations can lead to confusing the ideal with the real and consequently the perpetuation of stereotypes.

In order to arrive at a possible theoretical approach to counter-realistic Indo-Anglian writing, one needs to acknowledge that experimental works did in fact borrow liberally from Western models. Even a work such as G.V. Desani's *All About H. Hatterr* (a work which was ahead of its time, by both Indian and Western standards), owed much to the picaresque mode to create a work whose characteristics today seem remarkably similar to postmodern novels. Anita Desai's *Cry, the Peacock* is a stream-of-consciousness work whose formal origins can be traced to the West and to modernism. In fact, her works establish this link by persistent intertextual references to Western texts. And more recently, despite the foregrounding of Indian myths, *Midnight's Children* belongs to a line of magic realist works and establishes common ground with Gabriel García Márquez and Günter Grass, and even Laurence Sterne. To apply only a non-Western aesthetic to these works would be futile.

But Indo-Anglian literature is also insistently Indian. Its role is not as unequivocal or perhaps as political as it was, say, in Africa, but it is concerned with the quest for an Indian identity. The notion of separateness, of the need for self-identity, is evident as early as in Raja Rao's preface in *Kanthapura* where the author comments:

> We cannot write like the English. We should not....We,
> in India, think quickly, we talk quickly, and when we
> move, we move quickly. There must be something in the
> sun of India that makes us rush and tumble and run on.
> And our paths are paths interminable. (Preface)

His narrative is a version of the *Harikatha* and its characteristics include digression, repetition, and a leisurely circular movement.

The novel seems to work with the notion of *Rasa,* with Moorthy as an idealized figure, a devoted Laxmana to a Rama-like Gandhi, and other characters, from Lakshamma to Akkamma symbolizing various forms of *bhava.* The work is conceived mainly as an allegory, with colonialism analogous to the abduction of Sita by Ravana in the *Ramayana.* Without recourse to Indian forms of oral narrative, one could hardly comprehend the form of the novel. Its strength lies in its ability to sustain the narrative at the level of allegory. As the novel moves to a close, the honesty of the author demands ambivalence. Moorthy has second thoughts about his political struggle and non-violent resistance, and the supremacy of Gandhi is made deliberately ambiguous. If the notion of *Rasa* requires totality and a dominant motif, the complexity of the political struggle prompts ambivalence and plurality. *Kanthapura* straddles two worlds, the mythical and the political, and its function is not to stress the mimetic or the archetypal so much as to explore the ambivalence of sharing both worlds. Rather than ignore the audience, it thrives by dealing with concerns that preoccupy those who would read such works. *Kanthapura* is successful precisely because its self-consciousness sustains its multiplicity and enables it to be Indian in its sensibility without wearing the label of referentiality.

Even more than Raja Rao, Narayan has acquired the reputation of being the "quintessential" Indian novelist. His world of Malgudi, as the term implies, refers to the house of god. The struggle the characters enact is between the gods and demons. Even something metonymic, like the description of the printing press in *The Man-Eater of Malgudi,* takes on the force of metaphor when the press begins to look increasingly like a temple. And the transformation is not whimsical–it draws on the Hindu notion of sanctity that one associates with one's vocation. The novel itself is about the hubris of Vasu and his downfall, offering once again the recapitulation of the timeless battle between gods and demons.

V.S. Naipaul is trenchant in his criticism of Narayan, claiming, "there is a contradiction in Narayan, between his form, which implies concern, and his attitude, which denies it" (216). But in saying this, Naipaul fails to note the self-consciousness that pervades Narayan's writing, the need to reconcile a vision that accommodates both the timeless and the immediate. What Naipaul sees as the contradiction between form and content is in fact a synthesis between two world views that coexist in his writing. In short, a novel such as *The Man-Eater of Malgudi* is not simply an allegory about the hubris and self-destruction of Bhismasura. Nor is it entirely about the introduction of Western values into a feudal Malgudi. The two levels coexist and their symbiotic relation problematizes literary practice.

Narayan's ideological stance is fundamentally reactionary: he offers through his fiction a vision of stasis, a stratified, caste-oriented India, struggling against the encroaching values of modernism. To see him as a referential writer only is to miss the objectives of his work. There is a careful structuring in his fiction that distances it from referential writing. Contrary to popular belief, Narayan does not reflect the South India of his time. What he creates is the world he would like to see, and the ethos in which he would be comfortable.

In writers like Anita Desai, who hardly ever parade their "Indianness," this same sort of self-conscious fusion and fluidity are evident. If not for the indeterminacy of artifice, one would agree with Subha Rao that "no Indian author of fiction…is free from being anxious to earn credit by representing our life in an appealing manner" (Rao 23). An obvious example would be Desai's work *Fire on the Mountain*, a novel whose referentiality is made suspect from the beginning, partly by the ambivalence that surrounds Carignano and partly by the selection of characters who cannot be said to represent the average Indian. The novel is hardly a simple work of imitation, and the absence of closure, the introspective tone, and pervasive indeterminacy contribute to the artifice. What gives the novel its particular resonance is that it is both a rehearsal and a parody of the Hindu notion of *sanyasi*, with gender, guilt, and history being included within this framework to problematize it. Nanda's retirement to the hills is a version of renunciation, except that the terms within which she attempts that renunciation destabilize a time-honoured paradigm. A work that could have been accused of being elitist, solipsistic, and imitative becomes, from a Hindu perspective, a very "Indian" work that draws on prescribed Hindu patterns of behaviour.

Salman Rushdie's works, which are so often labelled postmodern and magic realist, have, according to the author, much in common with Indian traditions, particularly the twin epics and the oral narrative. As he points out in his essay "In Good Faith": "I was born an Indian, and not only an Indian, but a Bombayite—Bombay, most cosmopolitan, most hybrid, most hotch-potch of Indian cities. My writing and thought have therefore been as deeply influenced by Hindu myths and attitudes as Muslim ones" (404). *Midnight's Children* has too many parallels with *The Tin Drum* for Western influences to be ignored. In fact, this intertext is at least partly responsible for some of the subtleties of the novel. At the same time, the novel is also about Hindu myth, about Shiva, Parvati, Hanuman, and Arjuna. The reversal and parody of myth are crucial to the work and its total vision.

However, to insist on such "Indianness" does not deny the internationalism of so much experimental writing. And the experimentation is very much a consequence of writing from the margins. Indo-Anglian writing, in its experimental mode, is often the work of liminality. That several of the major writers, including Rushdie, Ghose, Suniti Namjoshi, and Amitav Ghosh are expatriates underscores the point that migration, exile, and marginality are often associated with the impulse to experiment. The consciousness that informs such writing arises from the cusp between what is acquired and inherited and so can hardly be called entirely Indian or totally Western. The authors belong and do not belong, although some tend to accept this predicament more readily than others. Thus Narayan would probably consider himself more secure within a traditional framework of values than, say, Suniti Namjoshi, who might perceive herself to be an outsider. But both are in fact "native-aliens," as are writers even like Zulfikar Ghose who were once suspicious of labels that circumscribe and limit their identity. Their narratives are essentially counter-narratives and, as Bhabha points out, "counter-narratives of the nation that continually evoke and erase its totalizing boundaries–both actual and conceptual–disturb those ideological manoeuvres through which 'imagined communities' are given essentialist identities" (300).

All the writers who chose to depart from or challenge the limits of the referential are less concerned with the quotidian than with meta-issues. Concerns with history, historiography, exile, decolonization, cultural complicity, ambivalence, etc. are among the preoccupations of this group of writers. Issues of feminism, sexual orientation, and patriarchy have become the foci of, say, Suniti Namjoshi. They all relate to the present but in a manner that eschews an immediate identification with a socio-cultural context. Their concerns are no less significant for that, but in their refusal to address what constitutes the immediate, the writers implicitly address a different audience and deal with the preoccupations of a particular group. This group includes the expatriate and the exile but also those for whom the process of decolonization has led to a greater sense of limbo, a greater sense of urgency about fundamental issues of identity.

The vision they project is marginalized, but nonetheless "Indian" and relevant. What distinguishes this tradition is, in addition to its internationalism and experiment, a mindset that refuses to accept totalizing positions–schemes that tend to fix the nation in self-sufficient and unambiguous paradigms. At the heart of this enterprise is a desire to question, to subvert and, in the end, to foreground ambivalence. Linking all counterrealistic writing is the consciousness of artifice, and the conviction that literature is, in the end, about itself.

Eclecticism, then, needs to be seen, not as experiment, not as a response to and mimicry of modernist or postmodernist impulses, so much as a mode that is sufficiently plural, parasitical almost, to express the voice of the liminal and the state of ambivalence that characterizes the nation. It is thus hardly surprising that Ghose, visiting Pakistan after nearly two decades, perceives not the referential, although it doesn't totally escape his observation, but rather an absence caused by a collective amnesia. Looking at the incomplete statue of the fasting Buddha in Peshawar, he comments:

> The missing parts of the statue appear to have a vital presence: the starved, absent organs—shrunk, withered, annihilated—throb bloodily in the imagination; that which is not there startles the mind with the certainty of its being; it is an image of amazing contradictions, and illustrates the ambiguity of all perception: reality can be composed of absent things, the unseen blazes in our minds with a shocking vividness. ("Going Home" 15)

The unseen has been unacknowledged, much to the detriment of the nation. The recent has been confused with the indigenous and the manoeuvring of historiography has been accorded the status of truth. If Indo-Anglian writing has a purpose and an audience, it must want to address these deceptions that have paraded as truth.

Literary theory about this writing thus needs to avoid totalizing positions. In a recent article on contemporary Indian fiction, Anita Desai draws attention to Rushdie's comment that his *Midnight's Children* was less influenced by magic realism than by the structure of the epic *Mahabharata*. She adds:

> Immediately there was a flood of younger writers delighted to return to the old style of story telling that was strangely the "latest" and "newest" style. In following his trajectory they found themselves travelling so far westward that, the world being the shape it is, they had arrived in the east again. ("Indian Fiction Today" 211)

That a lot of the Indian past has re-entered through the back door can hardly be denied. Tharoor's *The Great Indian Novel,* for example, is clearly a reworking of the epic *Mahabharata*. The complexity of

Ghose's recent work *The Triple Mirror of the Self* is that, while its form is clearly experimental and counterrealistic, the subject matter and the allegorical subtext are essentially Indian. If the novel is about the dislocation of the present, it is also about the spaciousness of the past. Adam Zameenzad's *The Thirteenth House* is, in its formal experimentation, very Western, but its preoccupation with religion is decidedly South Asian. Perhaps with a writer like Namjoshi, at the level of the text, Indian influences are sometimes more difficult to detect. But the questioning, the sense of marginalization, and the subversion are a consequence of social and cultural conditions in India. Counterrealism in Indo-Anglian literature looks both ways and locates itself on the crossroads of cultural intersection. Thus, totalizing positions are likely to be detrimental to the evaluation of a corpus of mixed parentage. If literature has felt comfortable in merging *Rasa* with magic realism, so too must critical practice. Literary histories that accommodate the notion of different traditions in the corpus of Indo-Anglian writing would eventually establish a critical practice that is less thematic in its methodology and less defensive in its approach. In fact, it would lead to a more fruitful pattern of analysis, not only in relation to other Indian literatures, but also more globally, along lines that Patrick Colm Hogan suggests in *Literary India*.[6]

Counterrealism, although unacknowledged generally as a distinctive strand, needs to be characterized as a tradition. Such a stance raises at least two questions: first, what is the relation between mimetic and experimental writing in Indian literature? Second, in what sense would it constitute a literary tradition? Despite the very real differences between the two, they are not entirely oppositional. There is too much ambivalence, too many shades of grey to keep them firmly apart. When the same writer moves from one to the other, the relation between the two is dialectical or even dialogic. When writers such as Rushdie commit themselves unequivocally to one mode, the relation between them and the realists is almost an acknowledgment of the different spaces they inhabit.

More importantly, does counterrealism constitute a tradition? Tradition implies a number of attributes, including those of continuity. Mark Williams, writing about New Zealand literature, speaks about "the debt a people owes to the cultural achievements of its forebears" (14) in a way that would be hardly applicable to Indian writing in English. It may be tempting to trace a genealogy that dispenses with ambiguity, but the fact is that the "native" and the "foreign" are partners in a literary enterprise. There is no clear line of descent, no originary moment except that all these writers share similar assumptions about the purpose, value, and inevitability of writing in English.

The tradition of experiment is obviously not as linear in its development as one would like it to be. An alternative literary history along these lines would be hard-pressed to find patterns of continuity or influence. From Desani to Rushdie there is a pattern of evolution and intertextual acknowledgment. Here again, it's important to stress that individual authors have not always been experimentalists. Of necessity, a study such as this, whose objective is to suggest a paradigm rather than account for every author, leaves out writers such as Arun Joshi who often located themselves outside realism. This study, which deals with six authors (namely, R.K. Narayan, G.V. Desani, Anita Desai, Zulfikar Ghose, Suniti Namjoshi, and Salman Rushdie), is intended to demonstrate, in some detail, a tradition that is distinctive in its narrative mode. There is no attempt to imply that counterrealism begins with R.K. Narayan. On the contrary, a form of fantasy was very much in vogue among the pioneers. In fact, Mukherjee, writing about the early novels, points out that "reality peeps through the chinks of the marvellous, reminding us of the tensions that created these novels" (*Realism* 67). Nonetheless, in the last five decades counterrealism as a self-conscious mode began to be employed by a number of Indo-Anglian authors.

After Rushdie, the experimental tradition takes on a more familiar pattern as authors borrow more often and learn from each other. But for the most part, this tradition has been noticeably indi-

vidualistic in its practice. At one end is, say, Narayan, whose counterrealism finds its sources in the structures of Indian myth; at the
other is the magic realism of Zulfikar Ghose that seeks its paradigms in Western and Latin American authors. What unites them is
their artifice and their refusal to be circumscribed by the conventions of realism. Once this distinctiveness is recognized it will
become increasingly clear that, contrary to what Naipaul has to say
about Indian writing in English, Shiva has not ceased to dance. But
then, neither should the educated reader look for an ash-smeared
Shiva dancing in the village cemetery.

CHAPTER 2

The Fabulator of Malgudi: R.K. Narayan

To invoke the work of R.K. Narayan as an originary moment in the history of counterrealism in Indo-Anglian writing is, admittedly, unusual, for his reputation as an author rests squarely on his penchant for truthful representation rather than experiment. Ever since Graham Greene in his famous introduction to *The Financial Expert*, written half a century ago, endorsed Narayan's contribution as a metonymist, as one who provides a window to India, the prevalent view has been of Narayan as a realist and that his Malgudi encapsulates the heterogeneity and religiosity of India in ways that are fundamentally authentic.[1] Among the older critics, Srinivasa Iyengar, William Walsh, and several others have seen in Narayan different reasons for serious attention, but all have been consistent in their assumption of the referentiality that sustains his work.[2] Edwin Gerow states that "Narayan's is *classical* art" (1) and Cynthia Van Driesen sees in his work the expression of "the Hindu concept of life and experience" (55). She goes on to add that "the Narayan hero in fact, impresses as a type of ordinary, average humanity. He is never exceptionally gifted, intellectually or physically. The primary impression is of fallibility and vulnerability–truly an Indian

version of Everyman" (58). Philip Scott goes further and suggests
that Narayan belongs to a long line of Indian nationalist writers:
"He is the torch-bearer of that more complimentary image of India
first seen by certain sympathetic Orientalist scholars and taken over
by patriotic Indians in the nineteenth century. Ultimately, he is in a
direct line of descent from men like Bankim Chandra Chatterjee" (96).

As spiritualist, mythographer, or satirist, he remains, almost by
consensus, a chronicler of the referential. Even in studies that
stress the mythic element in Narayan, such as Fawzia Afzal-Khan's
recent work on the Indo-English novel, the emphasis falls on the
manner in which "the demands of the mythic and the realist modes
often coalesce" (29). Afzal-Khan's reading of the mythic is primarily a religious one in which she perceives the seamless merging of
the sacred and the secular. One of the few exceptions among critics, perhaps, is Hadyn Williams, who draws attention to the element
of fantasy in Narayan's work when he claims that "Narayan's novels always combine realism with elements of fantasy" (1138). For
the most part, the notion of fantasy has hardly ever been dealt with
in any great detail, and even critics such as D.A. Shankar who fault
Narayan's evocation of the referent on sociological grounds are
careful to add that "there is hardly anything that is unreal about the
India that he presents in his fiction" (49). In short, the agreement
among critics is about the transparency of his work, the immediate
access it provides to the realities of India in general and South
India in particular.

An interesting departure from this line of thinking is the argument offered by Richard Cronin who sees a fundamental dichotomy
between the fabulist and the novelist. Identifying the allegorical
impulse as a form of fabulism, Cronin argues that the essentialism
that underlies Narayan's vision seeks recourse in fabulism, while the
author's honesty and objectivity lead to the novelistic mode to articulate unpalatable truths about the nation. Although the celebration
of Narayan rests largely on fabulism, Cronin points out that
"Narayan turns to the novel when he wants to evade the consequences of his fable and to the fable when the novel starts to drift

into dangerous seas" (63). Cronin's concern is with content rather than form, but he does acknowledge, implicitly, the presence of different modes in Narayan's fiction. The fabulism he alludes to, however, is that of the message-driven traditional fable rather than its more contemporary reincarnation.

Although Narayan's world is primarily mythic and is under-pinned by a religious vision, his awareness of the secular is a constitutive aspect of the *Weltanschauung* of India where divisions such as private and public, religious and secular do not exist in quite the same way as in the West. Narayan's perception of the everyday, the minutiae of daily occurrences, is often precise and arises from a nuanced awareness of detail. Ved Mehta's notable essay, among others, underlines the meticulous attention to detail that could be present only in one who *belongs* and is rooted in a way that several expatriate writers aren't.[3] Driesen is right when she says that "[Narayan's] picture of India is touched with that quality of intimacy, that perhaps only a native Indian, himself completely immersed in the kind of life described, could present" (51). There is clearly a commitment to a particular kind of truth, but one that needs to be carefully distinguished from modes of representation inspired by a particular vision.

The objective of this chapter is to reflect on the intersection of religion, ideology, and social practice in Malgudi in order to argue that Narayan's characteristic mode is artifice rather than expressive realism. The primary objective is not to fault or celebrate him so much as to demonstrate that his special strength lies in his artifice which works in tandem with his subject matter. Writing at a time when realism was the predominant mode in both literatures in English and in the vernacular, he chose to incorporate the conventions of contemporary fiction without subscribing to its ideological stance. His artifice is far more subtle than an ostensible representation of a somewhat essentialized holistic India. There is hardly any doubt that he believes in a particular ontology, and that vision shapes his fictive world. What he offers is an ideologically loaded, essentialist view that creates the illusion of the real.

Inspired by nostalgia rather than observation, his work reshapes the real in a manner that masks the experiment. In Narayan there is, for the most part, no conscious dislocation of the premises of realism, but the world he meticulously creates is sustained by a sense of artifice. It is this curious combination of the fictive and the referential that distinguishes his work and makes him a counterrealist writer. The myths he works with and even the hyperbole he is given to are not necessarily antireferential. Seen from the perspective of an Indian ontology, the supernatural does not distinguish realism from artifice, but the manner in which Narayan structures his referential world does. The unique contribution of Narayan to this tradition is that he combines the mode of Western realism with an indigenous world view in ways that are both real and fictive.

The idea of counterrealism is not necessarily synonymous with antirealism, although both are removed from the conventions of mimetic writing. Narayan's mode does not adopt an oppositional stance. The relation between contemporary forms of realism and Narayan's counterrealism is often a dialogic one in which the movement from one to the other is ambivalent. Since the issue is not probability, even the informed reader is likely to misread Narayan. The absurdity of a character such as Vasu in *The Man-Eater of Malgudi* or the factual incorrectness of Gandhi visiting Malgudi in *Waiting for the Mahatma* is not the occasion for counterrealism. A whole ontology gives Narayan the latitude he needs for enlisting an allegorical form and structuring his novels along the lines of religious tales. But the essence of his counterrealism, far less ostentatious than the writers who follow him, lies in the way he creates a parallel world–an alternative one–that pretends to be the real one. For Narayan the strategy serves the purpose of resistance, of turning away from contemporary realities to a world he is comfortable with. As with all counterrealist writers, Narayan finds this mode empowering in that it enables him to stand outside the everyday and, in the process, acknowledge the anomalous position of writing in English, and appealing to a middle-class westernized readership.

A more self-conscious departure from realism along Western lines can be found in Narayan, as in the latter part of *Waiting for Mahatma* where the old grandmother, who is pronounced dead, undergoes a resurrection of sorts, moments before she is cremated.[4] These incidents are not totally unheard of in popular myths, but they are closer to Tzvetan Todorov's notion of uncanny hesitation. They lead to a momentary pause, unsettling even for the reader who sees no disjunction between the real and the supernatural. It is surprising that Narayan expands the plot on the basis of such an occurrence, but here again the episode is hardly representative of the author's more characteristic use of a nonrealist form. The juxtaposition of the plausible with the imaginary in the manner of magic realism is less typical of Narayan than of later writers. But in *The English Teacher*, a whole section of the novel is devoted to the central character communicating with his deceased wife. Curiously enough, *The English Teacher* is not only the most personal of all his works but is also the one that would best work with the argument of counterrealism. Even within an Indian ontology, such a motif could not operate as the structural core in a work that is ostensibly realist. All the episodes involving such communication are likely to be seen as bordering on the fantastic. Ironically, the author himself does not defend the novel in any way except by invoking realism. In an explanatory comment, he says that "more than any other book, *The English Teacher* is autobiographical in content, very little part of it being fiction" (*My Days* 134-35). The occasion for the novel, as is well known, was the death of his wife, Rajam, within a few years of his marriage. The novel offers a deeply felt personal truth, and to use the work as an example of counterrealism would be ultimately self-defeating.

Narayan uses a more straightforward fabulist mode in *A Tiger for Malgudi*, which, if anything, goes to prove that artifice is never far from Narayan's consciousness. The novel is also unusual in his corpus, and is a mode that one hardly associates with his writing. The novel flaunts itself as an animal fable, and the perspective is, for the most part, that of the tiger. The suspension of disbelief that the novel demands makes the novel's tendentious quality all the more obvious, with the consequence that the artifice is simplistic. The novel deliberately orchestrates situations in order to reflect on issues of violence, nationalism, language, religion, and gender. In his introduction to the novel, Narayan himself claims that the desire to write from the perspective of a tiger was largely a whim—a desire to see what happens when a tiger is made the central character in a novel. In her review of the novel, Anita Desai rightly points out that "one is tempted to read the simple tale as a fable…following the traditional cycle of Hindu life in India" (9). The strategy is, however, one of naturalization, which prevents the novel from adopting the stance of self-conscious allegory. The novel paves the way for writers such as Suniti Namjoshi to write more elaborately in this fabulist mode several years later, and it certainly alerts the reader to the indigenous sources and systems of belief that shape his fiction. But very much like *The English Teacher*, the fabulism of this novel is also more of an exception than the norm.

Even *A Tiger for Malgudi*, one might argue, can be read outside the framework of a fable. The tiger's life—his roles change from the lord of the jungle to a performer in a circus and the friendship of a saint—naturalizes the four stages of life. The reader is struck not by the careful symbolism but by the logical flaws deliberately inserted into the novel. Why does the tiger that shunned human contact, even when its family was destroyed, seek refuge in a school in the middle of the day? Why does a trained hunter (who also has a lucrative business exporting tiger skins) get drunk and fall asleep after he is given permission to shoot the animal? The referentiality is arrested at such moments to allow for a range of issues to be invoked and eventually resolved.

There are earlier works that also arrest referentiality. For example, a number of episodes in *The Guide* and *The Vendor of Sweets* straddle the burlesque. (And an Indian reader encountering such burlesque might hesitate at these moments that are characteristic of what Todorov calls the fantastic).[5] But such episodes appear as isolated moments within an otherwise referential text. More significant is the construction of Malgudi, which flaunts itself as metonymic while operating within the discourse of the experimental. Interestingly, Narayan himself appears to have conceived of Malgudi as a fictive construct despite the diligence with which critics have tried to locate Malgudi within a realistic framework. Says Narayan: "A certain English professor has managed to draw an intricate map of Malgudi with its landmarks laboriously culled out of pages of all my novels. To see an imaginary place so solidly presented with its streets and rivers and temples did not appeal to me, it seemed to me a petrification or fossilization of light wish-like things floating across one's vision while one is writing" (*Nightmare* 200-201). What he admits to is a sense of dissatisfaction with the imposition of spatial and temporal fixity on a fluid, imaginary construct, but the fact is that Malgudi is a microcosm and an expression of what he would like India to be.

The emphasis on Narayan as a significant figure in the tradition of counterrealism in Indian fiction ties in with the more general hypothesis that underlies this book. Narayan, like, say, Mulk Raj Anand, who began to write during this time, and K.S. Venkataramani who wrote before him, was aware of a specific audience that belonged to a particular class. But unlike Anand, Narayan does not assume a direct correspondence between the fictive world and the real one. The irony of the situation is striking. Anand deals with social ills that were becoming increasingly apparent. Narayan pretends that they don't exist. Curiously enough, readers such as Graham Greene did not see in Anand the capacity to provide a window to India in the manner that Narayan did. Narayan gave his readers what they wanted to see, together with the sense that what they were offered was realist. In that sense, Narayan's counterrealism challenges the boundaries of mimesis by turning the focus on fiction itself. If artifice is introduced self-consciously in later writers, in Narayan it is subdued and indirect, with the consequence that readers do not often see the dividing line between the fictive and the real.

Narayan's Malgudi belongs to Tamil Nadu, although he is always at pains to remove specific referential markers from his fictive world. Though there is sporadic signposting to suggest that Malgudi accommodates Karnataka as well, for the most part, the landscape, the monuments, and the language that the characters use suggests Tamil Nadu as the setting. Also, there is a translucence about Malgudi that establishes its working, its social dynamic as the typical. A wide spectrum of social types—all typically Indian—inhabits this space. Natural markers—the river, the forest, the animals—complement the social in ways that appear perfectly natural. The supernatural is always present as part of the natural—again in ways that are typically Indian. Yet what Narayan projects is a Vaishnavite, Brahminical world where religious practice depicts and embodies a world view. There is, for Narayan, a correspondence between cosmic and earthly harmony. Despite the ambiguities that inform his narratives and the indeterminacy that testifies to the integrity of his authorial stance, his vision remains a holistic and almost idealized one that achieves its cohesiveness by ignoring a number of referential realities.

Malgudi, which serves as the locale for almost all his novels, is what Mircea Eliade would call "sacred space." Against the profane world, which denies the existence of a sacred universe and relies on an individualistic and teleological view of human progress, the sacred world recapitulates its origins through a variety of forms, including rituals, the landscape, and myths. According to Eliade, "for those who have a religious experience all nature is capable of revealing itself as cosmic sacrality" (12). This is precisely the vision of Narayan, whose ostensible concern is with the profane while the real quest is for the sacred.

Narayan's Malgudi is a town that, according to the author, is fixed in pre-independence India, in the 1930s, at the time when the author began his writing career and published *Swami and Friends* and *The Bachelor of Arts*. Since then, much of his fiction has moved chronologically to include the time of independence and even the 1950s and '60s, although one can see why Narayan would make such an assertion of stasis as recently as 1989. With characteristic simplicity, Narayan maintains that temporal distance enables him to indulge in artifice, for he is in a position to subvert the dictates of realism if necessary: "My fiction is set in my own background, though Malgudi is imaginary. Malgudi is fixed in the 1930s, and that gives me extraordinary freedom. I can even put a lighthouse there if I want to, though there is no coast near Malgudi" (Graubard 234). Of course, Narayan never includes a lighthouse, or any other marker that would disrupt the internal cohesion of his world. The sheer proliferation of Malgudi novels demands that additions be included to suggest transformation, but there is never a reason to undermine the inner logic of Malgudi. While subverting realism serves a narrative intent, the reasons for creating his Malgudi are probably a lot more complex.

My reading of Narayan's work, particularly *The Man-Eater of Malgudi,* as counterrealistic fiction is not an attempt to force his writing into a mould where it does not belong. The aim of reading his work in the light of contemporary postcolonial theory is not to impose an arbitrary grid on a body of work that is redeemed by its humour, its wit, and its unpretentious narrative line. The vitality of his work has rarely been matched in Indian writing, and it is this quality that, to some extent, masks the ideological assumptions that underlie his work. Narayan offers through his work a system that is inherently hegemonic and reactionary, and since the structure, like most systems, flaunts itself as natural, the strategy he adopts is, appropriately, a version of realism.

But Narayan's narrative mode is a departure from realism, not in the ostentatious manner of Salman Rushdie, but in a more subdued form where the artifice carefully ruffles the surface of realism. Yet to insist on a direct correspondence between the world of his fiction and referential reality would falsify his project: there is always the danger of attributing to Narayan the views of his characters. Between an approach that speaks of literature in hermetic terms and one which insists on its capacity to mirror the outside world lies a grey area in which the real, the fictive, and authorial intention intersect. That interstitial space becomes a significant aspect of this study.

The "space" he creates does not always survive translation. For example, the decision to locate the film version of *The Guide* in Rajasthan rather than in South India may well be an acknowledgment that Malgudi is a fragile creation. The individual components of Malgudi—the houses, shops, statues, and the landscape—might seem truthful as representation but they are used non-mimetically. A Narayan text makes the flaw evident in any true/untrue binarism. Narayan sets the stage for "secular" rituals that are created by him to reveal "truths" whose importance lies precisely in the illusion they create.

Perhaps the more obvious aspect of Narayan's counterrealism, but one that needs emphasis nonetheless, is that his fiction shares the same conventions of religious texts and epics. Although pulp fiction flooded India at the turn of the century, it doesn't seem to have influenced Narayan. A.K. Venkatachalapathy's research shows the cultural, political, and economic nexus that allowed for the large-scale local imitation of Western pulp fiction in India. Driving home his point, Venkatachalapathy comments that "novels were so popular that the District Magistrate of Tiruchirapalli, surveying the sort of reading materials available to people in the Swadeshi period, found no less than 114 Tamil novels in a reading room in the small town of Lalgudi" (56). Narayan appears to have been less affected by this trend of writing which based itself on Western forms of popular writing than on ones that were primarily indigenous and nonrealist. All the writing at the turn of the century, including texts written by South Indian authors, did not make the slightest difference to Narayan's own practice. Since the "great tradition" of Indian writing—epics, puranas, long poems, etc.—is fundamentally religious in outlook, a preoccupation with the transcendental is possible only by invoking a form of nonrealism. The aesthetic conventions that determined ancient writing required nonrealism. Fables, myths, and legends, often included in such texts, were primarily nonrealist. The rules that determined such writing, however, were not arbitrary. Although it wouldn't take much to invalidate the truth claims of such stories on rational grounds, within the ideological frame of the tale, certain nonrealist conventions were deemed acceptable. The poetics of Indian literature, such as the *Natyasastra*, easily accommodates forms of antirealist representation, and for Narayan, who was well-versed in this tradition, its conventions were very much a part of his intellectual makeup.

Unlike the traditions of Sanskrit literature, local or vernacular traditions functioned within essentially nonrealist conventions. Thus the conventions that determined the form of *Sangam* poetry (that is, Tamil poetry during the first three centuries A.D.), with its elaborate mapping of "aham" and "puram" (to correspond to "inner" and "outer"), probably had little to do with the realities of love and war in that region. The Tamil epics such as *Silappadikaram* and *Manimekalai* (circa 4th century A.D.) were similar in adopting conventions that were nonrealist. Here too, these forms structured their work in a complex manner, but the forms themselves lie outside the dictates of realism. In short, any author who taps into the vernacular tradition would be completely at home in a highly conventional and stylized form of writing.

Narayan works with a world view and a taxonomy that are mythical and cosmic. It is a world that places equal emphasis on day-to-day activities and on fables, superstitions, fairy tales, rituals, magic, and so forth. The ambivalence of the ending of *The Guide* or the sheer farce of a short story such as "A Horse and Two Goats" is possible only because the world in which these are set does not perceive any disruption to reality from how the tale unfolds. Like the Hindu epics—which, incidentally, were rewritten by Narayan—these tales are not intended to conform to notions of realism.

But Narayan does not write parables or fables per se. The form he chooses is decidedly Western and the language he uses is alien to the people he often describes. And the stasis he achieves through his fictive Malgudi is part of the counterrealism of his work. What he achieves is a combination of ideology and counterrealism, always mediated by his unique brand of humour. If he hasn't had any recognizable followers (with the possible exception of Kiran Desai) it is because no one has attempted precisely what he did.[6] In short, Narayan's singular achievement lies in his successful adaptation of local forms, with all their ideological functions, to Western forms of writing. And for the same reasons that ancient texts are not often read for their ideological content but seen as documents of universalism, Narayan's novels have been seen as reflectors of a holistic India.

Narayan's fiction rarely alludes to the well-documented political changes that were taking place in a country that was conscious of moving towards independence. Apart from *Waiting for the Mahatma* which deals specifically with the politics of the Indian National Congress and the career of Mahatma Gandhi, and some of his essays, the politics of decolonization have hardly ever been foregrounded in his work, although incidental comments remind the reader of the outside world. Narayan himself is aware of the gaps in his work, his failure to address certain issues, and has stated categorically that he is unconcerned about such a "lack." Asked about the social relevance of his work, he replies: "Critics say that I don't talk of the aspirations of the people, of the political agony we have gone through, and of all those plans for economic growth. I am not interested in that" (*Nightmare* 234). Since social realism is not his forte, one can hardly expect in his work the sensibility that informs the work of overtly didactic writers such as Mulk Raj Anand. But Malgudi does provide the basis for a syncretic world that reveals the social and cultural pluralism of the nation. Malgudi is an imaginary construct but not an improbable one. In fact, its artifice enables him to achieve a synthesis, as in the first paragraph of *The Man-Eater of Malgudi* where Hindu, Muslim, and Christian elements are invoked to demonstrate the allegorical and representative dimension of Malgudi. This fictional town offers itself as a mirror of the nation. A descriptive opening paragraph also serves as synecdoche:

> I could have profitably rented out the little room in front
> of my press on Market Road, with a view of the foun-

tain; it was coveted by every would-be shopkeeper in our town My son, little Babu, went to Albert Mission School, and he felt quite adequately supplied with toys, books, sweets, and any other odds and ends he fancied. My wife, every Deepavali, gave herself a new silk sari, glittering with lace, not to mention the ones she bought for no particular reason at other times. She kept the pantry well-stocked and our kitchen fire aglow, continuing the traditions of our ancient home in Kabir Street. (7)

Every aspect of the paragraph achieves precisely what Narayan does in all his fiction: it creates a structure that is balanced, representative, and inclusive, but one which also privileges the ideological stance that flaunts a hierarchical system as an egalitarian one.

The very fact that for critics the distinction between a fictive Malgudi and a real South India is blurred is itself an indication that Malgudi represents the real. Narayan's departure from realism enables the artifice that is crucial to his vision. And yet the desire to make his artifice appear natural compels the experiment to remain unostentatious. Cronin, in his discussion of Narayan, observes that Naipaul's disillusionment with Narayan is of a mask that slipped: "when [Naipaul] had read Narayan's novels in Trinidad and in London he had not doubted that connection: when he read *Mr. Sampath* in Bombay, in Delhi, in Kutch, his sense of it snapped. He could not connect the India he read about with the India he saw around him" (59). Naipaul's dismay was brought on partially by his own subjectivity, but the point can hardly be refuted.

That Narayan is at pains to project his fictive world as a real one is evident in his refusal to create schematic characters who fall on one side or the other of the moral divide. There is constant change, a dynamic tension that humanizes his world and lends it a measure of credibility. And the irony and wit for which Narayan is well-known are means by which the narrator identifies himself with the narrative and also remains detached. This capacity is what makes the narrator trustworthy and the world of Malgudi both fallible and believable. No Indian writer has so consistently sustained a capacity for satire as has Narayan, and that has given his work an apparent referentiality that few others have been able to emulate.

The issue, then, is not whether or not Narayan creates a believable world so much as the principles that underlie his carefully constructed world and the ideological purpose it serves. The complexity and heterogeneity that underlie his writing are religious and ideological, and since these are congruent with a colonial and Brahminical agenda, he remains, for many critics, very much the quintessential Indian writer in English. But most don't recognize that, in the process of recreating India, he has offered a vision of the nation that is orientalist, binary, caste-bound, and essentialist. One of the few writers to see this aspect of Narayan is, strangely enough, V.S. Naipaul, who insists that in Narayan's work "too much that is overwhelming has been left out; too much taken for granted" (216).

Naipaul's more general critique applies to all Indo-Anglian writers, with the sole exception of Ruth Prawer Jhabvala, who, in his view, has avoided the shortcomings of all the others. He singles out Narayan–probably because at this time Narayan was better known in the West than most writers–arguing that Narayan is "forever headed for that *aimlessness* of Indian fiction" (216). And he elaborates: "There is a contradiction in Narayan, between his form, which implies concern, and his attitude, which denies it, and in this calm contradiction lies his magic which some have called Tchekovian" (214). Naipaul's observation is astute, but he mistakes the humour and satire as lack of commitment, a failure to address with any seriousness the realities of Indian life. Contrary to what Naipaul claims, Narayan's sense of the ironic and his vision of the nation do not cancel each other out. They complement each other because the humour is a form of social critique and a defence against obvious valorization of the values he celebrates. In Narayan, it is often not the characters who are funny. The humour is the prerogative of the narrator and thus it speaks of authorial position.

For pedagogical convenience, postcolonial critics tend to group regions on the basis of distinctive traits, so if the Caribbean, for instance, is framed by the notion of exile, India is described in relation to religion. To a large extent, that description is true, despite the move towards secularism in the period after independence and the stated policy of leaders who chose to model India along the lines of secular western states. Regardless of official policy, religion is, as T.N. Madan points out, "constitutive of society" (116) and its presence and influence are felt not only in ritual but also in the conflicts that arise from religion.

Narayan's choice of the term Malgudi (literally, the house of Krishna) is itself an indication of the religious frame that encapsulates all aspects of life he deals with. Whether his novels are located around the temple as in *The Guide* or whether the plot focuses on festivals as in *The Man-Eater of Malgudi*, religion as everyday occurrence (i.e., not in any philosophical sense as in the writing of Raja Rao) is a central concern in his novels. And this is in keeping with a basic sense of Indian identity. Whether in celebration or in opposition, religion is never far from the consciousness of Indians.

Religion, for Narayan, is the organizing and overriding principle of his fiction. It is not the religion of abstract ideas but rather pragmatic. If his characters exist in secular time, they are held together and governed by religious time. Thus in *The Man-Eater*, the machinations of Vasu, the taxidermist, are necessarily a blip in cosmic time, and his eventual destruction is predetermined. And this cosmic system is part of a whole interlocking social system that privileges an orientalist notion of Aryan Hindu India and filters down to determine social relations and establish notions of social acceptability and purity. What it amounts to is a Brahminical notion of India, underpinned by the Vedas and religious texts and kept alive by a whole system of worship and ritual that encompasses a significant body of people but preserves a strong sense of hierarchy. To subscribe to one part of the system is to participate in a whole ontology. To reject this is to venture into an existential wilderness. And since the upper stratum of this hierarchical system, namely, the upper castes, had significant access to the colonial system, it found itself in the enviable situation of controlling both secular and religious life in the country. As M.S.S. Pandian notes, "the Brahmin exercised his hegemony in the 'political society' through the authority structures of the colonial state and in the 'civil society' through his caste location; in negotiating power in each of these spheres, he privileged English and Sanskrit" (3).

In *The Man-Eater of Malgudi*, the printing press, the core of the novel, is architecturally in the form of a Hindu temple, with a lobby for customers and friends to meet, while the machine itself is located behind a curtain and no one except Nataraj and Sastri (the name is significant) are allowed inside. Vasu, the taxidermist who is consistently associated with meat and violence and immorality, is the first to desecrate the sanctity of that space; the novel is at least partly about the restoration of its purity. In Eliade's terms, Vasu, who inhabits a profane world, violates the sacred space of Nataraj, with the consequence that he is ultimately destroyed. The language the novel uses to describe the moment of Vasu's intervention is significant: "He came forward, practically tearing aside the curtain, an act which violated the sacred traditions of the press" (15). To invade that private space is to question the validity of Nataraj's social and economic claims. The symbolism of the novel is hardly problematic. Nataraj is the victim, the man of principle and the feminized figure of Sita who is abducted to the hills by Vasu, and so forth. And Vasu is the overreacher; he is *Bhasmasura* who challenges the gods and must be defeated. Add to this the significance of Vasu attempting to shoot an elephant, and a whole symbolic world is complete.

What is striking is not the allegorical structure so much as the way in which Nataraj and his world are positioned in relation to everyone else in the novel. The description of Nataraj at the beginning, his leisurely walk to the river, his ablutions, his moment of prayer to the sun—all these are suggestive of an innate purity:

> At the foot of the tree was a slab of stone on which I
> washed my dhoti and towel, and the dark hour resounded

with the tremendous beating of wet cloth on granite. I
stood waist-deep in water, and at the touch of cold
water around my body I felt elated. The trees on the
bank stood like shadows in the dusk. When the east
glowed I sat for a moment on the sand reciting a prayer
to the Sun to illumine my mind. (9)

This daily ritual is held up in opposition to the self-serving lawyer,
the avaricious landlord, the dishonest milk vendor, and others he
encounters each morning. A routine occurrence is in fact a carefully
constructed artifice that is both religious and ideological. Here is an
implied hierarchy, a manichean opposition that is casteistic, that
works with the dualities of purity and contamination, but is hardly
ever alluded to in straightforward terms. This whole episode,
leisurely, anecdotal, and almost inconsequential in the typical
Narayan mode, is precisely how the fictional world operates. Daily
activities, such as bathing in the river or selling diluted milk, are so
ordinary that vernacular literature would not mention them unless
they become the occasion for providing an abrupt twist to the plot.
For Narayan, these activities make up the narrative; not because he
is writing for the West, but because they are framed by an ideological vision. The notion of "purity" is associated with the river, the
sun, with prayer, and all these are seen as natural to Nataraj and set
up in contrast to everyone else he meets. The activities are quotidian. The positioning and sequential arrangement of these activities
within the larger narrative underscore the artifice. Nataraj's world is
an idyllic one, constantly confronted with a materialistic and dishonest one, but it remains untainted until Vasu arrives on the scene.
Relate such episodes to the life of his father, who during his final
days spends most of his time reading the *Ramayana,* or Sastri who
leaves early in order to perform the *Satyanarayana Puja,* and one gets
a picture of caste structure within which the novel works. And surprisingly, Narayan succeeds in invoking a complex network of
social relations without ever invoking caste. Almost always, his
characters seem to exist in a casteless South India. As D.A. Shankar

quite rightly points out, "caste, in fact, has little or no bearing on the psyche of Narayan's characters: there isn't any structural or organic relationship between the characters and their caste" (51).

Granted, Narayan hardly ever creates characters in neatly schematic terms, so Nataraj is often envious of the complete disregard for conventional morality that Vasu displays. But in essence, Nataraj is the educated man who prints books, saves elephants, organizes temple festivals to celebrate the marriage of Radha and Krishna, and maintains a nuclear family. All these activities create in him a balance of tradition and modernity that in turn project him as the ideal of the novel. He is the moral centre of the work, a centre made possible by elisions and gaps that obscure the essentialism of such a creation. When asked in an interview about where he likes to live in India, Narayan responds: "I like Madras because I was born there and because in Madras the ancient and modern coexist....Some Madrasis are very orthodox. There are parts of the city where people with a traditional background in Sanskrit are still living" (236-37). And it is this world that he creates in his fiction—one that justifies the secular by invoking the religious (a version of the religious that is hegemonic, that belongs to the past).

If the beginning of the novel establishes notions of purity and contamination in relation to the workplace, the rest of the novel also demarcates the private sphere, as, for example, when Nataraj's wife does not admit the temple dancer Rangi into her house. The private space is sacred—hardly a place for untouchables like a temple dancer. Sastri, for strategic reasons, invites Rangi into his house and elicits information, but that in no way compromises his sense of purity. Sastri remains untouched by the various goings-on in the novel and disappears when the press is invaded by the police and others associated with the investigation of Vasu's death. The novel does not tell us why Nataraj does not admit Rangi into his house or the complex network of identities that establish her ambivalent position as a temple dancer and a prostitute. She is a stereotype, very much like several of the marginal characters in the novel whose positions within the world of Malgudi are left unexplained.

Nataraj is the liberal humanist, the benevolent middle-class printer who thinks nothing of not admitting a temple dancer into his house. By the same token, the Muslim trader becomes the subject of satire. They belong to the margins and appear as caricatures rather than characters.

Similar to the private space, the landscape too becomes a valuable trope in the assertion of a particular world view. The river, the forest, animals, and birds are all part of an overarching tradition in which myth, legend, and fable converge to establish dichotomies. It is significant that Nataraj finds the river a source of purity and the jungle an embodiment of evil, because the dichotomy draws its symbolic force from a range of religious and secular texts, particularly the *Ramayana*. In Narayan the natural landscape is never a backdrop; it is always a necessary part of the cultural makeup of the world he projects. In other words, nature has an archetypal rather than contemporary significance, and the mapping of nature enhances the artifice of his work.

A number of episodes which are memorable for sheer comedy are embedded in a framework that tacitly alludes to other texts and thereby invokes another level of meaning. A case in point is the "kidnapping" of Nataraj by Vasu, and the former's response: "I was struck with a sudden fear that this man was perhaps abducting me and was going to demand a ransom for releasing me from some tiger cave. What would my wife and little son do if they were suddenly asked to produce fifty thousand rupees for my release? . What was to happen to Sastri? If my wife appealed to him would he have the sense to go to the police and lead them to the tiger cave guarded by this frightful man with a dark halo over his head" (34). Beneath the humour, the intertext is the *Ramayana*, so the episode then becomes a retelling of the abduction of Sita by Ravana, the demon king. The myth not only underscores the dualism, but also gives both the characters and the event a symbolic significance that works in tandem with the comedy.

Critical studies of the novel have also drawn attention to a possible allegorical reading that sees the central conflict between tradi-

tion and modernity. Such an analysis would imply quite rightly that
a simple binarism would hardly suffice in a work that consistently
reveals the indeterminacy of the central character who finds himself drawn to the hedonism and "impurity" of the taxidermist.
Fakrul Alam's psychoanalytical reading of *The Man-Eater of Malgudi*
is devoted to establishing the villain as in some ways the alter ego
of the protagonist.[7] The conclusion of the novel makes that identification crucial to the narrative movement. Nataraj's admiration
for Vasu is based on Vasu's liberal attitude to sexuality, his devotion
to science and progress. Thus these values are an acknowledgment
of a colonial inheritance rather than a concession to the marginalized. In *My Dateless Diary* and elsewhere, Narayan makes it very
clear that he sees no real gap between the values of the West and
his own. The essentialism that underlies his work is in no way
affected by the ostensible admiration for the virtues of the West.

It is difficult to generalize about the period that becomes the
subject of Narayan's work. Even if one were to assume that he is
in fact recreating the 1930s, one needs to recognize the sweeping
changes and challenges that were taking place in South India. The
Dravidian movement, which began at the turn of the century as a
counter to the hegemonic control of the brahmins, was gathering
momentum, and assumptions about religion, and the whole caste
structure that upheld it, were being questioned. Even more significantly, the Self-Respect movement, spearheaded by E.V. Ramasamy,
was questioning the foundations of Aryan and caste superiority. As
Pandian notes, at this point, "the Movement could address a wide
range of issues by problematising a number of inferiorised identities. The newly opened up terrains of conflict was what ensured
the Self Respect Movement a basis for mass politics" (10). Anti-
colonial struggle was becoming increasingly complex with caste
and class affiliations being shown to be complicitous in various
ways. Even a cursory reading of Eugene Irschik's work on the
Dravidian movement would reveal that Narayan has been
extremely selective about the extent to which social realities would
be allowed to enter his fictional world.[8]

To insist that a writer must deal with these issues is to force an agenda on literature. And Narayan by his own admission is not interested in sociological relevance. But the Malgudi he presents masquerades as the real India with a clearly identifiable social and religious structure. As Anita Desai rightly maintains: "The bedrock is no longer made up of the old orthodoxies of religion, caste and family; everywhere are fissures, explosions, shatterings" ("Indian Fiction" 208). And none of this complexity is brought home in *The Man-Eater of Malgudi*. Narayan does not overtly champion a casteistic society. His integrity as a writer enables him to reveal the various contradictions in his world. But he is committed to an ideal that is in fact hegemonic, and the gaps in his narrative reveal his complicity in the orientalizing tendency of his work. His artifice–his counterrealism–lies in his capacity to naturalize a particular vision of society. He does not get the facts wrong. What he presents–admittedly, in a benign fashion–is a world that he is comfortable in.

Narayan is a complex writer, fully aware of the convergence of many contradictory forces in his world. Although his vision is static, he writes with an awareness for change. Work such as *The Dark Room*, as Teresa Hubel points out, "seems far more a call for change than serv[ing] as a panegyric to cosmic harmony" (127). Gayatri Spivak unpacks the wealth of cultural detail embedded in novels such as *The Guide*, but concludes by saying that the novel would fail to satisfy serious readers "precisely because the limpid prose would seem a bit 'unreal'; a tourist's convenience directed toward a casual unmoored international audience" (129-30). Narayan's world, then, is an imagined one, a fantasy generated by nostalgia for a world that probably never existed. But it is a world kept alive by a whole tradition of ancient writing that he draws on.

It would be futile to seek in Narayan departure from realism in the manner of Western writing. His counterrealism is a product of at least two impulses. The first is that he draws from a tradition that sees reality as a combination of the natural and the supernatural. The other is his careful selection of material to circumvent the referential in favour of a world that is ideologically determined–one that does not often acknowledge the multiple intersections and contingencies of colonial and postcolonial India. The conventions of realism are retained in part, but his success lies in his capacity to mask his artifice within the conventions of realism. And the fact that he writes in English enables him to work with an audience that is a willing participant in the subtle shift from one form to another. When Rushdie, writing in the 1980s, draws self-consciously from Indian epics and the tradition of orality, he advertises the fictiveness of his construct. It is only through defamiliarization that he deconstructs the real. Narayan does the reverse: he blends the traditions of the past and naturalizes his fictive world to uphold a Brahminical and patriarchal world.

CHAPTER 3

H. Hatterr and Sauce Anglaise: G.V. Desani

All About H. Hatterr begins with a prefatory "warning" that includes an anecdotal account of a disgruntled peasant who tries to derail a goods train because his house had been burgled, and a short dialogue about the status of this novel as gesture. This is the first indication that G.V. Desani's only novel challenges conventional notions of realism. Metafictional in intent, the dialogue between the surrogate author and reader ends with the author conceding that the limits of the novel can be stretched to include the present work, although it should probably be labelled more accurately as a *gesture* rather than a novel:

> *Indian middle-man* (to Author): Sir, if you do not identify your composition a novel, how then do we itemise it? Sir, the rank and file is entitled to know.
> *Author* (to Indian middle-man): Sir, I identify it a *gesture*. Sir, the rank and file is entitled to know.
> *Indian middle-man* (to Author): Sir, there is no immediate demand for *gestures*. There is immediate demand for novels. Sir, we are literary agents, not free agents.

Notes to chapter 3 are on pp. 191-92.

> *Author* (to Indian middle-man): Sir, I identify it a novel.
> Sir, itemise it accordingly. (12)

The author/narrator remains deliberately vague about the precise definition of the terms, thereby letting the work speak for itself. Among the few critical articles and one monograph on Desani that have appeared over the last five decades, Syd Harrex's analysis of *Hatterr* focuses on the notion of gesture as performance. As he puts it: "consider the word 'gesture' as it applies to physical actions and expressions of personality, consider the very theatrical qualities of Desani's writing, and it follows that *Hatterr* is aptly described as a dramatic gesture. Desani has virtually turned the novel into a performing art, just as his characters perpetually make performances of their own lives"[1] (215). A gesture is also a truncated form of action, an act that is less dependent on a temporal framework than the multiple intersections of the moment. Desani's artifice thus becomes an act of combining various modes, of accommodating the visual and the dramatic properties of drama within the framework of the novel. At the very end of the novel, in what serves as a mock-defence of the work, Rambeli (alias Beliram) argues that motive, moral, and plot are essential aspects of each chapter, thereby implying that, unlike Mark Twain who said about his work that "persons attempting to find a motive in this narrative will be prosecuted, persons attempting to find a moral in it will be banished, persons attempting to find a plot in it will be shot" (309), this novel does in fact conform to those features that define a conventional novel. But obviously, the very assertion also admits the opposite.

In terms of genre, the difference between a novel and a gesture is also illustrated, albeit obliquely, through analogy in which a causal link between the two episodes pertaining to the peasant is conspicuously absent. According to an unnamed Anglo-Indian writer in the novel: "Melodramatic *gestures* against public security are a common form of self-expression in the East. For instance, an Indian peasant, whose house had been burgled, will lay a tree across a railway line, hoping to derail a goods train, just to show his opinion of life. And the magistrates are far more understand-ing" (12). If at one level the whole incident of derailing a train could be read as a parody of abstruse psychoanalytical theories of motive, it is also a way of saying that causality along traditional lines of realism is not the objective of this novel. Put differently, the judge who understands the reasoning of the peasant is no dif-ferent from the discerning reader who perceives the necessary dis-junction between one action and another. Causality along empiri-cal lines, which would be a characteristic feature of realism, is hardly the mode of this novel. *Hatterr* begins with a binarism that equates the novel with forms of causality and linearity, and a "ges-ture" with properties that are associative, synchronic, and coun-terrealistic. The distinction that Cronin draws between Narayan as novelist and fabulist finds an echo in the self-reflexive comment with which *Hatterr* begins.

If one were to look for literary precedents and followers for Desani's novel, the texts would probably be modernist rather than the mimetic works of the nineteenth century. The references to "Shanti," given with the English translation, suggest the presence of T.S. Eliot and the final section of the novel ends with a refer-ence to Kurt S., an obvious intertextual reference to Conrad. The allusion to Conrad is particularly significant, for Desani's work too is a quest narrative about a character who, like Kurtz, decides to "go native" only to discover that an imagined "other" offers no easy panacea. In fact, at least two reviews that appeared soon after a revised edition of the novel was published [by Farrar, Strauss and Young in 1951] discuss both this novel and *At Swim-Two-Birds* by Flann O'Brien as inheritors of the tradition of Joyce. Delmore Schwartz sees both texts as examples "of a new mood and indeed a new tendency in fiction" (577) and adds that "both authors owe something to Joyce" (578). The comparison with Flann O'Brien is, however, a fruitful one, not only because both texts share a sense of wild humour and linguistic play, but also because both reflect something of the modernist sensibility of Joyce. The spirit of modernism—the pervasive sense of despair, the loss of faith in traditional systems of order, the awareness of multiple layers of consciousness—are all intrinsic to Desani's work as well.

More specifically, Nolan Miller comments that "Desani is presenting, by auto-inoculation it would seem, the portrait of a man—but a very special man, a man of the East, coping with a rational adaptation to the West" (240). The literary culture that affected him would be much clearer if we had a comprehensive account of Desani's life in England. But the details of his life are scanty, and apart from the facts that have appeared in occasional essays, nothing very much is known (although it is evident that in the 1930s he was a lecturer at the Imperial Institute in London and a broadcaster for the BBC).[2] We do know that writers such as Mulk Raj Anand who had begun writing in the 1930s were influenced heavily by the literary and intellectual climate of Britain, and it is only plausible that someone as erudite as Desani, living in the West, would have been cognizant of the cultural practices around him.

Alternatively, it is possible to argue, as Amitav Ghosh does in a note written soon after Desani's death in November 2000, that the novel takes an oppositional stance, in two ways, both of which are linked. According to Ghosh, *Hatterr* is, in fact, a sustained and complex interrogation of modernism; by the same token it is also a "profoundly resourceful defence of certain non-Western spiritual and metaphysical ideas" ("Regarding" 1). In short, the overarching ontological assumptions of modernity are pitted against a very different Eastern spirituality. In terms of narrative mode, Ghosh maintains that the "opaqueness of *Hatterr*," unlike the magic realism of recent writers, arises from the desire among writers "to make themselves heard in an idiom that barely acknowledged their right to its use" ("Regarding" 1).

It is possible to maintain that *Hatterr* is reminiscent of eighteenth-century fiction, particularly of Fielding, in the direct commentary of the author and the picaresque mode of having Hatterr go through a series of adventures, or of Laurence Sterne in its linguistic play and self-consciousness, but the more immediate prece-

dents would be the modernist writers. For critics, the issue of literary precursors has been a problematic one. Molly Ramanujam, for
instance, says that "the repetitive episodic rhythm brings it close to
Candide, except Desani tends to be non-dualistic. The representative allegoric nature of the narrative brings it near the medieval
morality play" (21). D.M. Burjorjee agrees but moves further: "it is
an Everyman allegory, a symbolist novel of quest, a *Bildungsroman*,
a cultural and social satire and, above all, a philosophical dialogue"
(216). In a work that is self-consciously subversive and densely
intertextual, precedence is hard to establish with any degree of
accuracy. If the tone of irreverence reminds one of Cervantes and
Sterne, the sheer exuberance of word play reflects the influence of
James Joyce or even Dickens.

Equally important is the evocation of Lewis Carroll and the
deliberate parallel with *Alice's Adventures in Wonderland*. The extreme
precision of the novel's structure serves as a reminder that Lewis
Carroll was a mathematician. More importantly, the notion of nam-
ing the central character Hatterr is the surest way of establishing an
intertextual link. H. Hatterr is really a combination of both Alice
and the Mad Hatter. The expulsion of H. Hatterr from the club is
the symbolic equivalent of falling down the rabbit hole. The parallels between the two texts are many: Mad Hatter's preoccupation
with time finds an echo in H. Hatterr's own failure to fulfil his quest
because time operates in a very different manner in the world he
encounters. The fairy tale jettisons logic and problematizes the relation between language and reality. Similarly, caught in a world he
does not understand, Desani's character is forced to recognize that
language creates its own reality, and identity is indeterminate. As in
Alice in Wonderland, in this novel the referent is also always suspect.

In Indian writing there is very little to establish, at the level of
narrative form, a link between Narayan and Desani, or for that
matter, with those who followed Desani. One of the curious
aspects of Indian writing is that, unlike in the Caribbean or in West
Africa, where one has a sense that writers were being influenced by
each other (facilitated, no doubt, by the presence of influential

local journals) there is no sense of a literary tradition that allows for influence and emulation. Even efforts such as P. Lal's Writer's Workshop were intended to facilitate publication rather than create a structure to enable a literary tradition. By the time Desani started writing, Indian literature in English was more than eighty years old, yet none of it appears to have impinged on Desani. Narayan drew on multiple traditions, Eastern and Western, cutting across genre in the process. But there is very little to link Desani with Narayan, not even the humour which arises from very different impulses. Narayan's humour, for instance, is germane to the Indian way of life. It is the humour one encounters in private and public and arises naturally out of everyday life. Desani's humour is often literary in that the artifice provides the context.

And yet the movement from Narayan to Desani is a logical one, not because it facilitates a temporal model necessary for establishing a tradition but because they were both testing the limits of a spiritual India. Narayan positions himself as an insider, in the same way Anita Desai does later, and to some extent Suniti Namjoshi after that. Desani locates himself as an outsider, in much the same way as Rushdie and Ghose do a few decades later. Narayan projects an imagined world to consolidate a static India; Desani does the same thing to deconstruct the idea of a spiritual India. The relation between the two finds a parallel in Fielding and Sterne. Despite the very different narrative modes they use and the mutually incompatible conclusions they reach, they do subscribe to the idea of the "literariness" of fiction, and belong to a tradition that is very different from that of, say, A. Madhavaiah, K.S. Venkataramani, or Mulk Raj Anand.

In terms of form, it is Rushdie (who admits, somewhat belatedly, the influence of Desani) and later Allan Sealy who write in a manner that establishes a line of continuity.[3] Even more than Rushdie's work, Sealy's *The Trotter-Nama* (1988) is a direct inheritor of the Desani mode and content.[4] In general, however, *Hatterr* remains a somewhat quixotic and digressive work, and D.M. Bujorjee rightly makes the claim that "the synthesis in H. Hatterr's case required a new form, something which in its totality never before existed in either English or Indian literature" (219).

One of the first aspects that most critics, including Anthony Burgess in his introduction, draw attention to, and one that is the most conspicuous feature in the text, is the language which Hatterr himself acknowledges as a blend of different registers: "I write rigmarole English, staining your goodly godly tongue, maybe" (37). Language has been, and continues to be, a preoccupation among postcolonial authors, with experiments ranging from the nativism of Okot p'Bitek to the orality of Raja Rao and the dialect of Sam Selvon.[5] In each case, the departure from standard English becomes a way of articulating a particular local reality. The language of *Hatterr* is a hybrid of the archaic, the local, the Babu, and the colloquial. As Burgess points out in his introduction to the novel, "the colloquialism of Calcutta and London, Shakespearean archaisms, bazaar whinings, quack spiels, references to the Hindu pantheon, the jargon of Indian litigation, and shrill babu irritability seethe together" (10). The language raises interesting questions, mainly because the use of English is inevitably artificial, given the social context of the novel. But mimetic writers tend to have it both ways: they create characters who speak and behave in ways that are Western, but the context makes them Indian, thereby creating the illusion of a mimetic representation. In Desani, this illusion is very deliberately dispelled when the diction borders on caricature. Often in its mélange of voices, it is totally artificial and insistently intertextual, and the effect is one of artifice. Conventional usage gets pilloried with relish as the British, the Indians, and the Anglo-Indians are given a language that amounts to burlesque. Characters hardly ever speak to each other in a manner that approximates natural forms of speech, be it British, Indian, or hybrid. Instead, the language of formal utterance, of heightened speech, and hyperbole, is used to the point of parody. Here, for instance, is a dialogue between Hatterr and his friend Bannerjee:

> "Damme, Bannerjee," I confided in my pal, "I am in a
> hell of a trouble!"

"Is in the morning the pharaoh's spirit really troubled, as
the Good Book says? I am deeply sorry."
"Damme, old feller, you don't understand! I am in a hell
of a mess. A woman is enamoured of me!"
"I don't mind, Mr. H. Hatterr. Good luck to her.
Whereas, I deplore and deprecate sensual Leda-and-
Zeus love, I am wholeheartedly for romance. Is her
name Priscilla, or is it Daphne?" (42)

A whole range of voices, each reflecting a particular class affiliation, permeates the text and becomes one of its most distinctive
attributes. In that sense Spivak is right in singling out this trait as
something that sets the novel apart from other works of Indian literature. As she puts it, *Hatterr* is "a virtuoso novel where 'English'
attempts to claim its status as one of the Indian languages (belonging to a national underclass) through the technique of sustained literal translation of the vernacular rather than islands of direct mon-
strous speech in a sea of authorial Standard English" (128).
Desani's language, instead of creating the illusion that it is the "natural" idiom of the characters, thrives on its artificiality.

It is hardly surprising that a novel which self-consciously draws
attention to its language should also explore the relation between
language and reality. Since the novel constantly highlights the
deceptiveness of reality, the language, too, becomes an instrument
of deception. Each register, from the pompousness of the British
to the fake spirituality of Indian gurus, serves the purpose of
detracting from the truth. In a mode that has been popularized to
a great extent by Rushdie, the local idiom is translated literally and
juxtaposed with standard English to reinforce the absurdity of
what occurs, and to flaunt the notion of performance and artifice.
The curious combination of an idiom that is almost always recognizable as Anglicized Indian, with a richness of texture that goes
beyond the characters, is yet another aspect that prompts a comparison with Joyce. As Schwartz perceptively identifies, "the effort
to unite all the richness of intellect and learning with the common

speech of the people" (578) is one of Desani's major achievements. Of course, the diction is intentionally artificial, but it draws heavily on the idioms used by a particular segment of society.

Along with the defamiliarization and the obvious intertextuality of the dialogue, one gets a sense of how Desani's novel operates, and for that matter, the Indo-Anglian novel that belongs to the counterrealistic tradition. Even more so than Narayan, Desani sets the tone for this tradition. Despite Narayan's admiration for the West, he remains deeply rooted in India. Although what he projects may well be a construct, it is based on an imagined India where certain hierarchies were intact and a classificatory system for society was firmly entrenched.[6] Credibility is central to Narayan's writing. Desani on the other hand was, in many ways, an expatriate writer who had spent decades in England at the time of writing this novel. He reflects the diasporic sensibility that one perceives in Desai, Namjoshi, Ghose, and Rushdie. To make this point is not to establish a schema that identifies "native" with realism and "diasporic" with counterrealism. The distinction between the two is a matter of sensibility rather than migration.

It is conceivable that, for migrant writers, the everyday event becomes more distant with the passage of time, but the issue is how writers configure the relation between texts and the world rather than the biographical circumstances of exile. Vernacular writers have always worked with non-realist forms, particularly when they felt that realism would not suffice for what they sought to express. Allan Sealy, for example, spends a great deal of time in India, but that hardly alters the fact that his sensibility inevitably leads him to non-realist forms. Desani, having left India in his teens, was to return to India after more than thirty years, and that too only for a short span before moving to Burma and then to the USA. His sensibility was shaped by living on the cusp, the hybrid sensibility about which Rushdie speaks in *Imaginary Homelands*.[7] A special issue of *The New Yorker* in 1997 published a portion of Desani's journal, begun after the publication of the novel. This is how it begins:

> I am going back to India. I expect to return. I am leav-
> ing all my things—books, manuscripts, clothes, every-
> thing. I can truthfully say that all my ambitions and
> expectations from this city have been fulfilled. Yet, I am
> not happy. This is a defeat. I am ashamed to admit it to
> anyone. (62)

And the final lines: "I imagine myself a man of reason, yet I cannot think what I am doing *here*, in India, in this third-class queue,
unless it is for the plain hell of it." (68). This is the dilemma of
migrancy; one can neither stay nor stay away, sees too much and
too little, and one's characteristic location is the cusp.

What Desani sees is Nirad Chaudhuri's India, a Circe that beck-
ons and destroys; more specifically, he sees Naipaul's India, the
been-to version with all its confusion, corruption, and lack of
vision.[8] The journal essentializes the subcontinent and resorts to
stereotypes in a way that shows how the rhythm of everyday life is
alien to the author. For the most part, the excerpt from his journal
reads very much like *An Area of Darkness*, which, with all its desire
for honesty, remains unaware of a complex social fabric. What he
sees is not necessarily false, but it remains a perspective that
belongs to the insider-outsider. All the accolades notwithstanding,
the novel is often trapped in essentialisms, about which little has
been said (although Harrex moves in that direction when he says
that "the final laugh is at the expense of the absurdist author-hero
who, while creating fantasy situations and manipulating fantastic
gestures, in a fictive universe, has no power to control life's events,
and consequently resorts to satirising other and mercilessly ridicul-
ing himself"[9] [237]). In a different context, Spivak maintains that
"if literature is a vehicle of cultural self-representation, the 'Indian
cultural identity' projected by Indo-Anglian fiction...can give little
more than a hint of the seriousness and contemporaneity of the
many 'Indias' fragmentarily represented in the many Indian literatures" (127). The comment is particularly applicable to a novel such
as *Hatterr* with its limited social spectrum. Nonetheless, the novel is

redeemed by its abundance, its capacity to expose and lampoon the very premises that served both imperial domination and nationalist pride. The central tenet that informs the work and all the encounters of Hatterr is the notion of "contrast" which surfaces in various contexts, and is affirmed at the end in Beliram's exposition. Contrast implies binarisms, the coexistence of opposites. Or, as Beliram puts it, after a lengthy discussion, "the conclusion drawn from the above puzzles, iterations and frustrations, is, that, Life is full of *opposite circumstances*" (293). At one level, the ideal of contrast seems to imply that amidst all the trickery that pervades the land, the fundamental decency of Bannerjee remains a constant. But more importantly, there is a curious irony in the fake gurus going to extraordinary lengths to find a victim, in being totally comfortable with two incompatible stances. In Desani's world there is often no middle ground, no redeeming virtue, no shades of grey; one of the limitations of a work that invokes writers such as Rudyard Kipling and Joseph Conrad is that its discourse works with orientalist assumptions.

That Desani's sense of India is hardly simplistic is evident as much in the novel as in his subsequent work *Hali* which is a collection of myths, fables, and stories. Initially published two years after the novel, *Hali* demonstrates a range that is not always evident in *Hatterr*. "Hali," for instance, is myth, retold not in the way that Narayan retells the *Ramayana* but rather as symbolic discourse in which a creation myth gets narrated to accommodate and synthesize a wide range of dualities. A reading of "Hali" along structuralist lines, or even within a religious and philosophical frame, offers insights very different from those of *Hatterr*. For one thing, the tone is far more solemn, with hardly any sense of burlesque or subversion. The myth itself is carefully structured to reveal multiple layers of meaning. Primarily a "personal allegory" (according to Ramanujam), "Hali" (with obvious echoes of "Hari") works with notions that are fundamentally opposed to male-centred myths of origin. Various forms of transgression occur as Hali moves from one developmental phase to another. The reconciliation that concludes the myth closes off the possibilities of fragmentation and open-endedness in a manner that is familiar in the retelling of myth. "Hali" is not anti-myth. It is, rather, a reshaping of traditional myth that offers new perspectives while preserving the old taxonomies. In Desani's corpus, the works seek to reaffirm and consolidate rather than question and destabilize. Ramanujam makes the insightful observation that "Desani's distinction is not that he is the creator of *Hali*, but that the writing of it transformed the writer" (98). If one were to trace a pattern of continuity at the level of subject matter between Narayan and Desani, it is to "Hali" rather than *Hatterr* that one would turn.

Far removed from the mode of the myth, *Hali* also includes stories such as "The Barber of Sahibsarai" which work within the structure of a quest narrative–although clearly as parody. It establishes several binarisms, including village and city, dull and shrewd, young and old, etc. It is satire, gothic tale, cautionary narrative, all within the general framework of mimesis. Clearly symbolic, its allusions to castration, phallic symbolism, and ignorance can hardly be missed. The story is a reminder that realism (although bordering on the Gothic) is not entirely unknown in Desani's corpus. Because he drew from a tradition of orality for this work, we know that the counterrealism of *Hatterr* was a conscious choice.

Neither entirely realism nor counterrealism, "Since a Nation Must Export, Smithers" belongs to a completely different genre, one that is much closer to what Todorov identifies as the uncanny. Having discussed the indeterminacy that distinguishes this mode of writing, Todorov claims that "in speaking of an *uncanny* event, we do not take into account its relations with the contiguous events, but its connections to other events, remote in the series but similar or contrasting" (91). As ostensibly diachronic movement holds the story together, it is the synchronic element, including patterns of repetition that accounts for its texture. If the story is "about" anything, it is probably about how the Other gets configured within a colonial framework, and how the native and the colonizer become willing participants in a process that fetishizes the country. This tale is about transforming human beings into mummies, into little Gandhis, which are then exported, since a nation, in order to survive must export. Such stories belong to fantasy or magic realist forms of antirealism and display the kinds of self-reflexive characteristics that Linda Hutcheon discusses in her work, *Narcissistic Narrative*. While *Hali* has generally received very little attention, it certainly merits some, both in its own right, and as a frame for reading *Hatterr*.

There is a prodigiousness about *Hatterr* that was not repeated until Rushdie arrived on the scene. But while Rushdie's vision is predominantly political, Desani's is largely mythical, or structural in Bruce Lincoln's sense of the term.[10] Patterns that provide cohesiveness and stability to society are introduced at different moments, but always with a sense of provisionality. An underlying ambivalence both ridicules and empowers the eponymous protagonist of the novel. There is also a strong visual quality imparted by the language and that invokes the sense of performance. And very much like ritual, Desani works with structures that define the nation in order to interrogate the epistemological assumptions behind Indian discourse. Thus the various meetings between Hatterr and the saints need to be seen not only as farce or an encounter between East and West, but as ritual (with all its ideological assumptions), subverted and satirized.

If *Hatterr* marks a watershed, it's at least partly because it is the first major Indo-Anglian work to look at Indian realities through the eyes of an Anglo-Indian. The Anglo-Indians, like the Burghers in Sri Lanka, were often the first victims of the colonial project and postcolonial nationalism. They are visual emblems of a syncretism that neither the rulers nor the ruled wished to acknowledge. They do not belong in the land of their birth, although they cannot really belong anywhere else. Nirad Chaudhuri, who speaks very disparagingly about this group whom he calls "half-caste" has this to say about Anglo-Indian men: "As for a man of Eurasian origin, it was virtually impossible for him to marry among the pure British. He could not even mix with them in society on an equal footing. The

British in India showed yet another similarity with the Hindus in thinking that the Eurasian who knew his place and kept to it was a better man than the Eurasian who wanted to pass off as an Englishman" (290). Unlike other groups that may have benefited under British rule for strategic reasons, or were wooed by the majority in the post-independence era for various political and symbolic reasons, the Anglo-Indian never found a niche. Having served as junior administrators, railway officials, journalists, and the like, they found themselves at the crossroads as the British made preparations to leave. They spoke a language that branded them as outsiders but their identity continued to be, willy nilly, Indian. A movie such as *Bhowani Junction*, produced in 1957, captures all the ambivalence and pathos of this group that neither the colonized nor the decolonized imagination wished to acknowledge. It is within this context that the novel needs to be seen. When Schwartz, for instance, maintains that the novel possesses "no inherent logic of narrative structure, no necessary movement and conclusion" (578), he fails to perceive that the novel cannot be fully understood except in relation to a very specific historical context. From trivial incidents (such as the naked Hatterr being given an Indian railways towel to cover himself) to the larger architectonics of the novel, the narrative of an Anglo-Indian has a particular valency.

The format of each discrete chapter (loosely connected by the presence of Hatterr in true picaresque fashion) consists of Digest, Instruction, Presumption, and Life-Encounter. This itself mimics and mocks the various stages associated with learning, with the progression of life, and with the premises of caste where a classificatory system is invoked. Reminiscent of medieval philosophical systems and the more recent triadic systems, the novel offers a structure that holds out the promise of understanding. Particularly the guru-shishya mode which is central to the learning process, and the stages of listening, thinking, and understanding are put in almost reverse order. As in chapter 1, the Digest offers a series of mock-serious questions rather than answers. The Instruction, given by the sage of Calcutta to his disciple, is in the form of a fable (with sufficient ethnic and religious markers to indicate both temporal proximity and distance) ending with a moral that is both insipid and anticlimactic. Then there is a brief exhortation in the Presumption that anticipates the moral or the Life-Encounter. The Life-Encounter is almost a *mise-en-abyme* of the Instruction, with the difference that it is contemporary and relates to Hatterr. In terms of structure, the parallels are intentionally similar.

The format immediately dispenses with conventional notions of plot and the epistemological assumptions that underlie such paradigms. The mode frustrates the reader who looks for a cohesive narrative thread, but the intention of the novel is to demolish those structures that offer the promise of meaning. The "ideal" reader of the novel recognizes the arbitrariness of what purports to be normative and also learns the symbiotic relation between a digressive, fragmented narrative and a subversive version of a spiritual India.

In chapter 1, the Instruction is about a king who makes love to his chambermaid and is rudely interrupted by a voice that cries "Stop Fool." Failing to identify the caller and convinced that the injunction was a divine message, the king finally offers a huge reward to anyone who identifies the god who had spoken. The reward is then claimed by a Muslim potter who says that his parrot was abducted by a hawk which, when it passed the king's palace, had really shouted at the hawk and not at the king. The truth, however, is that the injunction was made by the queen who used her powers of ventriloquism to foil the plans of the king but is unable to own up to it. The potter thus becomes the beneficiary.

In contrast to this fable is the Life-Encounter which involves Hatterr's amorous involvement with his washerwoman, his subsequent dismissal from a British club, his decision to go native after his total disillusionment with the British, his new job as a journalist, and his encounter with a sage who steals all his clothes. The sage and his disciple, we find out, are in the business of selling second-hand clothes and the unsuspecting Hatterr, who is sent to interview the sage, returns empty-handed and naked, except for a towel that belongs to the Indian Railway. In both instances, the marginal figure becomes the victor and the triumph has a peculiar appropriateness to it although it lies outside the realm of moral rectitude.

Framed by pseudo-philosophical utterances, the two narratives make up the chapter and the first of Hatterr's many adventures. Each encounter deals with a different aspect of Indian society, but the overall objective is akin to ritual. Each story has a paradigmatic aspect that invokes patterns ensuring the basis of society. The sage and disciple run through both, although kingship defines one and the British club defines the other. In both cases the expectation is one of stability, disruption, and the restoration of stability. But in both instances, the reverse occurs. The Maharaja (presumably Hindu) loses half his kingdom to a Muslim potter. The Anglo-Indian Hatterr is relieved of all his clothes by an unscrupulous sage. The potter and the sage are trickster figures who succeed in subverting established patterns of power and hegemony. Anecdotal, digressive, and full of elisions, the chapter forces a rethinking of the conventions of realism.

Given the framing and *mise-en-abyme* method of the chapter, it is hardly possibly to associate the novel with conventional realism. The action is more true of ritual than of mimesis. The crucial difference is that ritual here only serves to establish easy binaries and reinforces essentialisms–Bannerjee as the well-meaning Anglophile, Hatterr as the dupe, the saint and his disciple as rogues. Images that have resonance within a cultural context are chosen randomly, emptied of their meaning, and placed in different situations. Thus the hawk abducting the parrot is a caricature of the abduction of Sita by Ravana. Hatterr shedding his clothes is a version of the Congress plea to Indians to stop wearing clothes manufactured outside the country. The good, honest, but poor worker being rewarded by the king is yet another instance of how legend accommodates the marginalized within the social structure. All these are introduced, but in contexts where the signs are emptied of their meaning and given new ones. Within the narrative, all these images take on a new level of meaning that ridicules established norms. In the special issue of *Daedalus* devoted to India, T.G. Vaidyanathan shows in great detail the ways in which the guru-shishya system works in both its ideal and more mundane forms.[11] For him, all aspects of Indian life are framed by this basic hierarchical principle. Desani's chapter is the very opposite of this principle. If Hatterr learns anything at all as a result of his calamitous encounters, it is in spite of gurus rather than because of them. The Digest, which promises to be a summary, lists a series of questions, none of it in any logical sequence, but each one suggesting the success of duplicity. The Presumption, which precedes the Life-Encounter, advances an ethical basis for misogyny. It serves as a framing device for the story that follows.

Obviously aware of the potential for misreading or total incomprehension, Desani adds a subsequent defence, not by the sympathetic Bannerjee, as one would expect, but by Rambeli (an interesting name with multiple connotations), the lawyer now turned spiritual leader and Vedantist, who feels the need to defend Hatterr. If one were to give this section an allegorical reading, one would be struck by the irony of a spiritual leader and purist defending a very hybrid Hatterr who had been totally duped by spiritual leaders.

Offered as a defence of the book and of Hatterr by Rambeli, this part is in itself a critique and parody of literary criticism. The objective of Rambeli is really to advance his own credibility as a critic and scholar, and to this end he provides a wide range of allusions, personal anecdotes, footnotes, etc. that reflect his own erudition. Also, in Rambeli's defence, the quest is for a narrative closure and a moral conclusion to the novel. Various theories are advanced, all leading to a fairly universalist position that everyone should love each other. There is often a deliberate contradiction in Rambeli's point of view: and he begins by saying that the work is autobiographical but later claims that it is about moral values and the need for universal love. The notion of contrasts which is advanced leads to easy binarisms, essentialist statements, and an obsequious deference to Western modes of inquiry. The whole section is wonderfully parodic as the following reveals:

> Nevertheless, the above conclusion being a philosophi-
> cal locutory, the question remains, how to apply this
> induction to the majority, the hoi polloi, the fille de
> chambre and garçon, in short, the popular ignorants, not
> minding the literati which understands such-like dialec-
> tic and deductions. (294)

If it serves any purpose, it is probably to warn the reader against over-hasty generalizations about the content of the book. Thus the defence turns out to be a long rambling affair with several micro-narratives. They insist on the futility of attempting a conventional mimetic reading of the novel.

Rambeli's attempt notwithstanding, the structure of the novel is still problematic. There is no alternative structure, as in, for instance, *Ulysses*, to encapsulate the various encounters that constitute the work. Spatially, it is possible to argue that Hatterr moves from one place to another, symbolically represented through the sage of Madras, Calcutta, Delhi, etc., until he is finally duped by a guru who represents the whole of India. The element that holds the novel together is not its teleology or, for that matter, a religious or secular order. In any event, the progression to sanyasin is constantly thwarted by the gurus who are themselves quite young. There is no ostensible social structure to make the novel cohere along traditional lines. In fact, there is no reason why one chapter should precede or follow another.

Desani himself offers little help in his prefatory comments. He claims: "I never was involved in the struggle for newer forms of expression. Neo-morality, or any other thing! What do you take me for? A busybody?" (17). Refusing to call it a novel, he refers to it as an "autobiographical" and a "mosaic-organon" and a "medico-philosophical grammar" in the title page. The playful refusal to classify the work underlies an insistent concern with taxonomy and a greater willingness to subvert rather than assert fixed and mono-lithic positions.

Hatterr is significant for its recognition of the artifice that is inherent in the Indo-Anglian novel. It uses its hybridity to full advantage by juxtaposing multiple signifying systems that became readily available within the colonial context. Thus Bannerjee's spontaneous gift of an imported all-in-one vest to Hatterr is at once a gesture of magnanimity and a supreme irony. The gift marks the absurdity of the mimic person and identifies Bannerjee as a potential victim of an alien system that is no less duplicitous than the local one, albeit with more authority on its side. Written at a time when India was moving from a colonized country to a post-colonial nation, the novel reveals the paradoxes inherent in the various claims made in the moment of transition. The change from colonialism to nationhood was seen as a seamless narrative, framed by a dynamic and empowering indigenous tradition. The counter-realism of the novel not only destabilizes the grand claims but also reflects on its own ambiguities as fiction. (Three decades later Rushdie was to do the same thing, for reasons that are strikingly similar.)

The novel remains very much a resistant text. At one level, it draws freely on orientalist images of India to offer various tales. But it is also a carefully structured work: the building blocks of the narrative entice the reader with a teleological frame, only to shape the narrative in different ways. If, for instance, the potter and the Maharaja refer to a period when one form of rulership was on the verge of giving way to another, the second one locates itself on the eve of independence. And in both cases, the trickster figures are implicated in the structures they subvert.

Despite the randomness that appears to characterize the work, *Hatterr* is far from fragmentary. Some aspects of the novel do not change. Bannerjee is always loyal to Hatterr; Hatterr never learns from experience, and the gurus never become spiritual. The pattern, then, is one of repetition with minor variations. Even the dog, Jenkins, remains constant in its cowardice. No one is particularly vicious. The predictability of actions thus becomes the norm. Given the year of publication, the novel adopts a particularly unusual form. Despite all the events leading up to the euphoria of Independence and the subsequent violence of the Partition, the

novel has very little referential solidity. If anything, it recalls a somewhat orientalist, timeless India, except that secular and material concerns eclipse any semblance of religiosity. The past and present are
thus juxtaposed in a manner that flaunts artifice.

Despite the discontinuous narrative, most episodes connect—even
what appears inconsequential, such as the narrative about Jenkins,
the dog (who is as much hybrid as its owner, but much more adept
at surviving in a land where the fittest survive). All the major
episodes involve gurus and the gullible Hatterr, but each episode
reveals a different facet of the overall preoccupation with contrast.
That the sages are named by different regions accentuates the differences among them. Thus the episode involving the Naga saint is also
an illustration of the familiar "diamond cut diamond" truism.
Hatterr begins with the grand ambition of seeking out buried
Mughal treasures, only to find that the Naga guru appropriates his
space, and also strips Hatterr naked and scatters his money. An obvious reiteration of the typical makes the sage a Naga and the quest
figure an Anglo-Indian; the juxtaposition prompts a historical/alle-
gorical reading of the chapter. Such episodes reveal the novel's overall strategy which the author himself explains early in the novel:
"Mimic me Truth successfully (that's to say, lie to me and achieve
belief) and I'd credit you with Art, Skill, Imagination, and intimate
Intelligence of Truth" (13).

Hatterr is a variant of the good soldier Schweik. He is part of a
world where he does not fully belong, but he's determined to test the
paradigms of wholeness with which this other world is legitimized.
He is a comic version of Conrad's Kurtz who is determined to go
native by seeking spiritual enlightenment. And what is more paradigmatic than the renouncer—the linchpin of a whole spiritual system?

The stage of the renouncer does not merely provide closure to the
four-fold system of human progress; the sage is also the emblem of
a spiritual system that stresses nondualism. Therein lies the framework for a form of realism. A whole ontological system gets valorized through the figure of the renouncer. Religious tales, including
the epics, the *Ramayana* and the *Mahabharata*, work with this figure

as the moral centre of a Hindu world. Despite all the instances of fake gurus, this figure holds a significant place in the minds of the people. The guru marks the culmination of a teleological narrative that underscores Hindu ontology. However idealistic this paradigm may be, it holds together every aspect of life. Subverting the guru demolishes the entire edifice.

It is thus appropriate that a text that subverts one of the foundational aspects of a Hindu world should be written on the eve of Independence. At a time when nationalist leaders such as Gandhi seemed to legitimize not only a renouncer figure but also one who could shape a nation's destiny while remaining untouched by material concerns, a novel such as *Hatterr* needed to be counterrealist. The renouncer was part of the realism of the time and this novel, which satirizes the saint figure, flaunts itself as a kind of counter discourse.

By writing in a mode that is distinctly counterrealistic, Desani points to the conventionality of the figure itself. That the testing must be done by one who is very much a gullible outsider to the Hindu scheme adds further irony to the monolithic and purist assumptions of a taxonomy. The parody is intentionally exaggerated, discontinuous, and episodic. But in the process it reveals the deep paradox of a secular world that validates its existence by invoking a spiritual ideal. The two are not entirely incompatible, but the renouncer is problematic, for he is supported by a system that he spurns.

Hatterr is an exploration of this paradox. The shishya in search of a guru provides the structural basis for the text. But the language mocks, defamiliarizes, and ridicules the process. If realism aligned itself with the nationalist claim, counterrealism here is stoking the fires of skepticism. As the "warning" says,

> Improbable, you say?
> No, fellers,
> All improbables are probables in India. (27)

From the moment that the washerwoman exploits Hatterr, to the infatuation with Rosie, and the narrow escape from castration at the end, the motif of sexuality remains a constant presence. Forms of sado-masochism complement this preoccupation. At the other end of the spectrum is the saint figure, the otherworldly recluse. These contraries are a constitutive aspect of a literary and religious tradition where the two are harmonized. Whether in the four-fold stages of *brahmacharya, grahasta, vanaprastha,* and *sanyasa,* or in the larger symbolism of a spiritual order, the secular and the sacred are held together. The assertion of an essentialist Indianness is made possible by this fusion. For those concerned with bhakti marga, the journey from one place to another in the form of a pilgrimage is not unknown.

For Desani, who was himself given to rigorous spiritual practices, this novel probably becomes an occasion to test one reality against another. A totally syncretic mode that combines both the traditions of the West and the East serves as the ideal vehicle for drawing attention to a space outside the pragmatic and the orientalist. Indo-Anglian writers who remain steadfast in their loyalty to realism run the risk of nostalgia and subjectivity on the one hand, or sociological accuracy on the other. Either way, the result is likely to be unsatisfactory. There is something inherently paradoxical about realist writing in English in India. Writing about Anglo-Indian novelists in particular, Chaudhuri has this to say: "Even the novelists on India have become purveyors of sociological data…and then three quarters in ponderous solemnity, and a quarter in cold-blooded self-seeking malice, they turn out works which are no more fiction than blue-books are fables. In fact, at times they are documented with such apparent solidity that they may even be laid as evidence before committees for foreign aid" (12). Some of this may well be applicable to Indo-Anglian realist writers who, in the process of addressing an unfamiliar reader, feel obliged to catalogue what, in regional languages, would be considered totally redundant.

Despite the relative newness of Indo-Anglian writing, very few concessions are made to the Western reader or, for that matter, to

any reader in Desani's novel. The sweep of the novel is ency-
clopaedic; its defamiliarization is constant and intentional. Unlike
realist writing, it does not mask its conventionality or create the illusion of transparency. The trait that distinguishes this work from
Desani's more surrealist short stories is that, here, the Dickensian
excess distances empirical reality without erasing it altogether. In
the process, the novel avoids fidelity to social and cultural realities.
It thus encapsulates a very different space from the realism of vernacular literatures. At the same time, *Hatterr* does not aspire to the
conventionality of the epic tradition or the formal posturing of
other artistic forms. It reshapes local subject matter, viewing it
through the lens of Western narrative forms, to draw attention to
meta issues about the ontological basis of the nation itself. If the
central figure acts like the proverbial Mad Hatter, it is hardly
because the novel is unconcerned with significant issues.
Counterrealism in Indian writing, unlike in the West, does not question the claims of a unified world view. Rather, it recognizes the
limitations and strengths of writing in English in a country where
the English language occupies a unique, if limited, space. If Ghosh
is right in his assessment of Desani, Desani's unusual silence for so
many years has a great deal to do with his understanding of what
was possible. As Ghosh remarks, "Desani was unique in that he
alone had the courage to follow his perceptions to their natural
conclusion–into the unreachable otherness of silence" (1).

CHAPTER 4

Slipper Dragging and the Silent Piano: Anita Desai

Anita Desai's novel *Baumgartner's Bombay* concludes with the death of the ill-fated, exiled, and powerless Hugo at the hands of Kurt, the drug-crazed German. By turns poetic, ironic, and tragic, the episode reinforces the complexity of the moment, the confluence of various motifs, which permeate the novel and culminate at this point. The ambivalence surrounding the depiction of this scene and its significance in relation to the preoccupations of the novel are acknowledged by the author who comments in an interview that "life is a muddle, even history is a muddle, and [she] wanted Baumgartner's end to have that quality" (Ball and Kanaganayakam, "Interview" 34). Appropriately, the passage is also insistently sexual, and death becomes a form of penetration when Hugo is transformed into a feminized figure raped by Kurt:

> Then, with great speed, he raised the knife, then bent, and plunged it in, deep into that soft tallow so that it shuddered and let out a kind of whimper, or just a gasp, but some kind of flutter. It had to cease, or it had to be made to cease. Withdrawing the knife, he plunged it in

Notes to chapter 4 are on pp. 192-93.

again, and again, and again. With increasing slowness,
and increasing weakness, till all movement came to a
halt—the rocking, the quivering, the flutter, the gasp, all
ended. (219)

The context of an insane German killing an exiled and helpless Jew
invites a historical reading, but it also invokes other forms of marginality that relate more specifically to the world of the novel as
well. The language, with its many allusions, superimposes the
notion of gender and sexuality, power and control, thereby adding
to the depth of the description, and the manner in which the novel
orchestrates its closure.

Despite the feminization of Baumgartner, both at this moment
and throughout the novel, one is struck by the choice of
Baumgartner as the victim, when other characters, including Lotte,
could just as easily have served the purpose. Having written largely
about women all her life, Desai makes the unusual choice of por-
traying a man (and an outsider at that) as the protagonist in the
most autobiographical of all her novels. About her decision to
foreground a man, Desai says:

> Having written for so many years and in so many books
> about women's lives, and about the restrictions and lim-
> itations that an Indian woman has, I wanted to break
> free of that and see if I couldn't step out into the open
> world and write about action and experience, and I
> found the only way to do that was to assume a male per-
> sona. ("Interview" 32)

Although *Baumgartner's Bombay* has autobiographical elements,
Desai's autobiographical work is no less textual than any of her
previous work. She has commented that the novel occupies "the
earliest and deepest levels of [her] consciousness" and that the
text "will not mean as much to any reader as it does to [her]"
("English" 9). Yet there is enough intertextuality in the novel to

blur its referentiality. Baumgartner's terrifying encounter with the deity in the subterranean cave, for instance, clearly recalls E.M. Forster's *A Passage to India* and the novel's depiction of the Marabar Caves.[1] Even the name Kurt is a deliberate narrative strategy to recall Conrad and the quest narrative of *Heart of Darkness*. No less important are the many references to the Bible, to songs, nursery rhymes, and a host of other texts and authors. This novel, like so many of Desai's previous works, is clearly textual in that it constantly draws attention to its own grammar as a necessary aspect of its structure. Even the most subjective episodes in the text are framed by allusions that achieve the effect of defamiliarization.

The textuality of *Baumgartner's Bombay* and the relation between understanding and grammar are evident even as Lotte opens "the door with fumbling, ineffective movements as though she had forgotten its grammar, her fingers numb, tongue-tied as it were" (1). Language is the gateway to meaning, and despite its resistance to fixity, its "spidery" quality makes it a "kind of skein or web" (3) that unsettles and thwarts the quest of the characters. Even the ending of the novel is about numbers and language, a juxtaposition that embraces both to suggest that while numbers, with their claim to objectivity, provide "clues to a puzzle, a meaning to the meaningless" (230), language opens up the multiple layers of experience while retaining its centripetal focus. T.S. Eliot's epigraph to the book is not merely the philosophical underpinning—it is echoed in the very structure, thereby invoking a particular literary tradition as well.

Regardless of the experiential dimension, the novel announces its fictive quality, not only from the epigraph from "East Coker" that claims "in my beginning is my end" but also because the novel links the end with the beginning in the description of Lotte's departure from the scene of Baumgartner's death. The juxtaposition is striking: the literariness of the prose is always made clear, and if the tragedy is turned into farce with the arrest of an innocent man, the death also has the mythical quality of the crucifixion. Its performative quality is evident in the description of Lotte:

> When every lock was in place, she leant against the door
> in the theatrical manner that came naturally to
> her–pressing a packet of letters to her breast as years
> ago she had pressed a flower against a bosom still plump
> and warm, flowered with white and spotted with red
> spots, singing all the while to the stage-lights, her mouth
> open, a tunnel of red from which might issue either a
> trill or a howl. (1)

The diction that insists on its artifice complements the experiential element in ways that define Desai's particular mode.

The confluence of various strands–an awareness of societal conditions, the role of history and politics, the marginality of women, and the fictiveness of the narrative–is what makes Desai's writing resistant to any easy taxonomy. On the one hand, very much like Narayan, the referent is never far away from her writing. Often drawn from the middle class, her characters are recognizable types drawn from a wide spectrum of occupations. (It is this referential aspect that ensured the popularity of the Merchant Ivory production of *In Custody*). In fact, in novels such as *In Custody*, not only is the referent always present, the concern with the relative status of Urdu and Hindi makes the text both topical and quite controversial. It is, of course, a nice irony that even in the only work, which has the potential to generate controversy, the central issue is language itself. But the novels are hardly ever driven by the plots, and often the causal element is no more than perfunctory. Desai's strength lies in her experiment, in the solipsism of her textual worlds, and not in her skills as a realist. When realism plays a dominant role, there is almost always a corresponding loss in the appeal of the texts. The artifice is thus far more intrinsic to her writing, although it does not proclaim its experiment in the manner of, say, Desani. Her position thus remains problematic, and among the critics who have tried to locate her work, one of the more convincing ones is Meenakshi Mukherjee who sees in her work a shift from the public to the private. Working on the premise that Indo-

Anglian writing flaunts a public face, Mukherjee makes a case for Desai's distinctiveness, although she still places Desai within a univocal tradition. Mukherjee's taxonomy implies a corresponding change in the narrative mode although the focus of *The Twice-Born Fiction* is on a shift in perception rather than form.

In the fall 1989 issue of *Daedalus*, appropriately titled, "Another India," Anita Desai undertakes the task of providing a survey and a sample of contemporary Indian fiction. The process inevitably involves selection and categorization so the author's views and choices reveal as much about her own writing as they do about the Indo-Anglian literary scene. The distinctions she alludes to in establishing the boundaries of recent writing necessarily involve both the past and present, colonialist and nationalist discourse, and their complicity in fostering an epistemology that is both hegemonic and orientalist. Drawing attention to the literary practice of flaunting an atavistic culture, she suggests the need to transcend the boundaries of "imagined communities" (Benedict Anderson's term) in order to probe realities that have not found adequate expression.[2] Having posed the question "what do the words Indian literature evoke?" in her essay, she provides an answer: "Above all, its antiquity, traditions that go so far back in time as to enter a primeval world that is arboreal rather than pastoral, a formal wilderness in which sages live and courtesans dance. But if such images were ever apposite, are they relevant now?" ("Fiction" 208).

Given that contemporary literature does not often project the obvious orientalism of sages and courtesans, it's a valid perception that the reality projected in art is often a product of an essentialist and ultimately fictive discourse. Having made this assertion, Desai adds that the present is characterized by fragmentation and disruption of the paradigms that held sway in the past.

The consciousness of destabilization in political and cultural life becomes a point of reference for Desai's classification of Indian writers. The authors who are included in her list are not entirely the most recent. She provides samples from G.V. Desani, R.K. Narayan, Gita Mehta, Salman Rushdie, Bharati Mukherjee, Amitav

Ghosh, Allan Sealy, Meena Alexander, and herself. Many of these writers are, however, in some ways experimental and subversive, and they belong to a tradition that departs, in perception and portrayal of socio-cultural realities, from the mimetic tradition of Mulk Raj Anand, Kamala Markandaya, Manohar Malgonkar, and Khushwant Singh. Desai demonstrates the distinction by focusing on the narrative mode. Rushdie, she claims, most forcefully and effectively revealed and popularized the process: "Immediately, there was a flood of younger writers delighted to return to the old style of story telling that was strangely the 'latest' and 'newest' style. In following his trajectory they found themselves travelling so far westward that, the world being the shape it is, they had arrived in the east again" ("Fiction" 211).

The preoccupation with the demotic that Desai points to was symptomatic of a larger process, one that involved an awareness of multiplicity, marginality, history, and historiography, and the complexity of the colonial and neo-colonial process. The experimental tradition, at its most obvious, marked a point of departure from the practice of realism, from the boundaries of referentiality. Its project was subversive, and its subversion involved locating itself on the margins of both referential and nationalist discourse.

In the process of identifying significant contemporary authors, Desai does not chart a tradition. She does not, except in the most general terms, point to connections among them. And significantly, she does not say where she stands in relation to writers such as Narayan who began to write before she did, and writers such Allan Sealy who began in the 1980s. She occupies a distinctive space, one that is not imitated even in the work of her daughter who published her first novel in 1998.[3] At the risk of simplification, one might say that Anita Desai creates a texture that accommodates the conventions of mimesis while questioning and subverting them in order to secure a perspective that is both ambivalent and open-ended, one that displaces the colonial and patriarchal in order to speculate on a possible space for the marginal and the oppressed. Afzal-Khan points out that, "it is such a pull between the aesthetic attractiveness of myth and the moral weight of realism that gives Anita Desai's fiction its tension and interest" (59). Afzal-Khan works with a particular reading of myth, but if one were to adopt the structuralist notion of myth as symbolic discourse, then the combination she refers to would be particularly appropriate.

The position of liminality, the need to create a space for the marginalized, complements the impulse to experiment. Hence the intersection between exile, native-alien, and the counterrealist in her writing. Desai's perception includes hidden agendas and essentialist identities in social and cultural norms, but her dominant focus is gender, the problematic space occupied by women on the Indian subcontinent. She is aware of the possibility and the temptation of adopting a universalist (and essentially male) position that is unsatisfactory; but its alternative is a stance, that, because of its potential to disturb, invites forms of censorship. In an essay aptly titled "A Secret Connivance" she wonders: "Should we be serving an urgent need or the eternal needs, the secret, instinctive needs too deep to name? Society demands one answer, the artist another. To listen to society is to have one's belief in art gradually eroded and destroyed" (976).

The instinctive response is often one of silence, suppression, and self-censorship. She rightly mentions that apart from a brief and uncharacteristic period of Emergency imposed by Indira Gandhi in 1975, India never actively censored the artist. It did, however, censor on the basis of gender. That censorship was subtler and more pervasive for it was sanctioned and imposed by the collective community. Both the colonialism of the West and the nationalism of India combined to establish male dominance. Says Desai:

> The myth keeps her bemused, bound hand and foot. To rebel against it–either in speech or in action–would mean that she is questioning the myth, attacking the legend, and that cannot be permitted: it is the cornerstone on which the Indian family and therefore Indian society are built. ("Secret" 972)

Desai's fiction, however, is less involved with "political" and controversial forms of suppression, with allegations of dowry murders, physical abuse, child marriage, and so forth, and more with the complex historical process that created in India a duality that made it possible for the male/female dichotomy to be exploited in both colonial and nationalist practice.[4] The referential context is not totally absent in her work, but it appears less concerned with protest and more preoccupied with mapping the palimpsest of oppression. The dominant practice for Desai is to distance the immediate and frame the specific with the symbolic in order to reinforce the fictive element without jettisoning the subjective dimension. Even an event as mundane as the postman walking up a hill at the beginning of *Fire on the Mountain* becomes the occasion to reflect on notions of privacy, patriarchy, and sexuality. The language remains faithful to the metonymic impulse but gradually steers the reader towards the metaphoric and symbolic dimension.

Desai's perception of the historical origins of patriarchy is often similar to the argument advanced by Partha Chatterjee. Tracing historical patterns, Chatterjee claims that within the binary structure of Orient and Occident, the oppressed and silenced woman soon acquired an emblematic significance for the colonizers: "By assuming a position of sympathy with the unfree and oppressed womanhood of India, the colonial mind was able to transform this figure of the Indian woman into a sign of the inherently oppressive and unfree nature of the entire cultural tradition of a country" ("Colonialism" 622). The suppression was sanctioned by myth, and its particular contours were drawn by foregrounding Brahminical texts and practices.

As Chatterjee explains, the nationalist project, having to negotiate between the essentialism that defined the Indian as spiritual, passive, and other-worldly and the need to absorb the rational, enlightened ideals of the West, created yet another binary structure within which women became the guardians of the spiritual and the traditional. Chatterjee provides a perceptive account of the practice of such an opposition: it cleared the way for women to participate in the outer world of modernity, to leave the confines of the home, while being burdened with the task of remaining the custodians of culture. Thus the peculiar dilemma of freedom and entrapment. Chatterjee comments: "The new patriarchy advocated by nationalism conferred upon women the honour of a new social responsibility, and by associating the task of female emancipation with the historical goal of sovereign nationhood bound them to a new and yet entirely legitimate subordination"[5] (629).

Desai's perception of the multiple forces that impede the creation of a productive space for women is subtle, although its expression is less experimental than the writings of, say, Suniti Namjoshi. (Namjoshi's art is metafictional, self-reflexive, and fabulous.) About her own work, Desai says, "It is to that silent piano one must dedicate oneself, when society becomes a gaoler, and forbids music" ("Secret" 976). Fanciful as it is, the image suggests something of the mode that characterizes Desai's writing. Certain motifs recur in her work, and recognizable traits keep surfacing. The major concern is clearly the role assigned to and expected of women, but the experiential and social dimensions of her work are always subordinate to the formal or textual aspects which determine the task of what she calls dedication to the "silent piano."

Desai's only work that could be called overtly psychological, one that self-consciously seeks to establish an associative structure, is her first novel, *Cry, the Peacock*, which, in its attempt to capture the language of psychological extremity, adopts a variant of stream-of-consciousness. Its dislocation of syntax, shifting point of view, disruption of linearity, and obsessive patterns of repetition often approximate a discourse of madness. In Maya one finds an insightful portrayal of hysteria, its resistance to totalizing and normative rules, its refusal to participate in a logic that privileges the masculine and marginalizes the woman. In this work more than in any other, Desai aligns herself with a predominantly Western modernist tradition that includes Virginia Woolf and James Joyce.

Cry, the Peacock is an important work for its awareness of the destructive force of sexuality, and for its ambiguous relationship

with the male world of Gautama. The novel seeks to create a private space for Maya, and in its exclusion, its foregrounding of neu-
rosis, its solipsism, lie its main strength and weakness. Despite its
probing exploration of mental collapse and hysteria, the novel
becomes self-serving, indulgent, and evasive in its antireferentiality.
Desai admits that she avoided what she ought to have been writing
about "by sticking [her] head, ostrich-fashion, into the sands of
what critics call the psychological novel, the subjective novel"
("English" 4). The novel demonstrates through Maya a stance that
Desai perceives to be an inevitable consequence of centuries of
oppression, one that manifests itself in tearfulness and moping: "I
myself have enjoyed, when in a certain mood, dragging my slippers
to make a dull monotonous sound that irritates the listener and satisfies the maker. I have done a great deal of slipper dragging in my
writing, and it irritates me now as much as it satisfied me then"
("Women" 27).

What redeems the novel is its depiction of hysteria, its moments
of ambivalence which connect the consciousness of Maya with historical and mythical patterns. Maya and Gautama as symbols of
illusion and enlightenment are invoked and erased at the end as
Gautama dies without any enlightenment. Gautama's metonymic
function makes him a representative of the Westernized, middle-
class neo-colonial while his metaphoric and figurative role gives
him spiritual, religious, and patriarchal dominance sanctioned by
tradition. His insistence on detachment, along with Maya's sensuous attachment to living things and her sensuality, complete the
mythical pattern. Related to this are other symbolic patterns which
involve Shiva, whose cosmic dance is often referred to, and Radha
and Krishna, who appear in various guises, from the chant heard
from the servant's quarters to Gautama's preaching about Gita to
the dubious lawyer Krishnan.

The tradition that traps Maya is hegemonic, evident in the priest
who controls Maya's future and the phallic symbolism associated
with him that connects male sexuality and myth. If the inner, spiritual world is under the control of the priest, the outer worlds of

politics, art, and law become the province of Gautama. The brief references to Independence and colonial struggle are linked with men, and Maya is politely and effectively excluded from this world. Between the world of the priest and that of the neo-colonial are the silence and complicity of the mother-in-law and the futile rebellion of Gautama's sister, Nila.

Cry, the Peacock marks a watershed in that it departs from the referentiality of the traditional Indo-Anglian novel. It foregrounds, albeit intermittently, a characteristic ambivalence, evident in the symbolism of the moon, which in its demonic and eerie aspect links with the albino priest (an interesting strategy combining the religious and the colonial) who controls Maya's fate. If, in its conventional resonance it connects with love, it also aligns itself with the resistance of Nila (whose name refers to the moon) and finally with the death of Gautama. In its capacity to transcend binaries of male/female, and good/bad, the fluidity of the metaphor establishes a disconcerting multiplicity that questions the more obvious binaries of the narrative. But for the most part, in its attempt to transcend a univocal genre that complemented the patriarchal underpinnings of the nationalist project, it retreats into a private space that fails to establish an adequate context for liminality. The solipsism of this novel is not one that Desai has returned to and stream-of-consciousness is hardly the defining mode of her counterrealism. *Cry, the Peacock*, very much like Salman Rushdie's *Grimus*, embodies all the key elements of the corpus, but (again like *Grimus*) demonstrates the inherent danger of retreating entirely into a narcissistic space.

Desai's recourse to the mimesis of *Bye-Bye Blackbird* as an alternative hardly resolves this issue, for here, despite the ostensible preoccupation with gender and cultural conflict, the rigidity of the form and the absence of any real dialogue lead to stereotyping and naive resolutions. Desai's comment that the novel "was based purely on observation rather than any experience" ("Interview" 41) hints at the limitations of the work. Ironically, a work that deals almost exclusively with marginal figures leads to no real perception, no real progress beyond irony and parody. If anything, the novel provides a reminder of the symbiotic relation between narrative and marginality. It demonstrates the inherent weakness of a critical stance that is most apparent in "been-to" situations. Within Desai's own corpus, when the focus shifts to observed rather than imagined realities, the writing falters. Even her most recent work, *Fasting, Feasting*, in spite of its obvious strengths, is weakened by realism and its straightforward binaries.

Desai's characteristic mode finds expression in *Clear Light of Day*, *Fire on the Mountain*, *In Custody*, *Baumgartner's Bombay*, and more recently, in *Journey to Ithaca*, where the premises of realism co-exist with a poetic, polyphonic structure. Neither totally discontinuous nor entirely referential, they are counterrealistic in ways that defy easy definition. While critical studies almost by consensus focus on the psychological aspects of Desai's writing as her trademark, it is the constant interweaving of the referential and the inaccessible that gives her work a counterrealistic texture.[6]

The interplay between the two and the consequent destabilization of fixity, of unalterable truth-claims, paves the way for the multiple spaces within the fictive worlds. The public sphere, the world of post-independent India, with its multiplicity, its upheavals, and turmoil is still a recognizable presence, but it is often invoked through a metaphoric process whose associative power subverts a monologic interpretation. Thus, in *Clear Light of Day*, Raja's sudden illness during the Partition riots serves the metonymic function of pointing to a larger disease in the body politic. Given the naive romanticism of Raja, his sickness becomes a parody of Gandhi's fast to end the riots. Finally, there is the irony of Raja's sympathy for the Hyder Ali family against the Hindus. Similar in its effect is the story of Hyder Ali, whose namesake fought valiantly against the British, and who now flees, ironically, not to Pakistan but to Hyderabad (literally, Hyder's city). The word play, particularly with Hyder Ali's daughter being called Benazir, is probably intentional. In a different context, had Hyder Ali left for Pakistan, the referential value would have been enhanced and the multiplicity would have been lost. Speaking about this, Desai observes: "There are so many books which have fallen into two halves—India and Pakistan—and that I was not interested in doing." Having dismissed the inadequacy of such binaries, she adds: "Besides, wouldn't it have been just too predictable? One must avoid clichés of the kind" ("Interview" 34).

The historical and the public, thus invoked through the indeterminacy of metaphor, lose their status as absolute truth and move towards their epistemological status as human constructs. In the process, what is dismantled are the hegemonic paradigms that derive from the unalterability of such constructs. Nanda's Carignano in *Fire on the Mountain* has a colonial past, but its colonial legacy and its attendant assumptions of cultural superiority and hierarchy are questioned by the Gothic framework within which the past is couched. One of the previous owners of Carignano was a lady with queer medical practices who "poked a fork into her cook's neck when he was choking on a mutton bone in the belief it would make an aperture for him to breathe through" (*Fire* 9). The Gothic thus displaces both the mimetic and the hierarchical to problematize the colonial past. By asserting an alternative reading that is obviously fictive, the author demonstrates that the so-called historical and hegemonic are equally fictive.

Nanda as occupant of Carignano now occupies an indeterminate space, and her role as victim of social expectations and male dominance is juxtaposed with her complicity. By displacing the colonial and installing the Gothic, the narrator questions Nanda's solitude and her assertion of self. This makes possible the decadent aestheticism of *The Pillow Book of Sei Shonagon* that she cherishes and the orientalism of her tales to Raka. Her withdrawal and silence are gestures of resistance, her protest against the role-playing imposed by the dual forces of tradition and modernity, but her liminal space is tainted by her own complicity in the structures she opposes.

The space she claims for herself is disturbed by Ila and challenged by Raka who occupy analogous but different spaces. The distinctions are reinforced by patterns of repetition and erased by patterns of indeterminacy. Thus in Nanda's perception, Raka "was the finished, perfected model of what Nanda Kaul was merely a brave, flawed experiment" (47). If Raka is specular, she is also a figure of ambivalence and fluidity that is acknowledged in the narrative itself. Her name suggests the multiplicity:

> Raka—what an utter misnomer,…Raka meant the moon, but this child was not round-faced, calm or radiant. As she shuffled up the garden path, silently following Ram Lal, with a sling bag weighing down one thin, sloping shoulder and her feet in old sandals heavy with dust, Nanda Kaul thought she looked like one those dark crickets that leap up in fright but do not sing, or a mosquito, minute and fine, on thin, precarious legs. (*Fire* 39)

At least a part of her consciousness is formed by the world Nanda inhabits, of patriarchal dominance, male violence, and marital conflict, but she is also a part of the Gothic world of darkness, beasts, and devils. She can despise the westernized and pampered world of the "Babas" that Ram Lal would like to consign her to, and with equal ease displace the myth of *Ahalikai* by invoking a folkloric parody of it. If Nanda is associated with a silence the suppresses and Ila with speech that conceals, Raka is associated with Raga, its purity and its associative power. The connection between the two terms is not whimsical because Raga is a metaphor for fluidity, for multiple configurations that are made possible in literature. Here again, Desai's comment is instructive:

> One is handed a certain number of notes at birth or through one's experience and then it's up to the writer or to the musician to play with these notes. To combine them in different ways, to improvise upon them and to somehow find a pattern to them. A pattern that has a meaning in literature or a melody in music. ("Interview" 36)

The structure created out of this consciousness resists closure, as most of Desai's novels do. Predictably, not one of her novels, with the exception of *Bye-Bye Blackbird*, ends on an unequivocal note. There is no epiphany, no enunciation, no tying together of ends to complete the underpinnings of an ontology. Instead, the reader is given a moment of uncertainty, a sense of threshold, like the ending of *In Custody* which shows Deven caught between two choices, neither of which promises the freedom he seeks.

When the dominant mode is symbolic, Desai's work dissociates itself from reflecting socio-political realities and re-enters the public world in a manner more ambivalent and dialogic. The text permits the indeterminacy of tropes, a prime example of which is the cow and the well in *Clear Light of Day*. The cow appears referentially when it is in fact drowned in the well. More importantly, its figurative presence is obsessive for the characters, and Bim sees the image of a cow floating in her cup of tea. In the narrative, a clay cow stares at Bim and Biswas as their attempts to cement a relationship fail. The children staring at their parents playing bridge are described in a language that conjures up a vortex, of peering into a well. Significantly, Mira, the child-widow, virgin-bride, and poor relation finds in the fate of the cow cause for empathy, and her attempt at suicide by drowning in the well is foiled, but when she dies in bed, we are told that she was "overcome by alcoholic fumes."

The description of the well, which deserves to be quoted in full, suggests its multiple meanings, meanings that involve birth and death, the female body, childhood, and nourishment:

> But there was no milk, the cow had died, drowned in
> the well. In that well, deep and stony and still, in which
> all must drown to die. The navel of the world it was,
> secret and hidden in thick folds of grass, from which
> they all emerged and to which they must return, crawl-
> ing on their hands and knees. (*Clear* 90)

The ambivalence of the trope, particularly in relation to Mira, leads also to the practice of intertextuality. Mira is connected, repeatedly, with T.S. Eliot's figures and the quote from "The Four Quartets,"

> Who is the third who walks always beside you?
> When I count, there are only you and I together
> But when I look ahead up the white road
> There is always another one walking beside you (*Clear* 41)

reflects her liminality. She is "invisible" in the social and sexual context of the novel, and she is hardly a resurrected Christ, despite her obvious sacrifices. Marginalized by tradition, class, and gender, Mira, ironically, recalls the lover of Krishna. In a novel where the names of the main characters–Bim, Tara, Baba–are deliberately stripped of connotative meanings, the intertextuality implied by Mira acquires a special significance. It affirms the combination of various texts whose ideological stances intersect in combative ways, thereby making connections between text, genre, and historical and cultural imperatives. The intertextuality both supplements and subverts, installs and dismantles, points to an engagement with immediate realities and a distancing that affords a view of hidden complicities. The intertextual references span several worlds–the colonial, the marginalized, and the feminine–to create curious and paradoxical combinations.

The notion of placing, of fixing identities, gives way to a narrative of multiple ironies that coexist, often supplementing the master narratives without being co-opted in the process. It is a fluid and dynamic space that resists binary constructs. Desai's narratives embrace multiple meanings in a manner that foregrounds provisionality. In the most unexpected moments, when class affiliations pre-empt a subaltern reading, the artifice points to layers of meaning that unsettle the narrative. For example, an episode as therapeutic and benign as the father in *Clear Light of Day* administering insulin to his wife, takes on disturbing connotations of sexual penetration and murder:

> Once her father had risen, padded quietly to her
> mother's bedroom behind the closed door, and Tara has
> slipped in behind him, folded herself silently into the
> faded curtain and watched. She had seen him lean over
> her mother's bed and quickly, smoothly press a little
> shining syringe into her mother's arm that lay crookedly
> on the blue cover, press it hard so that she tilted her
> head back with a quick gasp of shock, or pain—Tara saw
> her chin rising up into the air and the grey head sinking
> back into the pillow and heard a long, whimpering sigh
> like an air-bag minutely punctured so that Tara had fled,
> trembling, because she was sure that she had seen her
> father kill her mother. (22-23)

The physical space occupied by Tara, together with her perception
of her mother's "violation," underlines the idea of marginality,
regardless of the status or the role as daughter or mother.

The ironies within which the space of the marginalized is
asserted are evident in the strange inversions of a novel like
Baumgartner's Bombay in which Baumgartner possesses very little at
the end, and even the trophies that adorn his room and which
tempt Kurt are products of chance and hardly reinforce his dubious claims to ownership. The cats he surrounds himself with do
acquire a home, but they also underscore his own sense of home-
lessness. His death at the hands of Kurt, a fellow German, is in
keeping with the tragic ironies of the novel, about which Desai sar-
donically comments: "just when he feels safe, [the past] catches up
with him. You know about the man who survived the sinking of
the Titanic and then drowned in his garden pond" ("Interview" 35).

And yet, in a curious way, we are confronted with what is, in a
sense, Baumgartner's Bombay, and the description of his death,
which clearly recalls the crucifixion of Christ, underscores the
tragic irony. Baumgartner is hardly a native, hardly a redeemer, but
the space he claims for himself in the vast metropolitan city of
Bombay is not without validity, given the ambivalence that sur-

rounds the community of the novel (a community that reveals the fictiveness of historical and referential certainties). The mimetic function of Café de Paris, for instance, is undercut by its anagram, for the owner is a Parsi. The "history" that Kurt creates for himself, obviously orientalist and fictitious, is no different from other versions that underscore the "imagined communities." In the process of questioning certainties, the space of the marginalized becomes foregrounded and legitimated. It is particularly significant that Baumgartner remembers a "home" that spurned him, adopts one that incarcerates him, and ends his life in a manner that hardly resolves the questions of identity and home.

In Custody is one of the most "public" of Desai's works. It is about linear time, about historical process, the rise and fall of civilizations, the symbiotic relation between text and nation, and the role of the masculine as the creator and preserver of art and literature. The fundamental assumptions of the main characters are rendered problematic by the spatial arrangement of the novel in which Mirpore (symbolically representing Mughal resistance to the British, and in that sense belonging to the margins), now seeks to re-establish its status through Urdu. Language and nation are thus made interchangeable. The process of unification, however, is attempted by Deven, who belongs to both the centre and the margin: centre because he is a Hindu and margin because he feels alienated in the suburb of Mirpore. In the interplay of conflicting forces, certainties disappear and identities, including sexual identities, become vague and confused. Confronted with the "public" aspect, one is reminded of expressive realism. Afzal-Khan observes that "in matters of message, however, Desai is clearly on the side of realism, so she chooses to view myth and its attractions from, and ultimately to subordinate it (or at least balance it) within, the critical realist perspective" (96). Given the politics of language and religion in post-independence India, the novel's "public" dimension, and even its performative aspect, can hardly be missed. A realist reading, however, needs to confront the melodrama, the stereotyping, and the simplistic binaries that make up the novel.

Once the referential aspect is seen only as a necessary frame, the metaphorical and allegorical layers of the novel take centre stage. The challenge of the novel lies in the subjectivity of the characters, the contexts in which they locate themselves, and the narcissism of the narrative.

It is in this context that Imtiaz attempts to upstage and supplant Nur, but her assertions of self, cantankerous, polemical, and demonstrative, are dependent on the approval of Nur, Deven, and the former's decadent male audience. Her language is as futile as the silence of Sarla, for both, in the process of demanding a niche in a hegemonic construct that is trapped in essentialisms, become themselves prey to what they seek to displace. Asked about the marginalization of women in the novel, Desai points out:

> But from that marginalized position they tend to shriek and scream and have tantrums and demand attention in a way which I myself don't find attractive and I'm sorry that I had to present them in such a way....If women had been so suppressed, their needs, their desires, their wants never taken into consideration at all, always put out of sight, always put down, then that was the way they were going to behave. ("Interview" 37)

Within the boundaries of the novel, of the poetry of Nur and Imtiaz or the letter/confession of the end, gender stereotypes maintain their hold. The world of the novel is still steeped in the orientalism of the naked Sadhu with a snake round his neck, and the submissive and religious widow who feeds such hangers-on.

Desai is aware of the multiple possibilities and temptations of the marginal position. She is aware, as Bim and Tara are in *Clear Light of Day*, that to dress and behave like men provides the illusion of shifting the balance, but the overriding implications of the emperor's clothes remain intact. Real change will challenge and destabilize. As Trinh observes, "being able to read and write, a learned woman robs man of his creativity, his activity, his culture, his language" (19). Or she might, like Ila Das in *Fire on the Mountain*, recite "The Boy Stood on the Burning Deck" or like Bim, teach a linear and hegemonic history. Neither withdrawal from history nor an identification with universalism resolves the dilemma. Instead Desai advocates an imaginative fusion of the two that both participates in socio-cultural realities and distances itself at the same time.

The fact that a strong social stance cannot be extrapolated from her fiction has been a concern among many critics. Desai herself is not free of the self-doubt that most postcolonial writers, men or women, must at some point face. Why is she writing fiction at a time when the euphoria of nationalism has given way to a profound disillusionment, and faith in a tradition that survived centuries has given way to a hopeless uncertainty? Says Desai: "what are you, an educated woman, doing writing novels, fiction? And I have no answer because a part of me agrees that yes, I should instead get together those beggar children and teach them to read and write so they could earn a better living than begging" ("Secret" 976).

To participate in forms of social activism uncritically is to wear blinkers that eventually trap and deceive. To distance oneself is to negate realities that are often unfair but always present. Desai's writing offers no easy solutions, but it provides a salutary reminder that, in moments of political and cultural upheaval, hegemony masquerades as egalitarianism; if one does not see through the false camaraderie of those who wield power, one is condemned to repeat the mistakes of the past. Desai's counterrealism is thus an unusual hybrid that acknowledges the local without concerning itself with the specific, works with the causal while insisting on the synchronic, alerts the reader to the power of metonymy while demonstrating a penchant for the allusive and the associative. The opening paragraph of *Fire on the Mountain*, given below, is written in her characteristic mode that observes the conventions of expressive realism while alerting the reader to a metaphoric dimension that suggests multiple layers:

> Nanda Kaul paused under the pine trees to take in their
> scented sibilance and listen to the cicadas fiddling invis-
> ibly under the mesh of pine needles when she saw the
> postman slowly winding his way along the Upper Mall.
> She had not gone out to watch for him, did not want
> him to stop at Carignano, had no wish for letters. The
> sight of him, inexorably closing in with his swollen bag,
> rolled a fat ball of irritation into the cool cave of her
> day, blocking it stupidly: bags and letters, messages and
> demands, requests, promises and queries, she had
> wanted to be done with them all, at Carignano. She
> asked to be left to the pines and cicadas alone. She
> hoped he would not stop. (3)

Given the location of Carignano, the scene is perfectly plausible, almost mundane in its description. Nanda seeks solitude, in true ascetic fashion, so even the presence of a postman becomes a source of annoyance. The language offers the perspective of the character, but moves beyond it without ever denying it. The multiple negatives of the diction lead up to the sexual imagery and to the whole issue of language which remains the main concern of the passage and the novel as a whole. The realities constructed by the language are suggestive and synchronic, and they both supplement and supplant the tenuous realism of the passage.

Journey to Ithaca (1995) is probably a useful example of the precarious balance that one associates with Desai. Using memories of the 1960s when the West converged on India as the source of spiritual wisdom, the novel deliberately invites a parallel with Aurobindo and the presence of the foreigner as a central figure in the Ashram. Even the names such as Matteo are meant to reinforce such parallels. But as a retelling of familiar narrative, the novel is both inadequate and redundant. As an enactment of Hermann Hesse's *Journey to the East*, the novel walks on thin ice. There is a certain exuberance about the way in which the narrative invents plots to maintain its teleological movement. The overall movement of the novel is not intended to be diachronic. Even at the beginning when the two children enact a parodic version of the quest, one is struck by both the childlike innocence of the performance, and the sexual, incestuous undertones of the play. Here is "reality heightened and raised to a pitch" (110-11) that transforms the quotidian into the symbolic and the mythical.

The quest narrative is constantly interrupted, not only by the shifts in temporality, but by images that subvert the very process of the novel. Take, for instance, the episode in which Matteo follows the Mother and her devotees to witness what seems like a breath-taking—and totally exoticized—scene: "The scene was utterly *extraordinary* to him—she seated in purple beneath the orange-flowering tree, the air and sky saffron about her, and beyond her the vast riverbed, shimmering in the afternoon light" (110, italics mine). Soon after, the Mother takes them to another grove, which is the abode of the yogi who has lived underground for fifty years or more. Just when that whole episode is going to be dismissed as pure fantasy, the saint emerges from his underground cave. Whether this is real or entirely orchestrated by the Mother is unclear. As surrogate author of sorts, she leaves everything in a state of ambivalence, and Matteo as implied reader responds with total acceptance, largely because he is predisposed to such a reading.

The meaning of this episode, like so many others, remains deliberately ambiguous, not out of a desire to deny meaning so much as to offer an accumulation of images from very different contexts that, taken together, would suggest certain patterns of experience. The image of Eden with which the novel begins, together with the garden at the end, make up a cluster of images that reveal structures of meaning. In that sense Desai has done what many counterrealists strive for: she draws attention to the dangers of totalizing meanings. Even as the novels use their subjective dimension to draw the reader into their world, the language, with its autonomous associative power, defamiliarizes and distances the texts.

As a linear narrative predicated on Aurobindo and the Mother, the novel creates a deliberate challenge for itself, with, according to

Makarand Paranjape, unfortunate results. Paranjape's erudite reading of *Journey to Ithaca* acknowledges at the very beginning the strengths of the novel. He concedes up front that Desai's intention is not to hurt or malign. But that said, he goes on to point out that Desai, in her acknowledgments and in her use of names, clearly intends the reader to be aware of the many parallels with Aurobindo's ashram. He adds that "it is amply clear…that the real Mother of Pondicherry was a far vaster, greater, and superior being than the one that Desai has created" (407). By extension, the metaphoric allusion to India by invoking Ithaca and the quest as being ultimately a chimera appears to Paranjape as both false and unfair. Ithaca and India, according to him, are hardly analogous, and to use them as interchangeable symbols of individual quest is to misrepresent history. He is blunt about his overall response to the novel: "Ithaca, then, is an objective correlative of Desai's fictional limitations.…The style, the sensitivity, the poetic appeal of the language, ultimately, reveals an impoverished soul, a heart of lesser depth and wisdom, merely a well-intentioned modern mind, limited in range and understanding" ("Journey" 410).

The failure of Ithaca as a trope points to a specific kind of reading which the novel often invites. Such specificity is not incompatible with counterrealism, as Rushdie has so amply demonstrated. But its major challenge is that it provides the opportunity for the reader to bring to the text certain kinds of knowledge. The realist writer thrives on that assumption whereas the counterrealist seeks to provide a measure of distance. Paranjape's critique is an important reminder of the author's responsibility when certain referential markers are invoked in the text. However, the novel could be read differently, even while acknowledging the valency of Paranjape's argument. *Journey to Ithaca* includes a wonderful episode of Sophie, in a voyeuristic moment, watching the Mother as she feeds a flock of peacocks. Sophie's role is that of the reader, skeptical, seeking a univocal meaning, as the Mother indulges in what could be seen as either a perfectly normal or self-consciously exotic gesture. As the Mother and Sophie look at each other, they turn away, embarrassed. And then Sophie looks back at the incident:

> On Sophie that improbably, dream-like encounter with the
> Mother had an effect she was hardly able to articulate even
> to herself. There had been revealed to her both the myth-
> ical figure who could summon peacocks out of the wilds
> as she did devotees from the world over, and the aged,
> solitary woman with sparse hair and a faded nightdress.
> Against her own expectations and intentions, the para-
> doxical, contradictory image stayed in her mind. (130)

It is a particularly striking moment in that the two images which are ostensibly oppositional are held together in a curious balance. Not even the Mother acknowledges that one image does not negate the other. The real and symbolic coexist in a world made possible by fictive representation. The episode, characteristic of Desai's metaphoric mode, serves as a metonym and a microcosm of the novel.

This is precisely what Desai's counterrealism seeks to achieve: a heightened consciousness that participates in and partakes of the realistic without being bound by it. The artifice provides the translucence that makes possible the simultaneous perception of the referential, the subconscious, and the mythical.

CHAPTER 5

The Art of Enchantment: Zulfikar Ghose

Zulfikar Ghose's recent collection of short stories, *Veronica and the Gongora Passion*, includes a story called "Lila of the Butterflies and Her Chronicler" which was originally written for inclusion in a special volume honouring Gabriel García Márquez, published by the *Latin American Literary Review* in 1985. The story is, given the occasion, overtly intertextual, its ostensible imitation intended as a tribute to a major exponent of magic realism.[1] An important aspect of the story, however, is that it ends with a quotation from *The Winter's Tale*, included almost as an aside, with the obvious suggestion that if one were to look for the origins of magic realism, one could go back to Shakespeare. The allusion to Shakespeare suddenly alters the intertextual field, revealing that if certain moments in the story are reminiscent of *One Hundred Years of Solitude*, others emphasize the presence and influence of *The Winter's Tale*. Once the comparison is made, the story becomes both a tribute to a major writer and an act of subversion, not so much to deny Márquez the reputation he enjoys so much as to signal to the reader the multiple sources of Ghose's own literary tradition.

As a descriptive term, magic realism has been immensely popular with critics as a way of characterizing Ghose's writing. The combi-

Notes to chapter 5 are on pp. 193-94.

nation of subject matter that is often located in Latin America and a
narrative mode that is clearly outside the tradition of expressive realism has a great deal to do with Ghose's work being described as
deriving from or beholden to the magic realist tradition. The label
has curiously not been courted by Ghose, although he has, on various occasions, drawn attention to Latin American authors in laudatory terms. In his critical works, particularly *The Fiction of Reality* and
The Art of Creating Fiction, the references to major and minor writers
are, predictably, numerous. He has unreserved praise for Machado de
Assis, and laudatory references to Unamuno, Borges, and several
others, but among Latin American authors, Márquez is referred to
only sparingly.[2] In fact, the references are often to Proust, Flaubert,
Joyce, Henry James, Beckett, Faulkner, and so forth, all of whom are
shown to be innovators in their own right. By the same token,
Hemingway, Greene, Bellow and, on occasion, D.H. Lawrence are
shown to be much weaker than they have been made out to be.
Curiously, Eastern influences are minimal in Ghose's corpus,
although there is some reference to Urdu sources in his early poetry.
Vernacular traditions–epic, puranic, or oral–are hardly ever present in
Ghose's work. The artifice in Ghose is shaped by occidental rather
than oriental sources.

Regardless of how convincing the final result may be, the concern
with subject matter, according to Ghose, can lead only to inferior
writing. Remarkably unconventional and often wilfully provocative,
Ghose's views about fiction are dictated by the conviction that a loss
of artistic worth is in direct proportion to the literary pursuit of transparency. Adopting a very uncompromising stance in his criticism, he
maintains that realist representation is best left to journalism, television, or political rhetoric. Literature concerns itself only with language and never with empirical realities. His own work does not
entirely abandon the outside world, but his uncompromising stance is
often a way of signalling to the reader that he has no patience with
criticism that uses the outside world as its sole criterion.

In 1989, *The Review of Contemporary Fiction* devoted a special issue to
Ghose and Milan Kundera. The appropriateness of putting these

two writers from very different backgrounds together has become increasingly evident in the last several years. Despite the ostensible differences in their narrative strategies and subject matter, the two writers share a penchant for seeing themselves as participants in and contributors to a literary tradition rather than as proponents of a particular belief. The dictates of history may be unavoidable as elements of the plot, but the artistic pursuit is neither subservient to nor shaped by it. In fact, history and art adopt oppositional stances. As Kundera puts it, "because of its personal nature, the history of art is a revenge by man against the impersonality of the history of humanity" (16). Speaking of the line of Rabelais, Kundera adds that "the novel as butterfly is taking flight, carrying the shreds of the chrysalis on its back" (3). Ghose's work captures something of that sense of exuberance.

Although form has been a persistent concern for Ghose, he is often much less fascinated by narrative mode *per se* than with style. Language is far more significant as a necessary tool than form itself, although there is a symbiotic relation between language and form.[3] In fact, he even mentions that working with "isms" such as surrealism does not call for any great depth of understanding. "There is nothing more easy" says Ghose, "to contrive in writing than the surreal image: it is the favourite device of writers who would like to be considered avant-garde" (*Fiction* 65). Of course, the struggle with language to express a particular vision of reality ultimately resolves itself at the level of form (hence Ghose's propensity to experiment with different forms throughout a career that has spanned over three decades). It is difficult to come across a writer, postcolonial or otherwise, who has worked with as many different forms as Ghose. From realism to metafiction, there is hardly any form that he has not, at some stage, used to explore different facets of experience. Yet he has remained unnoticed in Indian literary histories.[4] Until the special issue of *The Review of Contemporary Fiction* appeared in 1989, there was no real awareness of Ghose as an Indian or postcolonial writer.

Born in 1935, Ghose lived for the first seventeen years of his life in Sialkot and Bombay, which makes him very much an Indian writer. His early poetry (*The Loss of India*), his autobiography (*Confessions of a Native-Alien*), several short stories in *Statement Against Corpses*, and his first novel *The Contradictions*, are all set in India, but these texts have been eclipsed by his more recent ones that carefully avoid the subcontinent. In the last few years, critical perception has changed to some degree, and he is now seen to be a significant Pakistani writer. A recent anthology of Pakistani writing in English is entitled *Dragonfly in the Sun* and the title of the work derives from one of Ghose's poems. His identity as a diasporic Muslim writer has much to do with such identities, but he belongs firmly in the tradition of Indo-Anglian writing.

Perhaps more than any other writer who is discussed in this book, Ghose has demonstrated in his own writing the complex relation between form and experience in Indian writing in English. All other writers have, for the most part, remained loyal to a particular mode, and if they have digressed on occasion, it is only to return more emphatically to the preferred mode.[5] For Ghose, the practice has been to discard forms once they have been used, for the obvious reason that the potential of a given form to encapsulate a specific order of experience gets exhausted at that point. His second novel, *The Murder of Aziz Khan*, published in 1967, is located in Pakistan, and belongs very firmly in the tradition of realism. Incidentally, it is also the only work that was republished in Pakistan in recent years.[6] After that, his writing steered away from India, for more than two decades, until he wrote *The Triple Mirror of the Self*, which goes back to the India of his childhood. Obviously, there are significant differences in the subject matter between the two works. *The Murder of Aziz Khan* is about a farmer who refuses to sell his land and the local businessmen who eventually destroy him. The recent novel is at least minimally autobiographical–a *Bildungsroman* of sorts–and deals with a young Muslim boy in Bombay and his encounter with the growing religious fanaticism that accompanied the Partition and Indian independence. That said, the crucial difference is not in the plot, but the narrative form that separates the two. One work is sociological and the other personal, but both have to do with (to use the author's phrase) a "memory of Asia," and that makes the formal differences between the two a matter of considerable interest.

The objective of this chapter is to look at the two texts in order to examine the relation between form and experience in both novels. The formal differences between the two point to the intersections between the postcolonial experience and the role of the Indo-Anglian author. Ghose himself was impatient with such formal categories. As he puts it, "you should never think of realism, but always of reality. There is no such thing as realism, or naturalism, or, for that matter, surrealism, or symbolism" (*Art* 147). But the comparison between the two novels is necessary and useful, particularly when similar material is traversed twice, each time from a different perspective.

Although it is unclear what the origins of *The Murder of Aziz Khan* are, except that it was inspired by a news item about the eviction of a farmer, the novel belongs very much in the company of the referential postcolonial novel. It is not difficult to see parallels between this work and dozens of other novels from India and elsewhere. But to affirm its conventionality is not to claim that the novel was imitative or that it wasn't well written. The fact that it was republished in Pakistan indicates its appeal to a certain readership. But it does conform to a typical pattern in Indian writing. The novel is intended to be metonymic, with the title suggesting much more than the death of a single farmer. Given the various upheavals that Pakistan underwent in the first two decades, the title suggests political preoccupation, although the work turns out to be concerned with social rather than political realities. But the types, the class divisions, the moral spectrum—all these are present, with sociological accuracy.[7]

The novel fulfils all the expectations generated by a particular mode. There is, for instance, the use of the omniscient narrator, a very nineteenth-century fictional device, but one which works well for a narrative that is framed by a religious and liberal world view. Despite the spatial and temporal shifts that take place in the novel (it moves from Lahore to London, for instance, and flashbacks are interspersed with the chronological movement), there is no real disruption in the narrative. The teleology of the novel, the manner in which the social ethos is evoked, the spectrum of characters, and the economic underpinning, are all calculated to achieve a great degree of transparency. That is, the reader sees no difference, or is not intended to see any distinction, between the narrative and the "real." While it is true, as Richard Walsh claims, "fiction never presents an immediate reality, but only the discourses within which it is inscribed" (9), the novel is a way of experiencing the "real world" second-hand.

Although such novels are not inherently inferior to experimental fiction, it is all too easy to overlook how they are probably also a product of a long tradition of novelistic writing and owe as much to this tradition as to immediate socio-political conditions. And even political conditions function within the framework of certain conventions. The paradigms of the innocent victim, the rapacious landlord, the corrupt policeman, and the adulterous wife, all of whom appear in *Aziz Khan,* are types who belong to a tradition. Hence, such novels demand to be judged on the basis of fidelity to truth rather than the integrity of the text itself. When the author himself is removed from the world that he is describing, and when the readership is also unfamiliar with the social context, the novel operates only within a frame of expectation. In other words, the referential novel succeeds only on the basis of certain expectations being fulfilled. And for the readers, the expectations are based on the tradition of the local novel rather than the conditions of Pakistan that the novel seeks to describe. Consequently, the novel achieves two things: it depicts the multiple realities of a world the author is familiar with, and it shapes that world in ways that are meaningful to a Western reader. The combination of the two often proves to be the undoing of the Indo-Anglian novel.

Aziz Khan, like so many other novels that belong to the same formal category, tells a great deal more than it shows. Or to use the terms that David Lodge employs in his discussion of fiction, there is a much greater sense of diegesis than there is of mimesis, although the fundamental impulse behind the novel is mimetic. Lodge rightly maintains the need for balance. "The classic nineteenth-century novel" he claims, "followed the example of Fielding and Scott in maintaining a fairly even balance between mimesis and diegesis, showing and telling, scene and summary" (31). The implied readership of the Indo-Anglian novel makes that balance all the more difficult, a condition that is true of *Aziz Khan*. For the most part, the narrator's voice fulfils the role of omniscience without drawing attention to itself, but there are moments when the ideological stance of the narrator becomes intrusively evident. For instance:

> "It's bad, very bad," Akram said, frowning and looking at a bazaar print of Mohammed Ali Jinnah, the founder of the nation who is spoken of in Pakistan with a similar degree of reverence as is reserved usually for the prophet himself; disdaining idols, Islam accepts verbal idolatry. (105)

On more than one occasion when the subtext stands outside the reach of the Western reader, the narrator interjects in a manner that sets him/her apart. But even at other times, the third person narration is the preferred mode with a limited use of direct speech. The first section of the novel, entitled "Argument," consists almost entirely of third-person narrative, as a form of prolegomena to the novel. Aspects of character and plot, transitions that are difficult to accomplish but necessary, devices that anticipate or prefigure future actions, are all controlled by the narrator. Not that *Aziz Khan* lacks multiplicity: in a spirited defence of realism, Raymond Tallis maintains that "the realistic novel can present a polycentric universe, tossing the reader from consciousness to consciousness without adjudication, closure or spurious resolution" (57). For the Indo-Anglian novel, this is always a challenge, particularly when the subject matter lies outside the experiential reach of the implied audience.

The strategy of omniscience is in itself nothing new in the history of the novel. Omniscient narrative in the nineteenth century was a staple feature of authorial distance and the pretence of objective truth. The increasing presence of a limited point of view also coincided with a diminishing sense of certainty and a greater reliance on diegesis. With the Indo-Anglian novel, the difference lies in the purpose for which the narrative voice is used. When George Eliot uses the omniscient narrative voice to describe a character, the reader gets access to what is unique about the person. Ghose, on the other hand, feels the need to use narrative voice to express the typical as well. Dorothea in *Middlemarch*, for instance, does not conform to what one initially expects of her, so the reader needs the wisdom of the narrator to shed light on aspects of her character. Aziz Khan and his wife are types, and information about them is not always necessary to those who are familiar with the milieu in which they function. But because Ghose's readers are alienated from the scene, extensive narration is needed to fill the large gaps.

The distinction between diegesis and mimesis that Lodge draws attention to becomes blurry when the novel itself walks a fine line. To let the characters establish a multiplicity of discourses through their own voices is what one would expect of a referential novel. But in *Aziz Khan* only a few characters speak English. As for the others, the only way to establish differences among them is to have them speak in a manner that assigns them the status of stereotypes. Faridah speaks with a very pronounced accent, and that establishes her as shallow and snobbish, and very much a part of the new rich. Hussain's dialect identifies him as a sleazy broker. Officials speak a variety of standard or Babu English. Afaq and Javed use diction that one would associate with their counterparts in the West. Zarina reveals all the sentimental jargon of someone used to a diet of Harlequin romances. None of this is "real" but it establishes transparency to the Western reader who is no longer alienated by the "difference" of the text.

The challenge of the author/narrator is to capture the diversity of a whole social ethos through language, while always being aware of the conventionality of the endeavour. The note with which the novel begins gives an early indication of the author's awareness of the fundamental dilemma posed by the novel: "*The Murder of Aziz Khan* is set in that part of Pakistan where Punjabi and Urdu are the principal languages spoken; but since it is an original work of fiction in the English language, I have made the characters use accents and modes of speech which suited them best." For Western readers, the characters must appear both different and similar. But the difference lies in the language, for identity cannot be divorced from the language used by a person. To describe a farmer in Kalapur as eating chapati and speaking English is to create the Other in the image of the West. In this context, the role of the author is that of sociologist or anthropologist, with the stance always running the risk of appropriating local material for a Western audience.

The realism of the Indian novel is often based on the premise of *mise-en-abyme*.[8] What happens in Kalapur–the exploitation of the farmer, the power of industrial giants, large-scale corruption–is intended to be metonymic. And there are markers—sometimes trivial as in the reference to the movie *Bhowani Junction* or the more substantial reference to East Pakistan—and in both cases temporal and spatial coordinates are established. But much of the actual economic struggle is also sacrificed in the process of preserving a sense of the real while working with the conventions of the Western realistic novel. The trade union attempts in Kalapur, easily crushed by the Shah brothers, serve a novelistic purpose, but they hardly allow for the complex history of the trade union movement in Pakistan. The transparency of the novel is as much a strength as a potential weakness.

No writer, working within the confines of realism, can do justice to all the issues without the narrative itself being transformed into a social documentary. When the selection of what is told and what is implied is made with the Western reader in mind, there is both distortion and appropriation. And often this is not a matter of choice. The Other is seen to be interesting only because the other is constructed within the frame of a recognizable reality. The events that lead to the destruction of Aziz Khan are perfectly plausible, but the actual paradigms that frame the novel belong to the tradition of the Victorian novel.

Even at this early stage, Ghose is clearly aware of the limitations of his narrative stance. Where there is a juxtaposition of different forms of diction, or where there is a combination of reported speech and interior monologue, the reader recognizes an attempt to transcend the confines of the mode. When the linearity is arrested to present a version of interior monologue, combined with omniscient narration, the whole scene gets distanced, almost divorced from subjective particularities. These instances do not offer much more insight to the reader. The gesture towards a measure of inwardness plays off one kind of quest against another. Whether the sporadic attempts achieve much or not is probably of less consequence than the attempt at defamiliarization. It is almost as if the author is uncomfortable with the predictability of the paradigms he has invoked.

More significantly, there are at least two other occasions in the novel when self-reflexive comments are introduced to allude to the form itself. The first occurs when Afaq, after a particularly humiliating experience, is called upon to narrate a story. His story of the monkey is a familiar one, deliberately introduced to invoke immediate parallels, but the listeners (who are children) are more interested in the plot than the nuances of meaning. The secondary listener—the surrogate critic as it were—has different expectations because she brings a different frame to the act of narration and is unhappy when the story fails to conform to her preconceived notions. She expresses disappointment, and in fact comes back to the tale on more than one occasion to make sure that it satisfies her sense of closure. For Afaq, the tale is more metaphoric than metonymic, and even if the symbolic element is predictably superficial, the open-ended structure is a necessity even if it disappoints his listeners.

The second occasion of self-reflexivity occurs soon after Pamela and Afaq see a production of *The Winter's Tale* in Stratford. Afaq is frustrated at the absence of logic and the violation of basic conventions of causality in the plot. Pamela's response is also a statement against realism. The argument between the two, predictable as it is, serves the ironic purpose of not only revealing the superficiality of Afaq, who is in any event more interested in the performance of his new car than in the subtleties of the play, but also the author's awareness of the limitations of the form within which the novel operates.

It is not surprising that critical accounts of the novel have stressed the thematic aspect of the work. Its transparency prompts such a reading. But the fact that Ghose has never returned to this version of realism is also worthy of attention. That is not to say that the book is flawed. Robert Ross, for instance, makes the claim that "the book holds a solitary and distinguished place in Pakistan's English language writing" (203). To say that a work of realism is, ipso facto, inferior would be to oversimplify what is a complex issue. It is possible to claim, as Richard Walsh does, that "innovative fiction does not abandon the conventions of realist representation out of adolescent posturing, glib nihilism or sheer frivolity, but the better to pursue something else: an *argument*" (42). But the argument (or artifice) is the main impediment in *Aziz Khan.*

Tallis makes the point that realism has been condemned for various reasons, of which one is that it replicates and validates the ideology of the state. Regardless of the gestures it makes towards protest, it is eventually forced to capitulate to the ideology of the rulers and gives in to the situation of naturalizing the hegemony of the state. He points out that for critics impatient with the endless moralizing of realism, "realistic fiction is therefore an important component of the Literary State Apparatus that works to ensure the reproduction of the means and relations of production" (51). Tallis, who disagrees strongly with this reading of realism, prefers a more complex role for realism. In this novel, there is clearly a debunking of the industrial empire of the Shah brothers. There is also an idealization of the Aziz Khan family and a final acceptance of defeat. In itself this is not a surrender to the dominant ideology.

One sees the inevitable triumph of the Shah brothers, but there is certainly no moral validation of their world. But the novel is trapped within certain conventions (Aziz Khan is himself a landlord) and if a certain moral vision informs the novel and its tragic closure, there is really no attempt to transcend the basic condition of which the Shah brothers are the ultimate embodiment. Put this way, as a social document, the novel hardly goes beyond conventional pathos.

It is hardly profitable to enter into a detailed discussion of the relative merits and weaknesses of realism as a narrative mode. *The Murder of Aziz Khan* works with easy binaries, with paradigms that are predictable. But it attempts to do what the vernacular author does with much greater success. If nothing else, the vernacular author does not have to bridge the distance between the "real" and the "fictive" in ways that the Indo-Anglian author must. The need to explain, to make the remote familiar, to invoke pathos and a sense of the tragic are all challenges that can place too much of a burden on the novel. It is likely that Ghose needed greater distance. As he says in a different context, "the fact that every writer believes that the book he wrote ten years ago would be better if he were to write it now implies that the further we are from our subject, the better equipped we are to create the language which best suits that subject matter" (*Fiction* 66).

In an essay entitled "Going Home" he speaks of his impressions of Pakistan by describing an incomplete statue of the Buddha.[9] The choice of a signifier without a recognizable and logical signified is the author's provocative way of alerting the reader to the danger of confusing ideology with history. Again it is important that the palimpsest is not foregrounded at the expense of realistic representation. The statue itself is not distorted, but what it implies through its incompleteness is really what concerns the author. About his own writing he is explicit in *The Art of Creating Fiction*, drawing attention to the mode, which is clearly at a remove from the obvious strategies of non-referential writing. Summarizing a story by Henry James, appropriately titled "The Real Thing," the author describes how, in order to create an illustration of the English nobility, the artist-narrator eventually decides not to use a genteel pair but a dwarfish Italian ice-cream vendor and a freckled cockney girl. The author forsakes the easy choice of selecting the "real thing" in favour of two others who are anything but genteel. Thus he arrives at the paradoxical assertion that "the only certain reality is that which is known to be an appearance" (21).

More often than not it is the language, with its potential to construct its own reality, that concerns the author. The relation between language and the reality it implies is an arbitrary one, so while the language persuades the reader of a certain truth, the relation for the author may well be different. The sign is thus indeterminate and the quest for some form of unalterable truth through language is likely to be futile.

Almost twenty-five years separate *The Murder of Aziz Khan* from *The Triple Mirror of the Self*, during which time Ghose consistently moved away from both realism as a mode and from subject matter that was identifiably Indian or Pakistani. Poems, occasional essays, and even the sporadic reference in fiction are reminders of the author's origins, but the bulk of the work is set, quite deliberately, in contexts that have no bearing on Ghose's life in England or in the USA. Here again, there are exceptions–his two novels, *Crump's Terms* and *Hulme's Investigations into the Bogart Script*–but even these which are set in the West have no direct connection with the author's life.

After having written the Brazilian trilogy and three other novels that are perhaps more characteristic of his corpus than anything else–he wrote the *Triple Mirror of the Self*, a novel that combines a form of antirealism with a subject matter that is specifically Indian. The novel is intended to be intertextual–there are references that bring to mind both *Aziz Khan* and his poetry, for instance. Incidental as it may well be, the reference to Mohammed Ali Road in both novels makes the connection for the reader.[10] Kalapur may not be Sialkot, but the fictiveness of one is always underscored by the reality of the other. Bombay, on the other hand, is "real," but its transparency is constantly destabilized by the fictions of, say, Suxavat in the first section of the novel.

If one were to concede that both novels are "about" something, then they do thematize the notion of "home," and are about nations and identities and individual quests that are part of the author's consciousness. The crucial difference, however, is that while the earlier novel takes the subject matter for granted, the other problematizes it by insisting that what the mind remembers or fabricates is essentially a construct. The fiction is a product of language, and the language, without denying its dependence on the referent, creates its own reality. The artifice retains all the trappings of realism, but it is the formal experiment, the struggle with language and form, that concerns the novelist. Even Pons, the somewhat fatuous creator of the text, grants that he must "reinvent the idea of reality after discovering that reality, poor thing, has no existence at all" (194).

In different ways, *Triple Mirror* alerts the reader to the paradox of creating an end-stopped narrative to encapsulate an ongoing process. The self that lived in India, the man who leaves for England, and the author who writes are all implicated in a process that makes any easy resolution to the quest narrative suspect. Shimomura writes in his notebook about "the startling intimation that while [his] mind and body were inevitably interdependent there was a third aspect to the self, being, which could assume a detached existence, as though it resided on a shore now become foreign" (124). In this threefold division, the mind both remembers and leaves, the body changes location, while the being remains in a land where it is now an alien. Given this particular configuration, a narrative that rejects indeterminacy is in itself false. Put differently: "You can't write about yourself and then say *The End*" (148). Regardless of what descriptive labels attach themselves to the three parts (e.g., native, alien, other or local, diasporic, and mythical) taken as a whole, truth becomes suspect. The novelist as ethnographer, sociologist, or investigative journalist are all shown to be inadequate. The novel ends, not with any conventional resolution, but with perpetual entrapment and struggle. Images of enclosure abound in the novel, warning the reader that all narratives which promise closure are in fact fictions generated by the yearning for certainty.

Once the possibility of any definitive resolution is rejected as implausible, in the vision of the text, the first casualty is realism itself. One of the striking strategies used for this is the presence of an author (curiously enough, a famous Latin American realist) whose own world confounds the reader and the narrator. The author Valentin Sadaba, having come across the incomplete manuscript of Urim, chooses not to complete it but to entrust the task to Pons who is not a writer but an academic (a mediocre one at that). Pons, with his puerile fascination with his camera (also an indication of his brand of realism) is much more literal-minded than Sadaba, and the juxtaposition between the two is intended to reveal crucial aspects of the relation between realism and the lived experience of the author. Sadaba lives in a world that is recognizable as the stuff of realist novels, but his own thoughts move in the direction of the symbolic and the fantastic. When referred to by Pons as the "maestro of realism" Sadaba responds: "And that is precisely why I keep nine-tenths of my experience to myself" (110). Sadaba has no patience with imitators of Latin storytellers, but his realism is a curious kind. Pons, on the other hand, is given to reading *The Ring and the Book*, but has no real sense of the relativism and consciousness that permeates Browning's poem. Pons becomes increasingly perplexed with Sadaba and in response to his question about the genesis of the manuscript, Sadaba offers a small gift:

> Just then a boy with a basket of fruit on his head was passing by the window and Sadaba shouted at him, "Pablito!"
>
> The boy came to the window. Sadaba gave him a coin and took a fruit from the basket, a guava, I noticed. Sadaba turned to me, held out his hand and said, "And here's another small present for you. You saw how I acquired it, but who can tell where it came from? (116)

Here, a central aspect of the novel gets articulated. The context of the novel is easy enough, but the origins of the work are a different matter altogether. The task given to Pons, which evolves into the novel, is central to establishing its difference from *Aziz Khan*. The "I" that begins the novel is the voice of Urim, different in texture from the "I" of the narrator, although both are used without any explanatory comments. When the narrator shifts to the third person, it is still not totally omniscient, but rather a different centre of consciousness. The latter part of the novel is seen through the consciousness of Roshan, despite the omniscience of the narrator. The device of collecting multiple sources of information (including Shimomura's English notebooks) in order to cobble together the narrative allows for diverse voices, none of which establishes a firm point of reference. Conventional as it may seem, the point being made is that no single author or consciousness provides the authority for the text; its validity lies precisely in its status as a verbal construct.

Quite intentionally, a whole chapter devoted to the disastrous quest of Isabel is called "Novella Isabella." By self-consciously invoking the name of Henry James's famous portrait, the author not only underscores a whole intertextual field but drives home the idea that he too is concerned with form, with artifice, with consciousness, and the complex relation between art and experience. While Pons recreates with fidelity what is purported to be inscribed in the manuscript, he too is probably immersed in the task of shaping the text. The reference to Isabel is not gratuitous, for when Pons is vexed with issues of textual accuracy, he restores "[his] mental balance by reading a few pages of Henry James" (193). Despite the obvious similarities between Isabel Archer and Isabel Valdivieso (both are rich women who move to the "centre" of culture) the objective is less to play off one novel against the other than to invoke the idea of a literary tradition.

Repeatedly in *Triple Mirror*, point of view alters or destabilizes the nature of the experience itself. For instance, when Alicia and Roshan, having climbed up the Malabar Hill, look down at the Chowpatty Beach, all of them, including the narrator, see three different perspectives. Whether the moment lends itself to a comparison with Keats's urn, or with some sense of sensual fulfilment, or even a vision of something primordial that even the character is only vaguely aware of, the perspective is still dependent, not on something "objective" so much as the associations that the viewer brings to the moment. The intensity of the episode is a direct result of a juxtaposition that brings together a mundane instance of infatuation with the aesthetic refinement of Keats's poem in order to warn the reader that while the plot cannot be dispensed with in a work of fiction, the objective of the novelist is not to follow the plot but rather to use it to draw the reader into a fictive world where a cluster of metaphors permit the illumination with which the novel is really concerned.

Hardly surprising, then, is the constant presence of reflecting surfaces, of mirrors, and images of translucence. Even Pons has his epiphany in a Mughal palace when he is surrounded by mirrors. In a hotel, Urim sees Pons's reflection as a fragmented embodiment of himself. As Ghose points out in *The Fiction of Reality*, "certain realities are only to be perceived in carefully placed mirrors, and if the reflection before our contemplation is ablaze with a riot of brilliant images it is probably because the angle of the light in that moment excludes all shadows" (33).

Having thus established the solipsistic aspect of the novel, the text still offers a curious challenge. The unity of the novel is probably the most elusive aspect of the work, although at a most rudimentary level it's possible to make connections, or even assert a teleology of sorts. At least one third of the novel prompts a referential reading, partly because the reader makes the implied connection between the author and the text. The narrative covers a period of approximately ten years (from ages seven to seventeen) in the life of Roshan Karim in Bombay, from the early 1940s to the early 1950s, all of which coincide with Ghose's own life. It is a comparison that the text deliberately invites, by using markers that anyone familiar with the biographical or cultural backdrop would hardly miss. Placed at the end of the tripartite structure, the narrative adopts the order of reverse chronology, forcing a rereading of the text.

The other two sections are less metonymic. The second, involving Shimmers and Isabel as they move from London to Arizona, and then Isabel's own quest in Peru, seems to contain elements of both realism and artifice. Very few of the events themselves are overtly antirealist, although the narrator's manipulation of text and character reminds the reader of the literariness of the endeavour. The author himself follows the trajectory of his character Shimmers, and names in the novel have a tendency to be ambiguous as his own, but beyond that the connection is tenuous.[11]

The first section, set in Suxavat, a village without national affiliations, almost suspended in time, is perhaps the most magical and mythical. Here again, magic in the form of a performance is gratuitously included to warn the reader against a hasty identification with the magical. In general terms, however, this entire section comes closest to mythical or symbolic discourse, where the conventions of realism still function without the benefit of referential markers. What happens in Suxavat may well have happened elsewhere, except that the village belongs to a forgotten past. This is where Urim, tormented by having become an outsider in three continents, arrives to share with the rest of the village the consciousness that memory is all that is left.

The challenge that the novel creates for itself is one of writing about personal identity without necessarily claiming the representativeness of experience, or not wanting to validate personal experience by invoking public events as an anchor. If the journey out can be plotted in spatial and temporal terms, the quest must operate at least partially as mythical discourse where images surface in a logic that confounds the reader and the characters themselves. Even after one recognizes the reverse chronology that links the text, the rationale of the juxtaposition continues to be problematic. As in myth, the rational and the causal are only aspects of a discourse that needs to be understood within a larger symbolic mode. Archetypes rather than types dominate the novel and the intertext is as important as the text. In that sense the novel is part of "great new novelistic culture characterized by an extraordinary sense of the real coupled with an untrammelled imagination that breaks every rule of plausibility" (Kundera 30).

In his critical work *The Womb of Space*, and in a later essay which appeared in the *Review of Contemporary Fiction*, Wilson Harris describes what he perceives to be a cross-cultural imagination that underlies Ghose's work. The stance he adopts is not altogether unfamiliar given his own endeavour in his novels to recover a Caribbean history and identity that has been obscured by successive invasions. Working primarily with Ghose's poetry, he points to the manner in which images, startling in their incongruity, reappear in the work, sometimes unconsciously to augment what the mind intuitively grasps.[12]

In *The Triple Mirror*, such references to "home" appear in the most unlikely moments. Even in the first section, Urim is suddenly reminded of Mohammed Ali Road in Bombay, or remembers General Dyer ordering his troops to fire on unarmed men and women in the infamous Jallianwalla Bagh massacre or even more recent events such as the storming of the Golden Temple during the time of Indira Gandhi. Even Urim is puzzled by the strange associations that insist on floating up to the surface. "How could I have witnessed those killings on Mohammed Ali Road, an improbable name for a street, I have not left this muddy abode under the rain forest, what could make such information so valuable I must assign it recognition? I do not remember being in the streets where knives sprang up in the air" (6). The random associations of violence are not necessarily part of a continuum, nor do they connect in spatial or temporal terms, but they are germane to the discourse of the novel.

In the same manner, there are oblique references to Buddhism, again an unlikely motif, particularly because of the total eclipse of Buddhism in India, and because the character's Muslim upbringing makes that all the more unconventional. But Buddhism is a constant presence, as in the description at the beginning: "A man sat under the tree of rebirth. He faced the lake in which swam watersnakes around the green disc of the lotus. Upon the lotus reposed the last surviving drop after the evaporation of the oceans" (12). Again for no particular reason, Roshan and Mona, a Muslim and Sikh, chant Buddhist slokas as they desecrate a Hindu kitchen. The motif of renunciation, the desperate desire to seek release from desire and transcend rebirth, are very much a part of the Buddhist frame of the novel.

The ongoing conflict is seen in the constant invocation of Eros, symbolized in the passion for women, which promises freedom from torment, but always turns out to be chimera. Horuxtla, Eliza, and Alicia are all versions of this quest, a literary metaphor to encapsulate a compulsive search for wholeness. Intentionally, Roshan's "ideal" is a woman called Miranda, and when he follows her home, he expects magical experience. What he discovers (in addition to the fact her name is Alicia), is that she lives in a filthy home, with totally licentious sisters, and the stench of excrement destroys whatever expectation he began with.

The whole episode has some parallels with others in the novel, such as the conditions around Sadaba's home or the rampant sexuality in the hotel where Pons finds himself. Alicia's suburb masquerades as "real" simply because other markers are known to be real, but the structure of events is dictated by a compulsion to find a cluster of images that would express a motif necessitated by the internal logic and vision of the novel. While the sequentiality offers a particular kind of meaning, it is the diachronic mode, the constant linking of related images, that ultimately reveals the design of the novel.

An interesting example of what Wilson Harris alludes to as the cross-cultural imagination occurs in the second section when Shimmers and Isabel, after a long drive, find themselves in a village that the map has forgotten to mention and whose inhabitants, having been severed from the sources of their origins and culture, recapitulate (very much like the monkey warriors who visit Suxavat), rituals that have ceased to be meaningful and now serve the purpose of mere entertainment. And Jaghes, having witnessed the travesty of the former ritual, exclaims: "Nothing comes back of the past, ceremony is dead in us, and though we inhale the smoke of the forbidden leaf and call to our brains to summon ancestral apparitions, no stimulant works, no dream awakens, nothing comes back of the past" (147).

When they arrive at Kailost and seek the way back home, Shimomura begins his question with the words "would you know how we can get to" (42) and Isabel, concerned with location and facts, says simultaneously, "there's no mention of this village." They both pause and then utter the same words, "Where are we?" Their responses are paradoxical, given their subsequent decisions, but more important to the artifice that surrounds the episode is that Kailost is an anagram for Sialkot, the place where Ghose was born. Cartographically, Kailost is, in fact, lost, while Sialkot is not. The transformation of the real into the fictive captures layers of experience in ways that are hardly possible in a referential work.

The novel is hardly about nostalgia for a lost world or a celebration of a remembered one. The crucial aspect that distinguishes the novel, and sets it apart from the realism of *Aziz Khan,* is the capacity and insistent need to create fictions that would provide access to the truth. The novel is at least partly a creation myth, emphasized by the section entitled "Puru Sa"–an obvious reference to the *Rg Veda* and the Hindu myth of creation. It is no surprise that the social stratification implied in the myth impels Tambour after the expedition to Puru Sa to establish an oppressive and hierarchical system in Suxavat. If, at some level, the first section is allegorical, the correspondence does not hold good in the second section.

More important is the myth implied when Urim is first described curled up like a fetus in a village that is surrounded by water. At the end of this part, Urim is seen with Horuxtla, surrounded by logs of fire. The metaphors of birth and death, combined with Urim's passionate desire for Horuxtla, who gives herself to him only after she had given herself to several others, is seen as both death and rebirth. As elsewhere, Eros, personified in Horuxtla, is always elusive and consummation with her becomes a form of death and rebirth. The only satisfaction comes with the recognition that the mountain range on the horizon, blinding in its brightness, is none other than the Hindu Kush.

Very different from Rushdie's work, Ghose's novel demonstrates in yet another way the process of transforming the legacy of a Western literary tradition in order to access local realities, and the reality of an alienated consciousness. The conventions that inform the work are, for the most part, Western. The fusion of a "native" consciousness with an "alien" mode not only explains the novel but also the impulse behind much of counterrealistic writing. The self-consciousness of working with two different systems gets transformed into a strength. Unlike *The Murder of Aziz Khan* which struggles to maintain the pretence of transparency, or his subsequent novels that avoid referential markers, here is a work that invokes the referential without conceding the need to establish fidelity to truth. The Bombay that is described may well intersect, intermittently, with the "real" city, but what is more important is the form that, through its own artifice, provides some access to what Isabel in the *Triple Mirror* calls "a source of infinite sadness" (162). The realism of *The Murder of Aziz Khan* tells a partial truth while creating the impression of totality. *The Triple Mirror of the Self* parades its artifice while pursuing aspects of truth which, although empirically unverifiable, are no less significant.

CHAPTER 6

Fashioning New Fables: Suniti Namjoshi

Suniti Namjoshi's *Feminist Fables*, first published in 1981, begins with a fable entitled "From the *Panchatantra*," which, among other things, serves as an introduction to the discontinuous mode of the book and as an acknowledgment of the Indian sources from which the author fashions at least part of her work. The story is not a retelling of a fable from the *Panchatantra*, but in its texture and its ideological stance, it could well be a parody of this collection of stories. Namjoshi's story is about many things: gods, brahmins, women, gender, patriarchy, and Hinduism, although the "plot" deals with a brahmin who desperately wants a son and with his daughter who, with equal desperation, wants to be a human being. At the end of the fable in which a woman is denied her request that she be given human status, the author/narrator sums up by saying that while Aesop's fables include only beasts, the *Panchatantra* uses both beasts and brahmins. The deliberate reference to animals in a story that includes no beasts points clearly to the author's perception of the status of women in the world depicted in Visnu Sarma's popular Indian text.

Obviously, the *Panchatantra* includes much more than brahmins and beasts, but the point made here is well taken. The text privileges both men and brahmins and de-emphasizes women to the point that they are denied their humanity and serve as appendages to a male world. In another tale entitled "Svayamvara" the traditional Indian practice of a bride choosing a husband—ostensibly an egalitarian and non-androcentric attitude—is interrogated to reveal that in fact a male code of prowess and valour is being valorized in the ritual, rather than the free will of the woman. Comic and parodic in turns, the fable ends on a positive note with the woman marrying the prince only when he concedes that he has been beaten fairly in a whistling match.

According to Namjoshi, *Aesop's Fables*, myths, fairy tales, and in fact a whole literary canon works within an ideological framework that privileges men. It does not matter, as she demonstrates in "Myth" (*Fables* 106) that gods and demons endlessly fight each other or that Brahma is complicitous in prolonging the violence. In the end it is the fault of the goddess—"she gave in" (106). Discussing both the patriarchal and misogynist assumptions in his introduction to *Aesop's Fables*, Robert Temple makes the point that in the world of Aesop, "women were relegated to such obscurity and powerlessness that they...were essentially slaves....Second, there seems to have been no general consensus that compassion towards one's fellow human beings had anything particular to recommend it" (xvii). Writing against this tradition has been Namjoshi's major objective, although the degree of satiric denunciation has varied over the years. In her many interviews, she has been candid about the ideology that shapes her work. For example, in a dialogue with Pratibha Parmar, she makes the observation that her consciousness "is a lesbian feminist one and an Indian one in some curious way" (20). Speaking to Brenda Brooks, she insists that women have eavesdropped on male discourse for a long time and had to find a niche in the gaps and silences of male-centred texts. She also believes that now feminists in their own writing must necessarily transform the power balance and write for a female readership, allowing men to eavesdrop if they choose to.[1] In short, her writing in the late 1970s and early 1980s was, like so much of the feminist writing and scholarship of the period, concerned with deconstructing a literary canon and an ontology that insisted on privileging patriarchy.

In a significant article, entitled "Poetry or Propaganda" she elaborates on the impulse behind her writing, and although she sees no purpose in literature that is purely tendentious, she has no qualms about writing with definite goals in mind.[2] One of the tales in *Feminist Fables*, which deals with Philomel, makes it clear that art for art's sake, despite all the assertions of the self-sufficiency of the text, is the consequence of having silenced the female voice. Philomel sings and is celebrated only because she forsakes the story of her rape and disfigurement: "She had her tongue ripped out, and then she sang down through the centuries. So it seems only fitting that the art she practices should be art for art's sake, and never spelt out, no, never reduced to its mere message—that would appal" (102). In many of her critical essays and reviews, on the writing of P.K. Page, Adrienne Rich, and Jay Macpherson, for instance, her stance is always evident.[3]

The curious juxtapositions in her work, however, point to the fact that her impulse to distance herself from a formalist approach is never really endorsed in her writing. While her consciousness as a feminist, lesbian, and diasporic author requires her to deal with issues, her sensibility as a writer responds to the aesthetic appeal of artifice. Even the most epigrammatic and concise of her fables is never entirely transparent. The duality that appeals to her is evident, for example, in the comment she makes about Jay Macpherson's *Welcoming Disaster* that "it is also about the human soul exploring hell" and adds that "the distance between the mythopoeic and the familiar is less great than might be supposed" (58). As in *Welcoming Disaster*, the everyday is never quite referential and the mythical does not always belong to the past. The capacity to shift myth and fable from orality to a literary mode and, in the process, redefine the function of myth in contemporary culture is one of the major contributions of Namjoshi. She is, in that role, a self-conscious myth-maker and mythographer. She creates myths and unpacks them at the same time.

Namjoshi considers herself to be more a poet than a fictionist. And this is not simply a question of genre, for she pays little attention to such distinctions in her mixed-genre works. It is also not a preference for poetry over fiction. But the impulse behind her fiction is poetic, and her mode of writing, in its texture, its penchant for avoiding context, and its personal voice, has the quality of poetry. Her discussion with Parmar affirms that she is "essentially a lyric poet, even the fables are the work of a poet" (20). It is this peculiar mixture of the poetic impulse with her fiction that accounts for so much that is unique in her work.

In the tradition of Indian writing in English, there are few precedents for Namjoshi. Poets who worked with myth (such as Sarojini Naidu in the early part of the twentieth century) are too literal, almost exotic in the unselfconscious manner in which they reproduce myths. Surprisingly, there are connections between Narayan and Namjoshi, although in terms of ideology they represent two ends of the spectrum. Narayan's world is brahminical and patriarchal, while Namjoshi's is feminist and lesbian. For Namjoshi, her brahminical background appears to be less important than her Hindu sensibility. Her upper-caste background figures intermittently in her writing, but the references tend to gravitate towards irony rather than celebration. But both writers do write fables. At least one of Narayan's novels, namely, *A Tiger for Malgudi*, is clearly in the mode of a fable. More importantly, both of them share an attitude to ontology. For both Narayan and Namjoshi, a Hindu sensibility is a way of life that incorporates but is not subsumed by religion. Both writers foreground an identifiable Indianness in their work. But there the comparison ends. Narayan's counterrealism serves the purpose of asserting a revisionist world view. Namjoshi's artifice uses the past as a foil to project her own perspective. If Narayan's work is circumscribed by Malgudi, Namjoshi's is far more internationalist.

G.V. Desani is probably a useful point of comparison, although *Hali* is more conservative in its retelling of myth than Namjoshi's work. (More specifically, the eponymous Hatterr in the novel *All About H. Hatterr* is more than incidentally connected to the curious namesake in *Alice in Wonderland*.) Both authors share a sense of a topsy-turvy world, although the slapstick in Desani is hardly the mode of Namjoshi's work. Desani subverts conventional wisdom by introducing paradigms that are later shown to be false. Namjoshi deconstructs by offering what Bonnie Zimmermann calls a "perverse" reading that, in the process of suggesting alternative interpretations, shows how the original is neither disinterested nor innocent.[4]

Desai is obviously a precursor to Namjoshi, particularly in her concern with gender and myth, but Desai hardly ever deals with fable in the manner that Namjoshi does. For Desai, myth is a necessary subtext that calls into question the significance of the real. For Namjoshi, myth is the raw material to work with in order to alter consciousness. The precedents for Namjoshi are really more ancient texts, particularly the *Panchatantra*, which provides the kind of framework that Namjoshi uses to good effect. Her work draws from Aesop, from the Bible, from the two Indian epics (namely, the *Mahabharata* and *Ramayana)*, and from a whole fund of myths, fairy tales, and legends. As myth-maker and fabulist, she belongs to an eclectic tradition that is both oral and written, and from these she fashions her own work.

Her counterrealism, then, does not necessarily conform to the notion of the "fantastic" as defined by critics such as Todorov. The uncanny is not totally absent: there is one story involving two sisters dismembered and joined together again where the conventions of what is acceptable are deliberately subverted.[5] Even in this instance, the precedent is there. For instance, the fifth book of the *Panchatantra*, as Chandra Rajan quite rightly points out, belongs to a twilight world where realism and fantasy intersect. Rajan adds that "inhabiting the blurred landscape between reality and fantasy, this twilight world also holds up a mirror, a distorting one that is disturbing" (xxxv). In order to explain such instances of black humour, Namjoshi sometimes falls back on a kind of essentialist or nativist defence, when she claims that such a sense of bizarre humour is part of her Maratha sensibility. In fact, she has consistently maintained that several distinguishing characteristics of her writing can be attributed to her life in Maharashtra and her identity as a Maharashtrian. Referring specifically to "Snow White and Rose Green" she says: "The irony, the malice, and the bizarre sense of humour are certainly characteristic of Marathi (the language spoken in Maharashtra)" ("Snow White" 15). Nonetheless, in such cases, there is a deliberate attempt to flout credibility in ways that her animal fables don't.

"Snow White and Rose Green" is a disturbing combination of the Gothic and the surreal. The pattern of reversal tinged with humour, which is her characteristic strategy, gives way to the kind of counterrealism that shocks and unsettles the reader. It does not matter, the story seems to suggest, what the specific details are. The binary schemes within which fairy tales, legends, and folk tales operate favour those who conform and acquiesce. The pig that goes to market is always shown to be more "moral" than the pig that doesn't, in much the same way the person who is straight is contrasted with one who isn't. As myth-maker, Namjoshi is determined to subvert this paradigm even if it means denying the happy ending the reader expects and defamiliarizing the text. "Snow White and Rose Green" ends with the victory of the "bad" sister, who, by persuading a surgeon to cut her and the "good" sister in half and reattach them to the wrong half, succeeds in erasing the arbitrary morality that determines what is right and wrong. In fact, the very title, *From the Bedside Book of Nightmares* suggests that the artifice is a consequence of probing the subconscious, the repressed, and the oneiric. While Desai, for instance, taps the subconscious by letting clusters of images subvert the metonymic reading of her text, Namjoshi achieves the same effect through a diction that is transgressive. In an explanatory comment about the book in *Because of India*, she mentions that her intention was to "explore the bloodier aspects of gay liberation and women's liberation" (83).

The transgressive and surreal impulse that permeates *Nightmares* is unusual in Namjoshi's writing. The characteristic mode involves animals and human beings, with the dominant tone coming across as ironic or playful. For the most part, the constant weaving in and out of animals in her work is, from her perspective, not counterrealistic, except in relation to the conventional notion of classic realism. For the reader who brings to the fables a Western frame of reference it may well be the case; as Bruce Ross points out, "the grammar of traditional animal symbols is absent altogether in postmodern art and literature" (ix). Namjoshi's point is that if one had grown up in an Indian or Hindu context, then the distinction between animals and humans is hardly of much consequence, not a result of a belief in reincarnation but in a whole cultural ethos in which identities are necessarily fluid. The quest for individual identity is, for Namjoshi, a Western obsession. The issue then is not the difference between being religious and secular. Within an Indian framework, such identities are arbitrary, and hence metamorphosis or the phenomenon of animals and humans talking to each other is not part of the fantastic.

From the reader's view, such conventions are, at least initially, counterrealistic. Within a tradition that defines realism along certain lines, anecdotal stories involving animals and humans must lie outside the referential. But once the convention becomes naturalized, it becomes more difficult to read the fables as counterrealistic. As far as some of the conventions of realism, such as causality and linearity, are maintained, and animals are given human qualities, the element of artifice begins to diminish. Once the premise of the fable is conceded, the world she projects becomes naturalized, although it remains a far cry from the tradition of classic realism.

The main difference, however, that sets her work apart from the fable tradition, is the relation her work establishes to a prior text. The force of the fable is largely a consequence of a prior text and context that the reader shares with the author.[6] If the prior text, with its own cluster of meaning, is readily assumed by the author and reader, the author is automatically in a position to work with more than one level of narrative. Fables assume a "shadow" text that complements and establishes a distance from the present one. So depending on how much the reader knows about the symbolic or allegorical context, the fable makes sense. When the fable works at the level of myth it presupposes a particular kind of knowledge; and when it operates at the level of allegory it draws on another level of understanding. Fable as allegory draws on binaries quite easily while fable as myth allows for multiplicity. If the fable is an "easier" form in some respects, it is because much of the referent is assumed integral to the narrative.

Working consistently with fable and allegory is more difficult than it appears for the writer whose objectives are subversive. Allegory works well when it operates in tandem with the reader's sense of the past. Greenfield makes the point that "allegorical reading is seldom capable of radicalism precisely because it provides a metaphoric mechanism of escape from any uncomfortable associations" (16). In short, when allegory performs the role of affirming the status quo or understanding the values or ideology about which there is consensus in a community, it encounters very few challenges. There is, then, a tacit agreement between author and reader about the symbolic role of allegory. When this agreement is ruptured, as with subversive forms of allegory, sustaining the interest of the reader becomes considerably more difficult.

Greenfield's observation brings to mind Fredric Jameson's well-known article that characterizes the entire corpus of postcolonial literature as national allegory, and claims that even the most personal and private texts have a public and national relevance. "Third-world texts" says Jameson, "necessarily project a political dimension in the form of national allegory" (69). In retrospect, Jameson's stance is no more than a broad generalization, but the notion that the oppositional and subconscious impulse in postcolonial litearature is anchored in allegorical writing is an important one. If Jameson's position holds true for at least some writing, then surely allegory is capable of radical thought.

The difference between Greenfield and Jameson lies in the manner in which allegory is invoked and built into the structure of a work. The kind of allegory that Greenfield works with advertises itself as allegory from the very outset, while in Jameson's use the markers are not self-evident. In Jameson's reading of postcolonial texts, the narrative establishes a measure of self-sufficiency even while it gestures towards a symbolic reading. It is the referential dimension that allows for the subversion. In Namjoshi, the referent is conspicuously absent, and the objective is to destabilize traditional structures that are hegemonic.

Allegory assumes a particular resonance in Indian epics in which the literal and symbolic levels coexist. When the referential is ambivalent and the morality is subversive, allegory can shift the reader's focus from individual motives and actions to ideology. The allegory here coexists with and complements the human or referential aspect. The combination of the two serves the purpose of accommodating the aleatory and making it acceptable to an audience that does not wish to focus on indeterminacy and compromise. For example, both in the *Ramayana* and the *Mahabharata*, there are moments when the actions of characters who embody god-like qualities become morally ambiguous. At such moments, the shift to allegory redeems the text and provides the rationale for the intransigencies of character. Because the prior text is, by common agreement, sacrosanct, individual actions are seen to be of less consequence.

For Namjoshi, the audience is hardly homogeneous, even when she writes for a feminist and lesbian readership. When she invokes a tradition, it's only to subvert and distort it. Rewriting traditional myths, as in the fable about the sage Gautama, and the rape of his wife by the god Indra, immediately recalls and realigns the frame of reference.[7] What she attempts is not merely a different reading of an old myth. Now a new myth is created in ways that create a kind of doubleness. The possibility of different versions underlines the ideological bias inherent in the myth. Each myth lends itself to a new telling says Namjoshi in *Building Babel*, and each such occasion provides the opportunity for a new reading.[8] But now the frame is not collective wisdom so much as the voice and perspective of the author. When the author intervenes in such a manner, the artifice also becomes evident.

In fact, the presence of the author is one of the more noticeable aspects of Namjoshi's work. In her early work, *Cyclone in Pakistan*, the editor makes the observation that the author requested that no biographical details be included in the volume. In *Feminist Fables*, the persona of Suniti begins to enter her fiction, and from *Conversations of Cow* onwards, not only is Suniti a constant presence, but the relation between the persona and the author is insistently emphasized. The details given in *Conversations*, for instance, that Suniti is Indian, is a university teacher, etc., hardly allow for any ambiguity. The combination of a recognizable author-figure and the mode of the fable, brought together, makes the work counterrealistic without dismantling some of the conventions of realism.

A recognizable trajectory in Namjoshi's fiction reveals ways in which the form itself changed over a period of time. Her two collections of fables share similarities; both are discontinuous, anecdotal, and satiric. The concerns are both feminist and lesbian and the formal strategy is often to either subvert traditional myths and fables or fashion new ones. There is both a sense of writing against and of rehabilitating old myths in order to posit a new frame of reference. They are often open-ended and they deliberately resist closure. The very eclecticism enables a defamiliarization and a sense of artifice. As Meigs sums it up: "*The Fables* are written in a special language, like a dream language...which Namjoshi has invented to express her thoughts, her anxieties, her griefs, her wit....The myths, the fairy tales, the bits of news or the real events she has observed have become parables" (66). While *Feminist Fables*, by virtue of its eclectic mode, tends to draw examples from a range of sources in order to deconstruct them, *The Blue Donkey Fables* works with the persona of the Blue Donkey, who, like the one-eyed monkey, is a marginal figure whose life and various encounters become a metaphor for a very different perspective and aesthetic. While the earlier text deconstructs, the next one moves in the direction of recuperation and a much greater sense of agency for the marginalized. However, even in *Feminist Fables*, happy endings that celebrate male myths are often retold to suggest alternative endings that are far more empowering to women. Thus Cinderella, for instance, walks out of her house after an argument with the prince: "'You married me for my money,' was the Prince's charge. 'You married me for my looks' was C's reply. 'But your looks will fade, whereas my money will last. Not a fair bargain.' 'No,' said Cinderella and simply walked out" (*Feminist* 118)

By the time Namjoshi moves to the novella, *Conversations of Cow*, a very different perspective begins to emerge. For one thing, the form itself is closer to the novel with something of a beginning, middle, and end. It is written within the framework of a novelistic tradition. Also, it is a work that examines the complexities of personal and collective identity within utopian separatism. There is no outright rejection of any position, no clear dichotomy, and no attempt to gloss over the problems of racial identity. In fact, Suniti's first act of resistance is against her name being shortened to Sue by her lesbian friends.

The reception to the novel has not been particularly favourable, partly because of its form and its mode of inquiry that moves away from the dominant mode of feminist utopian writing. While agreeing that "*Conversations* seems to deliberately defy categorization as a novel" Patricia Morris goes on to say that she was embarrassed by "the dialogue and plot" and adds that "the child-like allegorical mode, which turns painful adult problems into a simple narrative, is to blame"[9] (41). For many critics, the characteristics of such writing are bypassed in favour of very different mode of inquiry. Unlike the fables, the artifice is far more overt, largely because the sense of a prior text is juxtaposed with the conventions of realism. There is enough referentiality to ground the novella in a particular time and place, and the personal element is flaunted in a manner that demands a biographical reading. At the same time, the work rejects all the details of the tradition realistic novel. Namjoshi herself has commented that very little information about Suniti's (one of the major characters in the novel) background is given in the work and the sense of continuous present is maintained. But the mythical element is never lost sight of and the conventions of probability are subverted. Animals and humans talking to each other may be naturalized within a certain framework, but an animal renting a van or showing a partiality for scotch isn't. The attitude of skepticism that runs through the novel requires an experimental form that forces the reader to adopt new strategies of reading.

A *Bildungsroman* of sorts, *Conversations* is allegorical without ever claiming to be. Almost all the characters have a mythical resonance that draws in a whole field of intertextuality, including the ideological stance of feminist utopian separatism. At the same time, it is a diasporic novel involving a brown woman in a white society, with the consequence that the homogenization of feminist or lesbian identity is resisted from the very beginning. A binarism that borders on essentialism is deliberately invoked and even sustained, but neither Suniti nor the cow Baddy fit into any dualistic scheme.

The rituals that are available to the characters often invoke heterosexual paradigms and are sustained by a patriarchal framework. A whole typology is made on the basis of ideological assumptions. The novel is based on the dilemma faced by Suniti who discovers to her chagrin that her resistance serves only to recapitulate and strengthen these paradigms. The metamorphic element which enables Baddy to take on multiple identities reveals the extent to which counterrealism has a way of circling back to the referential in Namjoshi.

The ironies of the title notwithstanding, the novel is, quite literally, about cows and, to a lesser degree, about humans. Metamorphosis is taken for granted although Suniti, who is the character most concerned with identities, is not permitted the luxury of transformation. The timelessness of myth and the temporality of a contemporary referential work merge in the book, and that accounts for the counterrealism.

The novel begins and ends with a certain kind of Indianness. The invocation with which the novel opens deliberately offers an intertextual parallel with *bhakti* poetry, which consistently used the convention of secular love to religious ends. The heterosexual paradigm is invoked by a dissatisfied Suniti who seeks enlightenment and is visited by a goddess/alter ego who then becomes the occasion to test out all the options available to Suniti. The novel ends with the notion of a grand narrative and a cosmogonic myth, again along traditional lines. The difference, however, is that the myth of the novel celebrates a feminist world, with the qualified assertion of a separatist utopia. Written soon after Namjoshi's decision to leave Toronto and live in England with her partner, the novel is an exploration of the values she believes in and her skepticism about generalizations that recapitulate hegemonic paradigms.

The idea of a separatist world, which is suggested with all its complexities in *Conversations,* becomes the central concern of her next major work of fiction, *The Mothers of Maya Diip.* Certainly the first of its kind in Indian fiction, the novel, set in India, on some indeterminate island off the west coast, is entirely about a lesbian utopia, about a world that, for the most part, excludes males. Strongly reminiscent of postcolonial texts that use this mode to explore the various issues raised by colonialism and decolonization, this text works with a very specific focus. The only exception to the general assumptions of this island is in the person of Valerie, a heterosexual white woman, who dislikes patriarchy and would like to test the viability of a total matriarchy.

There is a relentless logic about the novel that makes the artifice less conspicuous than in *Conversations.* Except for a brief period when men, flying a helicopter in a parody of aliens, attempt to rescue Valerie (again a parody of a conventional patriarchal myth), the locations of the novel are naturalized. From the initial configuration of Maya Diip, where women are the subjects, to Asha Nagar where "pretty boys" adopt the role of women, to the final paradise where gallants spend all their time wooing women, the attempt is to test the viability of a world which excludes not only men but all the conventions of patriarchy.

The very naturalness of the novel becomes, eventually, a measure of its artifice. In ideological terms, the novel is perhaps a retreat from the optimism of the earlier novel, and there is a much greater acknowledgment of the complexities of a separatist utopia. The mode is conventional, but the fabulous is never abandoned. Even in the helicopter used by men to rescue Valerie, the person in charge is a "mother." The novel itself is about mothers and their relation to children, subjects, suitors, and so forth. The hierarchy of the novel is based on different kinds of mothers and their relative power. And with any kind of system, certain assumptions are built into the organization, and regardless of altruistic motives, the system replicates the moral assumptions that gave rise to it. Ironically, the novel is set in India where the maternal cult is woven into the very texture of life.

The "illusion" implied in the title of the novel–"Maya"–is an important aspect of the mode. In a work that, for the most part, conforms to the conventions of the referential novel, the strange presence of the blue donkey is a reminder of both intertextual continuity and artifice. The blue donkey as an animal does not disrupt the naturalness of the novel. What it does, however, is defamiliarize the text for the reader. Always the voice of reason and tact, the blue donkey ensures the ironic detachment of the novel. Interestingly, the prior text of bluebeard or even the patriarchal world view of blue donkey in many of the fables that are included in *The Blue Donkey Fables* do not operate in this work. The novel is a form of self-parody. None of the idealistic paradigms elaborately introduced in *Maya Diip* really succeeds. Sisters turn against themselves, lovers do not see common ground, "pretty boys" are not as harmful as they are made out to be. And the fictiveness of the text becomes a strategy of reappraisal without negation. The abstraction of a matriarchy that eschews all forms of competition and greed is tested out and found to be wanting. But that world too is an illusion.

Saint Suniti and the Dragon marks a point of departure, in ideology more than in form, although its mode too is striking in its artifice.

The text itself is divided into two sections: the first is the narrative of St. Suniti and the dragon and the second, the more traditional collection of discontinuous fables entitled "Solidarity Fables." Thematically the two are connected–preoccupied with the nature of commitment, the virtue of detachment, the impulse to move towards a fundamentalist position, and the intellectual history that validates a particular way of life. The "Solidarity Fables" share much with the author's earlier work, although the sense of ambivalence is often far more noticeable in the later fables.

St. Suniti's narrative, despite the self-reflexivity characteristic of the author, has less to do with feminist and lesbian concerns than any other text. The concern is with metaphysics, with the problem of fear and evil, with a profound sense of despair that any form of posturing–as a poet, or as a theorist–may not have the same valency as commitment and action. Despite all the trappings of the traditional morality narrative, this fable constantly weaves in and out of the public and private, from omniscience to autobiography, from past to present, and from contemporary documentary to fabulism. Poetry appears inevitable in a narrative that invokes Blake and Pound. Fiction, however, is the dominant form. The framing narrative is that of St. George and the *mise en abyme* subverts it by insisting that Suniti internalizes the dragon (read Fear) before starting on the quest towards sainthood. Grendel and his mother consistently appear as the forces of evil in abstract form, against which Suniti struggles by adopting various postures. At the same time, the manuscript itself is interrupted by contemporary events that mock the poet. In the section entitled "War Diary," immediately after the comment that "they bombed Israel again," the narrator adds: "I feel a little ashamed of 'St Suniti and the Dragon'–all that posturing and posing, however ironised. The moral dilemmas are carefully planned, carefully constructed to make them a little clearer. In the manuscript the pictures on TV are playfully conflated with a dream, and the dream with imaginary fields of battle" (23). Contemporary events thus question the artifice, forcing a reappraisal of the manuscript itself.

The absence of a social agenda thus causes an element of misogyny, causing Grendel to reappear in the text and recruit Suniti by establishing a sense of empathy. The conversation between the dragon and Suniti with which the tale ends is one more assertion that this resistant text recognizes the teleology inherent in each form and chooses to remain distanced from all. Self-consciously open-ended and almost a parody of popular melodrama and Harlequin romance, the ending affirms the need for artifice.

The narrative recalls Namjoshi's work on Pound and her essay on the notion of evil in Pound's *Cantos*.[10] Throughout her essay on Pound, she underlines his conviction that evil is not the existential condition of life on earth. The emphasis on harmony rather than discord, pervasive in Pound, is, according to Namjoshi, a constitutive element in the transformation of both teleology and ontology. The quest in *St Suniti* is a traditional one, expressed often in binary terms within the framework of a single genre. However, the text is defamiliarized and rendered ambivalent by deliberately mixing different forms. The juxtaposition of discursive prose and the lyric, for instance, paves the way for multiple meanings and for the subtle interweaving of recognizable context with fantasy and folk tale. The artifice is thus a necessary aspect of the manner in which the counterrealistic tradition defines its role and its location on the cusp of cultures and traditions.

The movement from the fables to *Conversations* and *Mothers* is a logical one, leading, inevitably, to *Building Babel*, a far more self-conscious, reader-oriented text that invites the reader to make up the final section of the novel. The collective effort of building Babel now includes the reader as well.[11] As all systems reveal their limitations, a biblical myth becomes a way of going to the past in order to test the possibility of achieving a resolution for the future.

The author's extensive introduction to the text is one of the clearest statements by Namjoshi about the role of the author as the creator of artifice without the need to jettison truth. In a clear exposition of the role of myth, the author describes her own project and her necessary ambivalence about the endeavour. Myth as symbolic discourse and as narrative about self-imaginings is what this work asserts from the beginning. Working through the various beliefs and influences that shape her writing, she arrives at her conviction that "a powerful metaphor is a source of revelation" (xiv) and that "building Babel is what people do" (xvi).

Building Babel is a perfect allegory for the task of the Indian writer in English. Multiple traditions, languages, social concerns, and agendas converge in the author's consciousness. The need for a kind of transcendence becomes paramount even as dissonant voices seek privileged status. Having explored both feminist and lesbian concerns, the author now turns from subversion to rehabilitation, to the possibility of constructing a common culture, whose very process would be a testimony to its strength and feasibility.

The convention of announcing her presence in the text is nothing new in Namjoshi's work, but in *Building Babel*, the author is not part of the text; she is the author—an individual who is both Indian and Hindu. This point is driven home to establish a kind of pantheism and to defend herself against any charges of blasphemy. To be a Hindu is to recognize the sacred in a particular way. It does not make her world view in any way superior; it is simply different. Her view of Babel would, then, inevitably involve what she calls a "literal[ism] of the imagination" (x). An imagined world—even an anthropomorphic one—is both real and fictive at the same time. That said, the work is not an individual project: the reader must participate, disagree, challenge, and nourish. An invitation to do this is given by the author and publisher at the beginning and at the end of the book. If building Babel is a process, then it would continue as readers fill in the gaps, suggest their own narratives, and reshape Babel to be more inclusive.

The self-consciousness and self-reflexivity of the text are very much along postmodern lines. The parody, the resistance to closure, the mixing of genre, the structural discontinuities, and the deliberate defamiliarization are all counterrealistic, although there is a certain transparency to the text. The overall format is of the fable or allegory with familiar characters such as Little Red, Black Piglet,

Cinders, Snow White, Rose Green, and Alice appearing together with classical figures such as Medusa and Kronos and allegorical figures such as Charity and Verity and Solitude. All of them suggest a prior text, which is a necessary aspect of the narrative. They provide the context, the sense of a past, although in their present reincarnations they lead different lives. Cinders has a very uxorious husband and two affectionate brothers. Little Red has married the Wolf, and so forth. Snow White and Rose Green are present but Bluebeard is not included. Alice is barely recognizable from Lewis Carroll's text.

The project of building Babel is tantamount to constructing a temple to Crone (clone?) Kronos. The classical figure who severed heaven and earth and ate his own children, is also the symbol of time, of memory, and continuity. While the associations are important, what the text grapples with are the notions of time, memory, and words. The interrelatedness of the three, very much like the relation between Charity, Verity, and Solitude, for instance, is necessarily ambivalent. Building Babel is in itself a contradiction, since time is never purely diachronic and memory is constantly transformed by language. The sheer idealism of building Babel is, from the beginning, undercut by the multiple points of view that are evident from the beginning. For example, while Rap believes that Babel belongs in cyberspace, Cinders contends that they are constructing the universe and Little Red interjects: "Can't we just construct civilisation, and leave the universe to its own devices?" (36). Having internalized values from very different contexts, they often disagree, until they realize that they are trapped in the language they use.

The unfortunate aspect of Babel is that as it begins to take shape, it begins to recapitulate the paradigms it rejected in the first place. Lady Shy mutates into Lady Shylock and appropriates power. The very language that had been used to promote fundamentalism and oppression is now used to fabricate history. As coups and counter-coups are enacted, new religions emerge and ideological stances become both fixed and stifling.

The whole section entitled "The Life and Death of the Black Piglet" ends with all the impulses it sought to avoid. Along the lines of Ovid's *Metamorphoses*, this section is a caricature of the real world and an acceptance of idealism's limitations. It is hardly surprising in the next section when Alice takes over Babel and begins to control thought and language, a new fundamentalism takes over. The Cat, who is now the narrator, quite rightly says: "I thought that Babel was getting cheap and tawdry and that with one swipe of my paw I could knock it down" (129). The only note of reassurance occurs at the end when Mad Med (Medusa) "sets off to inform the world that Babel is now open to touts and tourists, vagrants and visitors, friends and allies…and other pickers up of cultural artifacts" (181).

Building Babel continues the counterrealism of the earlier works, although the ideological stance of the earlier work now gives way to a preoccupation with language itself. The didacticism of the earlier work is conspicuously absent in the later writing that accommodates feminist and lesbian concerns but is more pointedly involved with metaphysical issues. The mode, however, continues to be experimental and mythical. Paradoxically, given all the difficulties in decoding her work, Namjoshi has insisted that the work was always meant to be clear and precise. Obfuscation was never the objective. And yet her extended fables offer little by way of signposting. The absence of realist markers poses a challenge, but her mode is probably inevitable for a writer who is less concerned with how things are than with how things are meant to be.

The most recent addition to Namjoshi's corpus is *Goja*, which, curiously, is also a text that connects with Ghose's *Triple Mirror of the Self* and Rushdie's *Shame*, both of which combine memory and autobiography with fiction. In all three the idea of invention is central and establishes lines of continuity. In this book, the stated purpose is to offer an autobiographical account of the author's life in India and the West, but as Namjoshi admits at the very beginning, fact and truth are, for a writer like her, problematic concepts: "This account is autobiographical in that my experience is all I have. It's fictional since any version manipulates facts. And it's mythical, because it's by making patterns that I make sense of all I have" (ix).

If, in the past, all mythical narratives included a recognizable "Suniti," the present book insists on the author's centrality while including large segments of artifice. In previous works, the reader begins with the assumption of the fabulous and gradually accommodates the referential and the allegorical; *Goja* begins as straightforward memoir and slips into a mode that occupies a middle ground between realism and fantasy.

The structure of the book is, in itself, quite straightforward. The three sections correspond to the three phases of the author's life: childhood and adolescence in India, leading to a position in the Indian Administrative Service and then a decision to leave for the West; life in the United States and in Canada, first as a student and later as a teacher and writer; and the move to England, which brings the text to the present. The subsections achieve an almost perfect balance with only the last chapter being slightly shorter in order to reiterate the open-endedness of any process of writing about one's life.

Within this conventional framework, the meditation takes on a unique texture. The three figures who dominate the text are the grandmother Goldie, the servant Goja, and the author. The grandmother and the servant are now dead but are resurrected to enter into a dialogue with the author who must resolve all the tensions created by and around these three. As the title suggests, the central figure is Goja, who, as a servant, becomes the occasion to reflect on class, injustice, gender, alienation, poverty, and despair. The author realizes that, despite all the privileges she enjoyed by virtue of her caste and class, guilt alone is hardly appropriate to achieve a form of reconciliation. Simple binaries leading to repentance will hardly do when the author herself has been both oppressor and victim in India. As the narrative progresses, even the grandmother narrates a story that exonerates her, at least within the logic of her life.

While the facts that are interspersed in the text allow for a linear mode in the book, the strength of the account lies in the recognition that revisiting the past is hardly a simple task. The author is wary of speaking for everyone, and the fusion of direct and indirect speech, of monologue and dialogue, becomes a way of preserving an authorial distance. With multiple perspectives, truth is difficult to arrive at, and even the multiplicity of voice becomes an impediment to the quest. Characters refuse to retain the parts assigned to them and identities keep shifting as characters refuse to conform to expectations:

> As I gather the *dramatis personae*, some are internal and some are external–they take on each other's faces–and some are both. They don't stay the same. They change their age. It's frightening to think, despite all this talk of sacrosanct identity and the integrity of the personality, that we are all composites, and we are all parts of each other. (41)

The author realizes that the only perspective that would make the quest meaningful is that of Charity, although the precise definition of Charity turns out to be elusive. As each attempt to find a vantage point fails, the text moves from one mode to another, fusing poetry with prose, documentary with artifice, and realism with fairy tale. As autobiography, the book is not so much about recording the past–in fact much of the information is available in her previous works–as mediating on how to understand and reconcile oneself to the past.

In his book of poems called *Handwriting*, Michael Ondaatje devotes a poem to his servant Rosalin, and after having described her with wonderful subtlety, concludes by asking "who abandoned who, I wonder now"[12] (50). *Goja* is, to a large extent, about this dilemma as the author, who, as a woman, lesbian, and Indian living in the West, empathizes with the struggles of Goja, but also wonders about compassion, recrimination, self-pity, indifference, celebration, and acceptance, all stances made possible by an artful use of language. Language is what the author has, and it is for language that she traded so much in life, and yet the access to reality through language is at best partial. As she puts it: "What worried and delighted me at this time was how language cloaked, altered and even fashioned reality, how there were multiple realities, and how it was possible to juxtapose these so that they resonated and shimmered and multiplied meaning" (79).

Admittedly, *Goja* reveals much about the author, her life, her choices, and their consequences. More importantly, the book is a thoughtful–and often brilliant–account about values and stances, about the process of revisiting and understanding events that shape one's life, and about people whose actions seem justified and inevitable, even when they oppress and hurt. What makes *Goja* different from many of Namjoshi's previous works is a tone of acceptance, a recognition that the capacity to live by one's convictions and yet avoid recrimination is made possible not by debate or argument, but by an abiding belief in charity.

As author and myth-maker, Namjoshi's status in the tradition of Indian writing is unique, indebted to an Indian world view that offers a rich mythological tradition, a variety of languages, a tone of voice that is both sardonic and solemn, and Western literary history with its fairy tales, fables, literary forms, and cultural values. The relation between the two is both oppositional and dialogic, leading to a vision that permeates both the poetry and the prose. The conflation of India and the West has resulted in the many experiments of Indo-Anglian authors; for Namjoshi the consequence is a sensibility that re-examines the most seemingly benign constructs and transforms them in a manner that reveals hidden agendas and oppressive ideologies.

CHAPTER 7

Fabulating the Real:
Salman Rushdie

 Paying a grand compliment to himself, Salman Rushdie, writing in a 1997 special issue of *The New Yorker*, refers to a short-lived but widespread virus called Rushdie-itis—a condition he claims affected many but from which Indian authors soon recovered to find their own voices.[1] Despite the vanity of the assertion, it is possible to speak of a particular kind of literary tradition or a movement in Indo-Anglian literature after the appearance of Rushdie. Rukun Advani, for instance, claims in an issue of *Seminar* devoted to contemporary Indian writing that "in the beginning there was Rushdie, and the Word was with him" (15-16). Admittedly, there are several contemporary authors such as Anita Rau Badami, Rohinton Mistry, and Vikram Seth whose work owes nothing to Rushdie and who function largely within a tradition of expressive realism, very much along the tradition of nineteenth-century fiction. They have been immune to the virus that Rushdie mentions, and they belong to a different but equally distinctive tradition of Indian literature.

Nonetheless, the predominant trend among the substantial number of Indian writers who emerged in the last two decades has been to lean towards the mode exemplified by Rushdie. A number of

Notes to chapter 7 are on pp. 195-96.

authors, both Western and Eastern, have found in Rushdie a writer worthy of emulation, and South Asian writers in particular are candid in their acknowledgment of Rushdie's influence. Rukun Advani, Shashi Tharoor, Rajiva Wijesinha, Adam Zameenzad, and Chitra Banerjee Divakaruni, to name a few, have shaped their writing in ways that clearly echo Rushdie. Authors such as Vikram Chandra have drawn from both traditions, moving from one to the other in order to project a particular kind of experience. In their critical comments, Anita Desai and the Sri Lankan author Rajiva Wijesinha, among others, have tried to explain why Rushdie provided new possibilities for writers.[2] Desai is lavish in her praise for Rushdie although her own fiction has remained stubbornly resistant to Rushdieitis. What Desai identifies as Rushdie's contribution is a return to the demotic, a way of writing that taps into the oral tradition.

Wijesinha's work is no less distinctive, but it owes much to Rushdie and magic realists in general. His major fiction, particularly the novels *Days of Despair* and *Acts of Faith*, were written when political circumstances were far from favourable for writers in Sri Lanka, and the mode he chose to adopt, partly for reasons of expediency and partly because the political situation made allegory the rational choice, was remarkably close to Rushdie. It is possible to speak of his fiction as the literary equivalent of Rushdie's work in Sri Lanka. In an essay he speaks of the significance of the Rushdie mode by saying that

> in the sort of society under consideration, the flow of information is generally restricted. As such, rumours proliferate. In the absence of credible monitoring systems, the exaggerated version of a story has as it were parity of status with the bare essentials. Correspondingly, the organs of the state arrogate to themselves greater licence simply because there are no objectively authoritative media restraints. Consequently, we live in a context in which excess has become the norm. (*Inside Limits* 39-40)

Hence, according to him, the tendency of "political" writers to gravitate towards Rushdie allows them to adopt a mode that encapsulates the valency of gossip and rumour as a way of interpreting the political scene. The qualities of exaggeration, parody, and discontinuity become extensions of a particular social and political ethos.

Yet another reading, no less original, has been offered by Milan Kundera, who, in his lengthy discussion of *The Satanic Verses*, links the particular narrative mode of Rushdie to the author's larger project of seeking the contours of identity, not through social and cultural context, not even through the unconscious, but through the psyche which encapsulates more than one civilization. "Where is the rupture in those roots and how far must one go to touch the wounds?" (22) wonders Kundera. In his elaborate typology that involves the process of creating fiction, novel, reportage, short story, poetry, and essay cohabit a common space. In Rushdie the privileging of subordinate categories ensures the "musicality" of the text and that explains both the form and the experience.

Until the appearance of Rushdie, it is almost impossible to map a clear line of descent and influence in Indo-Anglian writing. One cannot speak, for instance, of the "sons of Sargeson" as one would about literature from New Zealand. Despite more than a century of writing in English, there is very little by way of a teleology from, say, Bankim Chatterjee whose novel *Rajmohan's Wife* appeared in 1864, to the work of Nayantara Sahgal in the 1970s. Similarities among authors exist in preoccupations–the hegemony of the caste system, the disintegration of the village, the politics of the Partition, etc.–and in the formal strategies (the use of myth, realism, and so forth), but there is hardly a pattern of evolution or a conscious emulation or rejection of what was done previously. It is only with Rushdie that an "anxiety of influence" begins to manifest itself. Literary histories, particularly the monumental work of Srinivasa Iyengar, offer a detailed study of individual authors, but the structure of his history goes no further. Even the theoretical matrix established by a critic such as Meenakshi Mukherjee in *The*

Twice-Born Fiction, who perceives a movement from the public to the private in Indian writing, is more a response to external conditions than a collective decision by the authors themselves. It is likely that writers such as Forster, with certain subject matter (particularly in *A Passage to India*) and liberal ideology, were seen as worthy of imitation. But in Indo-Anglian writing per se, no writer before Rushdie had the readership or the charisma to initiate a following.

Vernacular literatures have always been quick to acknowledge influences and both follow and imitate when the need arises. A literary history of Tamil literature, for example, could well invoke a pattern of imitation and innovation in a way that is not available in English writing. From the turn of the century to the present, fiction in Tamil has observed certain recognizable conventions, and novelists have been quick to complement each other and make their intertextual lineage abundantly clear to their readers. Novelists feel far more obliged to locate themselves in a fairly self-evident way within patterns that are familiar to readers and are of relevance to their own practice. The presence of certain journals and literary groups provided the markers necessary to regulate forms of literary descent. The sense of a writing community is much stronger among vernacular writers, whereas writers in English tend to work in isolation, relying on whatever sources are available to them. A variety of factors, not the least of which is the location of the authors themselves and their readership, have been responsible for the sense of isolation that appears to characterize Indo-Anglian writing.

Rushdie himself seems to have been eclectic in his choice of reading and influences. In *Imaginary Homelands* he lists a wide range of authors, including Gogol, Cervantes, Kafka, Calvino, and Borges, all of whom, according to him, make up "a polyglot family tree" (21) to which he belongs. Among these he likes many and admires a few. About Calvino, for example, he says: "I can think of no finer writer to have beside me while Italy explodes, while Britain burns, while the world ends" (*Imaginary 261*). Add to this the number of authors he refers to in the various acknowledgments that appear in his novels and one has a much better sense of a broad (often European) intertextual field. Moving to Indian sources, he speaks of Desani, of the two epics, the *Mahabharata* and the *Ramayana*, folk tales, the oral tradition, and so forth that enabled him to write in the way he did. He is clearly aware of Indian writers, even makes subtle distinctions among them as in the article in *The New Yorker* where he speaks of Narayan as an Indian Richardson and Desani as his Shandean other. About influences he is less clear, although he admits that he "learned a trick or two from [Desani]" (58). The point is that he really did not learn from any single source and the only real Indo-Anglian influence on him was Desani. The more significant influences, among writers of fiction, appear to have been Western.

For Rushdie, the process of finding the right mode was not easy. Early novels were rejected or abandoned and his first work, *Grimus*, according to the author, bombed.[3] Had he continued to write in the manner of his first novel, the chances are that like Zulfikar Ghose, he too would have been known to and admired by a small group of readers. But the publication of *Midnight's Children* marked a watershed in his own work and in Indo-Anglian writing. And immediately, there was not only the recognition of the Booker Prize but also the unreserved praise of critics who claimed that here was the key to Indian reality. Valentine Cunningham appropriately titled his review of *Midnight's Children* "Nosing out the Indian Reality." Postmodernism, magic realism, surrealism, fantasy, historiographic metafiction are all terms that have been used at various times to describe Rushdie's oeuvre. There are times when the bewildering profusion of terms associated with magic realism causes more confusion than enlightenment. In fact Stephen Slemon makes the point that "in none of its applications to literature has the concept of magic realism ever successfully differentiated between itself and neighbouring genres such as fabulation, metafiction, the baroque, the fantastic, the uncanny, or the marvellous" (407). (A sustained study of the origins and evolution of magic realism is much needed.)

The consensus, however, is that his style is best characterized as magic realism. The number of times Rushdie is referred to in *Magical Realism*, edited by Lois Parkinson Zamora and Wendy Faris, is a fair indication of how much he has come to dominate theoretical accounts of the mode. Rushdie has not always been forthcoming about his allegiance to magic realism, but his comments on Márquez, for instance, are a clear indication that the configuration of Macondo in *One Hundred Years of Solitude* suits his own way of representing reality.[4] Patricia Merivale does a meticulous study of the relation between Günter Grass's *The Tin Drum* and *Midnight's Children*, and here again the lineage is made abundantly clear. Not only does Merivale firmly establish Rushdie as a magic realist, she goes on to add that "*Midnight's Children* owes its 'magic,' one could say, to García Márquez and its realism to Günter Grass" (329). In a letter written almost a decade ago, Zulfikar Ghose speaks of *Midnight's Children* as a "magic realist structure in which autobiographical experience is transformed into an exuberant and colourful mask behind which is to be glimpsed the author's own sadness" (10 March 1992). And Rushdie's total admiration for certain writers, including Thomas Pynchon, further underscores the kinds of influences that shape and structure his writing.

In any event, what constitutes magic realism itself—a term that Stephen Slemon rightly points out is an oxymoron—is far from clear.[5] When the term was coined by the German art critic Franz Roh in 1925, the intention was to separate a new mode of painting from both Impressionism and Expressionism. In an interesting distinction between the referential and the new mode, Roh says:

> A painter like Schrimpf, who attempts to create the exterior world with utmost precision, considers it very important not to paint outdoors, not to use a model, to have everything flow from the interior image of the canvas....Nevertheless, he repeatedly insists that the landscape be definitively, rigorously, a *real* landscape that could be confused with an existing one. He wants it to

> be "real," to impress us as something ordinary and
> familiar and, nevertheless, to be magic by virtue of that
> isolation in the room. (24-25; italics in the original)

The paintings chosen by Roh do not always bear this out or, for
that matter, reveal a consistent pattern. But the fundamental point
about the need for artifice even when the "real" thing is available is
a valid one which in more recent years Ghose draws attention to in
his critical writing.[6]

Twenty-five years after Roh, Alejo Carpentier wrote on what he
calls the "marvellous real," especially in Latin America, where,
according to him, "the strange is commonplace, and always was
commonplace" (104). Here the distinction is based on ontology
rather than form and angle of perception. Carpentier argues
against conscious artifice in order to depict reality. In Latin
America the unreal is a constitutive aspect of the real and so magic
realism is, in itself, nothing other than a faithful reproduction of
the real. His novels are, to a large extent, predicated on the notion
of a universe where such dualities are easily resolved. But Rushdie
himself, in one of his occasional comments, speaks of magic realism as a "development out of Surrealism" (*Imaginary* 301). By way
of bringing such various points of view together, Brenda Cooper
makes the valid point that the "magic realist writers have an urge
to...capture...ways of being and seeing that are uncontaminated
by European domination. But at the same time, such authors are
inevitably a hybrid mixture, of which European culture is a fundamental part" (17).

While any or all of these definitions may be true, it is also necessary to recognize that no two works by Rushdie are really alike,
despite all the similarities and continuities as he moves from one to
the other. *Grimus*, for instance, belongs to a mythical mode that
does not completely disappear in his work, but remains somewhat
apart from all his other novels. Almost all the future directions of
Rushdie's writing are prefigured in *Grimus*. But the novel "bombed"
anyway, probably because its mode does not suggest to the reader

an identifiable referent. *Haroun and the Sea of Stories* is probably the novel that comes close to the mode of *Grimus*, although its fantasy is configured in very different ways. The fairy tale mode, together with the quest narrative, point to an allegorical dimension in ways that are more accessible than *Grimus*. The intertextual references in *Haroun* are many, including the title which refers to an ancient Indian text called *Kathasaritsagara*, but it is a mode that, in retrospect, was ideal for the years immediately following the *fatwa*, rather than one which expresses the kind of vision that Rushdie works with. *The Jaguar Smile*, in keeping with the genre of travel writing, hardly ever strays from the referential. It is as close as he ever gets to straightforward realism. The particular combination of the real and the fantastic in *Midnight's Children* is the more enduring mode, but here too it is not always similar to the formal strategies of *The Satanic Verses*. To speak of one particular Rushdie mode is misleading, even when such generalizations are necessary and inevitable. For practical purposes, the combination of formal strategies that one associates with experimental writing–hyperbole, parody, excess, satire, fantasy–combined with the sense of urgency that characterizes so much postcolonial writing, has become the signature of Rushdie's work. He is very much the classic writer-in-exile, but instead of the nostalgia that usually permeates such work, in Rushdie there is satire and a willingness to interrogate both home and exile.

Not all critics foreground magic realism in relation to Rushdie. Regardless of all the self-reflexive strategies built into his fiction, his readers have often focused on what the author thematizes. In a sense, by moving away from the purely non-referential mode of *Grimus*, Rushdie does invite that response. Among recent critics, Sara Suleri, for instance, claims that the peculiar "complicity of comedy and shame" in Rushdie is a clear indication that it "descends from the jaunty adolescence of *Kim*" (178). Aijaz Ahmad is less convinced about the Indianness of Rushdie than his allegiance to a European cultural and literary context. Says Ahmad: "It has not been possible, though, to sustain this idea of quintes-

sential Indianness in the *form* of Rushdie's narrative techniques; the
lines of modernism and postmodernism are too numerous" (126).
He is less concerned with the minutiae of formal elements than the
perspective that emerges from the work. He places Rushdie in the
company of European exiles for whom not belonging was also tantamount to belonging everywhere. There is in them, and by extension in Rushdie, both despair and empowerment, and a rejection
that finds its voice in postmodernism.

Both Suleri and Ahmad have reservations about the ideology
that informs Rushdie's work. For various reasons, postcolonial critics in particular have tended to focus on the discourse, the various
layers of meaning, at the expense of ignoring the form that
imposes a necessary ambivalence. Particularly the publication of
The Satanic Verses, with the global backlash that followed, has had
the effect of obscuring narrative form in favour of thematic content. There is nothing inherently flawed in a preoccupation with
meaning, but it runs the risk of implying a precise correspondence
between fiction and sociological truth. Kundera warns the reader
of the negative effects of such an approach: "imperceptibly, inno-
cently, under the pressure of events, through changes in society and
in the press, literary criticism has become a mere (often intelligent,
always hasty) *literary news bulletin*" (24, italics in the original). While
it is impossible to separate the formal strategies from the vision
that permeates the work, it remains true that Rushdie marks the
culminating point of the counterrealistic tradition. It is hardly possible to dispute the claims of Rushdie as a literary phenomenon, as
an originary figure. As Todorov has rightly pointed out, "we grant
a text the right to figure in the history of literature or of science
only insofar as it produces a change in our previous notions of the
one activity or the other" (6). And changing our notions is precisely
the role played by Rushdie in his major novels. The rest of this
chapter will look closely at *Shame* in order to speculate on the place
of Rushdie within the counterrealistic tradition in Indo-Anglian
writing. Rather than engage with the political stance of the author,
my intent is to focus on one of his texts in order to test the coun-

terrealism he espouses. While any of his recent works, including *The Moor's Last Sigh* or *The Ground Beneath Her Feet*, would serve as equally significant examples of the Rushdie mode, *Shame* is probably where his particular brand of counterrealism finds its most succinct expression.

Shame is important for a variety of reasons. It is the first novel to establish Rushdie as a subversive and anti-establishment writer. While *Midnight's Children* has enough material that one might consider oppositional to state ideology, and probably enough to offend Hindus in general and Saivites in particular, the only person who took Rushdie on was Indira Gandhi, and it was over a matter that was quickly resolved. But with *Shame*, an entire system came under attack and the novel was banned in Pakistan and India. It takes aim at specific political figures, at the role of Islamic leaders, and at the culture of Pakistan in general. If postcolonial discourse began as an offshoot of nationalism and independence, it is also true that the collaboration was destined to end when the politics of postcoloniality came into conflict with the liberal values of the writers themselves. The defining stance of the writer thus becomes oppositional. On the one hand, there is the mode of writers such as Ayi Kwei Armah, which one might describe as a reflection of the chagrin of the insider; on the other, there is the despair of the outsider whose identity is, nonetheless, bound up with "home." *Midnight's Children* is playful, exuberant, and concerned, to a large extent, with the imagination that shapes a large body of material. *Shame* is more centrally about the nation, about its fragmentation, its failures, and its destructive impulses. It is about the postcolonial experience in Pakistan. Ideas of nation, politics, gender, history, and historiography, all seem to converge in the text.

Apart from the subject matter, the novel also perfects the Rushdie mode in ways that one doesn't encounter before or after. Obviously, this is likely to be a contentious opinion, since *Midnight's Children* continues to be a favourite for many Rushdie fans. *The Satanic Verses* is easily the most controversial. It is possible to argue that *Midnight's Children* has more magic in it and *Shame* has too much realism. By the same token, it is possible to make a case for his more recent novels. *The Moor's Last Sigh* is arguably his saddest novel in which a deeply felt sense of personal despair struggles to find an objective correlative through the distance afforded by artifice. Or it is possible to say, as Nick Prescott does, that *"The Ground Beneath Her Feet* is, among other things, an extended and breathtakingly allusive exercise in the creation of a parallel world "* (119). But *Shame* is probably the most self-referential, the work that insistently interrogates itself to establish its own narrative mode.

Despite all the inventiveness that goes into the novel, the author himself has always insisted that the world of the novel is a real one. In an early interview he claims that *"Shame* is a political novel and…behind the fantasized or the mythologized country in the book there is a real country, and behind the dictators in the book there are real dictators"* (*"Midnight's Children* and *Shame"* 15-16). Even to those with no more than an elementary knowledge of Pakistan's political scene, the identity of the major characters is always clear. In some instances the markers are very specific, but even where there is some defamiliarization, the connections are obvious to those who are part of that world. The political history of Pakistan becomes very clear in the novel. The assassination of Liaquat Khan, the coup organized by Ayub Khan, the war with India, the takeover by Yahya Khan, followed by the rise of Bhutto and then his fall when Zia takes over the country: Benazir, like many others, is always present to provide a sense of the country and its political history.

The micro-narrative of the narrator is firmly in the realist tradition. The composite picture of the narrator and his family, as it emerges sporadically, constitutes a text in itself, and deliberately problematizes the macro-narrative that involves the major political figures. The narrator's interventions are almost gratuitous and they flaunt an autobiographical element almost in deliberate defiance of the novel's counterrealism. But the surrogate author of the novel also maintains the opposite. The novel quite self-consciously addresses the issue of realism. It lists elaborately what might have been included had this been a referential work. The narrator then adds:

> By now, if I had been writing a book of this nature, it would have done me no good to protest that I was writing universally, not only about Pakistan. The book would have been banned, dumped in the rubbish bin, burned. All that effort for nothing! Realism can break a writer's heart. Fortunately, however, I am only telling a sort of modern fairy-tale, so that's all right; nobody need get upset, or take anything I say too seriously. No drastic action need be taken, either. (*Shame* 70)

Obviously, the intention of the author is to provoke, subvert, and antagonize. This is Rushdie's strategy of upping the ante, of usurping the realist territory without jettisoning the advantages of his so-called fairy tale. By recapturing the specificity of realism while always denying it, he succeeds in flagging both, not simply to deny responsibility, but to maintain a balance between both, to ensure that the real and the imaginary are seen as complementary. As the narrator puts it, "the country in this story is not Pakistan, or not quite. There are two countries, real and fictional, occupying the same space, or almost the same space" (29).

The novel does not seek to document in meticulous detail the story of Pakistan. One only needs to look at the work of his friend Tariq Ali, particularly the book *Can Pakistan Survive?*, to recognize that Rushdie did not set out to write a historical novel. But even Ali's "objective" narrative occasionally slips into the kind of burlesque that Rushdie's novel revels in.[7] But the comparison is an important one, partly because both authors work with similar ambitions; they seek to tell the story of a nation. Ali and Rushdie speak of origins and establish systems of classification for understanding the history of Pakistan. Both are concerned with discourse in the broad sense. And Ali's account offers a contrast with Rushdie's, for both deal with the same political figures. The story of Pakistan cannot really be told without acknowledging the roles of Zia and Bhutto. Ali and Rushdie seem to concede that. But if one were to grant that Ali's work is referential, then Rushdie's is not. The similarities between Ali and Rushdie are striking, for both are novelists whose careers trace similar trajectories. They have been supportive of each other and remain friends. Ali is no stranger to counterrealism, but his major novel *Shadows of the Pomegranate Tree*, a novel whose allegorical aspect is not unlike *The Moor's Last Sigh*, is predominantly referential.

The realistic novel is often about characters–about Jane Eyre, about Tess, and about Pip. But *Shame* is, according to the narrator, not about Sufiya. On the contrary, Sufiya is about the novel. In fact, the narrator wants it both ways: "This is a novel about Sufiya Zinobia, elder daughter of General Raza Hyder and his wife Bilquis....Or perhaps it would be more accurate, if also more opaque, to say that Sufiya Zinobia is about this novel" (59). The implications of this statement are interesting. When a novel is about a character, the context provides the canvas on which the character is drawn. The social ethos helps us understand why Pip is what he is. The method is to look at the character who serves a metonymic function in order to arrive at a larger picture. But here the objective is to look at the context and the character becomes a means of doing that. In other words, within the framework of realism, the context is the background and the character is placed against it. The relation between one and the other is metonymic. There is a complementarity between the two in that the details selected reflect broader social values and trends. As David Lodge puts it, "the appropriate response to the metonymic text would seem to be an attempt to restore the deleted detail, to put the text back into the total context from which it derives" (97). Reverse that and you have events dominating the canvas with the character being figured against it. The relation is necessarily metaphoric and inevitably problematic. The mode is that of documentary, travelogue, or history that is being appropriated to serve the interest of fiction.[8]

The distinction that the narrator makes is not mere obfuscation. In her own life, Sufiya both reflects and naturalizes the story of the nation. To understand what she does—when she beheads the turkeys or decapitates men after having sex with them—one does not look at her character; rather, one looks at the backdrop, the multiple examples of shame and violence and retribution, so her actions begin to make sense. For Omar, Sufiya's psychosomatic eruptions are the occasion to write "The Case of Miss H" (142). His parody of Freudian analysis turns out to be wholly inadequate, and the doctor, rather than cure the patient, becomes the victim, in more ways than one. Sufiya is an embodiment of various forces. In fact she is a reincarnation of different forms of shame, of adultery, of opportunism, of cruelty, and so forth. In order to understand why her immune system fails, one also needs to recognize that the nation as a whole is not immune from shame and that Sufiya's lack of defence is another version of the country's "defence" area that turns a blind eye to large-scale corruption. The inversion accounts for the palimpsest of history and also the layers that make up the multiple legacies of the psyche.

Having established the symbolic dimension of the character and the novel as a whole, the narrator adds that Sufiya is also a reincarnation of what the narrator claims to be three "real" incidents. Listing the origins of the novel in such a manner adds a further layer of complexity. The so-called real incidents take place in London. One is about a father who would, for the sake of honour, choose to kill his daughter who is suspected of having gone "all the way" with a white boy; the father lays her across a zebra crossing. The second is about an Asian girl who is harassed in the underground train and who would, if sufficiently incensed, lash out against the oppressors; and the third is about a boy who, presumably filled with shame, decides to spontaneously combust. These examples of the intersection of shame and violence are documented in ways that insist on a referential dimension. All three are victims of transculturation. The novel is an elaboration of these "truths," but to perceive them in all their complexity one must resort to a version of fantasy or the counterrealistic. Equally important is the need for these three characters to be reborn in Pakistan and for the issues raised by their victimization to be played out in different circumstances. The three "core" incidents have to do with migrancy, of being marginalized and discriminated against. In claiming three such episodes as the originary moments for a novel about Pakistan, the narrator immediately signals a departure from traditional realism.

But the novel itself is not about these figures in the literal sense, although references to them do occur. The text is not about the diaspora but about the history of Pakistan. The issue then, is, how one would tell the story of a nation from the perspective of one who must face the ambivalence of being an outsider everywhere. The very first paragraph establishes the element of allegory and fantasy that merge in the text. If the three sisters need to be read allegorically, Raza and Iskander need to be seen as both symbols and caricatures. There is a careful weaving in and out of recorded events that prevents any easy occlusion of real political figures. But in real life, as Ahmad points out, they were not buffoons but very shrewd and capable men.[9] And depending on who reads it, the text can be hilariously funny or in shockingly bad taste.

But surely, even with the recognizable figures, their fictive lives hardly coincide with what we know about them. There is exaggeration, parody, and what Janet Hospital appropriately called a "melange of tall tale, apostrophe and moral thesis." It is this curious juxtaposition that critics such as Suleri and Ahmad have taken issue with. For Suleri, the motif of a romance gone wrong, the orientalizing impulse, becomes the occasion for the author to exploit a local context in a particularly self-serving fashion. While masquerading as an interpreter, he embellishes, distorts, and essentializes in order to valorize his own partial perspective. In a damning indictment, Suleri claims: "in its attempt to reimagine Pakistani history, *Shame* seems guiltily aware that its lineage leads back in the direction of such influential texts as James Mill's *The History of India*, the first philosophical history of India written by an author who had never visited the subcontinent" (176). James Mill was part of a colonial (and hegemonic) enterprise. Rushdie occupies a different space on the cusp, but he too, according to Suleri, feminizes the land and locates his narrative within the paradigms of romance and marriage. Among the many examples that the text provides one could, for instance, recognize this motif even in the description of Karachi:

> By the year of the Hyders' return from Q. the capital had grown, Karachi had become fat, so that people who had been there from the beginning could no longer recognize the slender girlish town of their youth in this obese harridan of a metropolis. The great fleshy folds of its endless expansion had swallowed up the primeval salt marshes, and all along the sandpit there erupted, like boils, the gaudily painted beach houses of the rich. (118)

Even more trenchant perhaps is Ahmad's critique that Rushdie, while speaking from a position of immense privilege and influence, represents the country as a circus and its people as clowns. What he perceives is a clear failure to portray the everyday, the daily acts of heroism and compassion that make up the life of the nation.[10] As a general point of view this sentiment is shared by several major critics, including Kwame Appiah, who makes the point that "Postcoloniality is the condition of what we might ungenerously call a *comprador* intelligentsia: a relatively small, Western-style, Western-trained group of writers and thinkers, who mediate the trade in cultural commodities of world capitalism at the periphery" (348).

Against this view, there is the strident defence advanced by Kundera who, writing specifically about *The Satanic Verses*, sees the novel as symptomatic of a larger conflict between the rigour of theocracy and the heterogeneity of the modern era. As he puts it, "just as Iranian Islam was at the time moving away from religious moderation toward a combative theocracy, so, with Rushdie, the history of the novel was moving from the genteel, professorial smile of Thomas Mann to unbridled imagination drawn from the rediscovered wellspring of Rabelaisian humour. The antitheses collided, each in its extreme form (26).

The issue of locating Rushdie, then, has a lot to do with Rushdie's specific vision and its relation to the form he employs. Rushdie himself has commented that his readers in Asia tend to see his novels referentially while his readers in the West respond to the fantasy. What this binary implies is that the ideal reader would perceive a combination of the two. To seek out meaning while ignoring the form would do injustice to the novel, but flaunting the form as a way of evading the ideology that pervades the novel would be irresponsible. Rushdie's work insists on being read on its own terms, and to naturalize it would be as pointless as to valorize its sense of the carnivalesque.

For the South Asian reader, the non-real does not lie outside the real. Laws of nature can be violated without jeopardizing the sense of perceived reality. But when there is confusion about what belongs where, when that order is subverted, then there is fantasy. Rushdie naturalizes the fantastic, while always maintaining that the element of fantasy must be recognized to allow for literary artifice. What this enables, quite often, is access to levels of understanding that lie outside ordinary or referential discourse. Rushdie's mode does not appropriate the territory of the realist writer. Instead, he establishes different spatial and temporal coordinates that frame contemporary events in different ways. Hence, for instance, the need to look at *Shame* from a synchronic perspective, through motifs that establish different patterns of apprehension.

When Jameson writes about the third-world novel as being primarily allegorical, he has in mind a particular form of realism that mirrors the social and political conditions of the country being described. Rushdie's allegory, as in the beginning of the novel with the three mothers who give birth to Omar, must be taken entirely as artifice. The three women serve an allegorical function but they are, for the reader, fictive creations. All the episodes in the chapter that trace the early life of Omar belong to the fantastic. But beneath the fantasy lies the factual that is never lost sight of. Nishapur or Quetta conjure up a wide range of images and they form a subtext. The fantastic is offered and decoded at the same time. The exaggeration leads to a shock of recognition. Sometimes the hyperbole rings true, particularly when it takes a mythical shape.

It is important to recognize that Rushdie's counterrealism is not that of the Indian epics or the Puranas where the real and the fantastic blend without any disruption of the discourse. The epics are framed by a system of belief, of faith that is not questioned. One does not question Ravana's ten heads or Hanuman's ability to levitate. Within the ontological framework of the epic, such questions do not arise. But *Shame* is not of that genre. To a larger extent, *Midnight's Children* exploits the traditional notion of the non-real. Yet even here, the transcendental does not work in the way that it does in Narayan's fiction. Forms of digression and repetition may well seem to imitate the conventions of orality and folk tale, but the dominant mode remains within the terms of conscious artifice. Gods and demons may well engage in epic battles, but the novel makes sure by its tone, diction, and juxtaposition of events that the effect is one of defamiliarization. (A useful comparison here might be the serialized television version of the *Ramayana,* which was intended specifically to elicit a response that naturalizes the supernatural.)

Rushdie has, on several occasions, acknowledged the tradition of the epic as central to his own narrative mode. *The Mahabharata* is a sprawling epic whose teleology is framed by hundreds of digressions, the supernatural, the fantastic, the mythical, and so forth. All these reappear in Rushdie. The crucial difference is that the epics are naturalized and have remained so for centuries. They are not perceived to be "real," but they are not considered fantastic either. They may not be a part of contemporary reality, but they are a version of "truth." Rushdie's work does not occupy that particular space.

Shame assumes an educated reader. And given the relatively short time span of the novel, and the particular contours of Pakistan's history, it is hardly possible not to be aware of major events, such as the war with India, the secession of Bangladesh, or the rise and fall of Bhutto. In any event, the narrator steps in to fill the gaps and add a personal dimension to the narrative. Read in isolation, there is very little to differentiate these sections from any conventional work of realism.

Superimposed on this is a form of symbolic discourse, not unlike myth. In fact, the novel is a complete myth of sorts, beginning with the origins of the nation and ending with an apocalyptic vision. But myth, almost always, works within a system of belief. It offers a way of reconciling societal contradictions in the interests of maintaining a social norm. Rushdie's myth, on the other hand, is private, rather than collective and its objective is to deconstruct ideology, not uphold it. In myth the fantastic is made natural within a symbolic framework. In *Shame* the natural is made to look fantastic and surreal.

Allegory disclaims responsibility while remaining transparent. At its most obvious it says one thing and means another. For example, Chunni, Munnee, and Bunny are originary figures in the birth of Omar. Within the framework of allegory, they would stand for Hindu, British, and Muslim interests in the creation of the nation. Allegory of this sort is particularly noticeable in Rushdie. Its advantage is that allegory suggests so much more than the realistic. Analogically, Omar and the nation intersect, and the nation too, like Omar, is a migrant, depraved, corrupt, and given to excess.

The notion of allegory is invoked regularly in Rushdie criticism and there is at least one essay devoted to the exploration of *Shame* as apologue.[11] But the allegorical dimension continues to be an undertheorized aspect of Rushdie's work. In Rushdie's characteristic mode, the correspondence among the various levels of allegory is made uncertain. Iskander is clearly a version of Bhutto. He is not a type of corrupt and ambitious politician: he *is* Bhutto, to the extent that one wonders why he was not called that in the first place. In fact, Rushdie causes offence when those who insist on the transparency are shocked by the lack of correspondence between the "real" and the fictive. But Iskander must remain a fictive char-

acter, not only to transcend the dictates of realism, but also to facilitate the various layers of meaning that make up the text. In a very
erudite discussion of allegory, Carolyn Van Dyke makes the observation that "allegory as genre derives from one manifestation of
that tendency: syncretic statement, bearing simultaneous and
equally privileged reference to concrete particulars and to univer-
sals or intelligibles" (293). *Shame* does precisely that and in the
process also alludes to empirical and psychic realities. Iskander is
thus Bhutto, both as he is seen and how he needs to be seen. Critics
have not agreed on Rushdie's representation of Bhutto and have
pointed out that his subjectivity is self-serving and that he deliberately denies important figures any agency or dignity. That may well
be the case, but one can hardly dispute the necessity of the form to
achieve the kind of multiplicity Rushdie aims for.

Obviously, *Shame* is not allegorical in the sense of *Everyman*.
Here Iskander is insistently outside the referential without becoming quite fantastic. The indeterminacy affects the reader's understanding of the real Bhutto. Neither one is privileged over the
other. In contrast, Omar or Sufiya work at a different level. They
too are allegorical, but the referent lacks the fixity of Bhutto. In
fact, while discussing recent writers in relation to allegory, Van
Dyke comments that the "realistic referent is a perpetual chimera,
the seeking of which exhausts both characters and readers" (293).
If allegory enlarges the real, for Rushdie, fantasy insists on its
improbability. While characters may straddle the allegorical and the
realistic planes, their actions may well push them in the direction of
the fantastic. Given the status of the novel as myth, teleology is
inevitable. But episodes are not always causal and often insistently
random. The decisions that affect the nation are within a
diachronic framework but the forces that shape the text are con-
tingent and synchronic. Had the novel been entirely allegorical, one
would only need a template to understand the various strands. If,
on the other hand, the mode is realistic, then the text has to be seen
as metonymic. Rushdie deliberately fuses the two, thereby prevent-
ing any single reading. Hence the need to look for alternative strate-

gies, for motifs and patterns of repetition to establish layers of meaning.

Rushdie himself has commented on his strategy of motifs or patterns of repetition to reveal the structure of the novel. For example, there is the girl in London who did not go "all the way," compared to Bilquis who does. Good News Naveed refuses to marry Haroun, and Shabanou gets pregnant by being a substitute. The three mothers, all of whom conceive twice, reinforce yet another pattern. Iskander is a playboy who abandons his wife. Omar is given to debauchery but does not sleep with his wife. Other patterns exist: the slitting of the girl's throat to make her pure–like Halal meat: does this connect with the decapitation of the turkeys by Sufiya and later her dismembering the four men and finally Omar as well? Decapitation as a way of making pure coexists with a symbolic form of castration. And sexuality looms large in the novel. The novel begins with an act of sexual transgression. The wild party thrown by the three sisters is an act of resistance, of capitulation to Western values, of children against their father. It ends with a strange parody of the same impulse as the three mothers orchestrate the death of their son. The naked Raza carrying a fully-clothed Bilquis is a macabre repetition and reversal of how he found her. Then she was unclothed and he was in full attire. Omar's death is a form of consummation he never had in life. This time the sexuality is associated with death and apocalypse–all suggestive of a form of purification. Omar becomes the "bride" at the end, and Sufiya the masculinized beast.

The issue of gender is constantly referred to in the novel and its critical accounts. The novel is about the hegemony of a patriarchal order and its subversion in various forms. Framing the concern with gender is the motif of androgyny. From the time one sees Mahmoud the Woman and the tears-prone Raza, to the transformation of Raza and Omar into transvestites at the end, the recuperative potential of androgyny is made a constant presence. The androgynous figure of Shiva in Hindu iconography–the *ardhanareesvara*–is far more non-real than, say, the more conventional dancing Shiva. But the figure captures a particular truth. Such is the effect of androgyny in the novel, which subverts the rampant patriarchy but also establishes the artifice as an aspect of the design.

Granted, there is no one way to read Rushdie and no easy definition to capture the totality of the experience of the text. But what makes his particular form of counterrealism so effective is its elasticity, its capacity to adapt and change. Hence the number of variations among those who have learnt from Rushdie. There is a world of difference between Rukun Advani and Kiran Desai, but both work within a counterrealistic frame and both owe something to Rushdie. And then there is Tharoor who does something entirely different, but here again the influence of Rushdie is unmistakeable and in fact acknowledged openly in *The Great Indian Novel.*

Whether Rushdie pursues a particular vision of wholeness or appropriates the East to valorize his own condition of exile is really beside the point. The mode resolves the challenge of how to write when the writing grows out of an anomalous context. Clearly Rushdie feels the need to write about a home which is the source of identity but not necessarily a repository of consciousness. He must use a language that is virtually his mother tongue but one that has limited currency in India. He must write about the East for readers who belong to the West. For those who left fairly late in their lives—for instance, Vikram Chandra and Rohinton Mistry—the consciousness is still largely Indian, which in turn might explain the appropriateness of their realism. Equally true would be the circumstance of Bapsi Sidhwa or Shyam Selvadurai. For those who left early—Ondaatje, Ghose, and Rushdie—the concern is not often the everyday so much as the issues of identity and representation. To establish a certain translucence that allows the effect of a palimpsest is probably as important for the writer as it is for the reader. Even at the risk of generalization, it is necessary to insist that "magic realism" in Rushdie and his followers is not quite the same as in Grass or Márquez. At best, it departs from its allegiance to realism without jettisoning a concern for the real. At worst, it slips into essentialisms that lead towards the trap of orientalism.

The fascinating paradox in Rushdie is that the fragmentation and counterrealism coexist with memory and a longing for wholeness. In an interview given soon after the *fatwa*, Rushdie says: "many writers have sacred objects that they keep around them to help them work, and I have one or two as well, so I managed to get those out. I have a little inch-high block of silver, Indian silver, engraved with the map of the unpartitioned continent of India and Pakistan, which was given to me as a present by a friend of my father's when I was one day old" ("An Exclusive Talk" 48). The implied vision, which is one of unity and consolidation, ironically entails a fictional representation that is both fragmentary and counterrealistic.

CHAPTER 8

Midnight's Grandchildren

Salman Rushdie's *Midnight's Children* ends with the scattering of the gifted and ill-fated children. The final vision, partially redeemed by the token presence of the pickle jars and the birth of Ganapati, is less apocalyptic than that of his subsequent novel, less solemn than, say, *The Moor's Last Sigh*, but the pervasive tone is still pessimistic and despondent. The next work, *Shame*, more bitter and trenchant in its critique of the political scene, refers to itself as a novel of leave-taking, and here again the narrator/author's departure is juxtaposed with the destruction of both Nishapur and the novel's main characters. If one were to think of these novels as sustained allegories of India and Pakistan, then the collapse at the end of the novels would be a symbol of a more general collapse of the two nations. But contrary to what the novel foretells, India and Pakistan are alive and well, and not only have both nations made strides in their economic and social life, India's literature has taken centre stage, nationally and internationally. Never before in postcolonial India has literature in English flourished as it has in the last two decades. The literary efflorescence that occurred in the Caribbean and in Africa in the 1950s and 1960s took place in India and Sri

Notes to chapter 8 are on pp. 196-97.

Lanka in the 1980s, for very different reasons. Independence and its attendant nationalism appear to have occasioned relatively little literary activity among South Asian writers, despite the constant references to the political scene that preceded independence. In the 1960s and '70s the older authors in India continued to write with an awareness of social conditions, but were not particularly concerned with political upheavals and national recuperation. Even an event of magnitude such as the Partition has not been dealt with in more than a handful of novels. There is very little evidence to suggest a symbiotic relation between decolonization and literary activity in South Asia. While vernacular writers grappled with the complexity of emerging from centuries of foreign rule, Indo-Anglian writers were often content with observing conventional forms of social realism. With notable exceptions, this remained the norm until the transformation that occurred in the early 1980s.

The recent popularity and burgeoning of Indian writing needs to be seen as part of a more general cultural trend in the West to celebrate the fashions, artifacts, and cultural practices of the East. After a hiatus of three decades or so, India—of a particular kind—has now become trendy. Such fascination with an imagined Other is, in itself, nothing unusual. The 1960s, for example, were a time of considerable interest in the spirituality of India as a foil to the violence, alienation, and materialism of the West. A major difference, however, was that this interest did not manifest itself in as many forms as it has in the past two decades. The fascination then was largely with the prospect of spiritual enlightenment in the East. The reasons for the current attraction are as much political and economic as they are literary. Spurred no doubt by India's role as an economic power and as a potential market for western goods, the West has, in the last two decades, paid considerable attention to the subcontinent. Inevitably, such political gestures are followed by cultural interest, and one only needs to look at the range of films such as *My Beautiful Laundrette, Mississippi Masala, Fire, Kama Sutra, Bhaji on the Beach, Surviving Sabu, Sixth Happiness,* the experiments in art, and the hybrid forms of classical Indian dance to recognize that new forms of cultural expression are beginning to emerge out of the renewed interest in the East. The precise nature of this interest needs to be theorized more fully. Neither totally orientalist nor entirely pragmatic, the preoccupation is in fact a curious fusion of adulation and critical appraisal. Hollywood's depiction of India, as in the movie *City of Joy,* is an indication of the dualities that shape the West's attitude. The recent controversy in India about the screening of Deepa Mehta's *Fire* is yet another instance of radical changes in consciousness among artists and the complex relation between the conditions in the West and the imaginative exploration of the East. Nonetheless, the interest is real and the achievements of Indian authors are equally real: Jhumpa Lahiri's success in winning the Pulitzer Prize for her book of short stories entitled *Interpreter of Maladies* is perhaps a striking example of this new phenomenon.

The most noticeable change in international reception has been in the area of literature. Special issues of journals, such as *Daedalus, Modern Fiction Studies,* and *ARIEL* confirm the resurgence of Indian writing. Specific literary issues to commemorate fifty years of Indian independence, such as those brought out by *The New Yorker* and *Granta,* reflect a popular appeal and a substantial readership. Several anthologies dealing with new South Asian authors have appeared in the last two decades. Among contemporary authors, Allan Sealy, Shashi Tharoor, Amitav Ghosh, Adam Zameenzad, Gita Mehta, Upamanyu Chatterji, Kiran Desai, Chitra Divakaruni, Rohinton Mistry, Ven Begamudré, Arundhati Roy, Vikram Seth, Vikram Chandra, Farrukh Dhondy, Anita Rau Badami, Pankaj Mishra, and a host of others are now writing for a national and international audience. From Sri Lanka, there is Carl Muller, Rajiva Wijesinha, Shyam Selvadurai, A. Sivanandan, Romesh Gunesekera, Jean Arasanayagam, Yasmine Gooneratne, and Chandani Lokuge, all of whom have suddenly brought Sri Lankan writing into a new phase of growth. One only needs to look at anthologies such as *Dragonfly in the Sun* to recognize the surge of new writing among Pakistani writers.

In retrospect, Rushdie's role in this growing awareness and popularity can hardly be underestimated.[1] As an author and as a controversial figure he has been and continues to be an icon of sorts—a staunch defender of free speech and values of liberalism, and a victim of authoritarianism and religious fundamentalism. By the same token, he has been seen as the agent and voice of the West, the migrant who lacks the sensitivity and depth of understanding to articulate the East. From a literary perspective, however, the narrative modes he popularized have been followed by a whole group of writers, with each person shaping his or her fiction to suit the needs of different contexts. The counterrealistic tradition of writing, having found its most popular exponent in Rushdie, then moved in diverse directions, encompassing a number of authors from different nations.

To state Rushdie's contribution in somewhat simplistic terms, his experimental and magic realist form has provided the formal literary strategies that gain access to levels of experience not always available to earlier novelists. Ghose preceded him, and he too marked a point of convergence for multiple traditions. A strong grounding in British and American fiction, combined with an awareness of European and Latin American innovations, provided the literary mode for both of them. The difference between the two—and this explains the postcolonialism of one and the internationalism of the other—is the kind of allegory they worked with. Rushdie's work is unambiguous about the "nation," however disguised, that found allegorical expression while Ghose's remains implicit. But both writers are remarkably similar in that they were clear about the need to forge new directions.

Desai and Namjoshi, who are experimentalists, for example, do have their followers, and Narayan continues to be an admired Indian writer. But the dominant influence after 1980 appears to have been Rushdie. The combination of a much-needed antireferential mode with a remarkable sense of historical and cultural reality accounts for the special place accorded to Rushdie in Indian writing in English. In that sense, *Midnight's Children* did mark a watershed in Indo-Anglian writing, and its influence in the 1980s was perhaps as pervasive as E. M. Forster's *A Passage to India* was several decades ago. One would certainly agree with Rukun Advani that "irreverence, iconoclasm, and witty forms of subversion in relation to institutionalized, fossilized and dominant forms of thought and power characterize his fiction" ("Novelists" 16). If Forster provided a basis for consolidation, Rushdie paves the way for a fiction of fragmentation. If Forster served as a model for neo-colonial writing, Rushdie becomes the elder statesman of recent postcolonial literature. It would not be far-fetched to claim, despite all the exceptions that do exist, that the present generation of writers are in fact "midnight's grandchildren."

Forster's "Indian" novel has been the target of much vituperative criticism, particularly because of its ideological stance, its treatment of gender, and its failure to go beyond banality and stereotype. But Forster has remained a powerful influence in Indian writing, mainly as a result of a referential mode that absorbed a Victorian model and adapted it to an Indian environment. In short, he created a paradigmatic work for Indian novelists, who were then able to provide a wide range of combinations from the material and methodology of *A Passage to India*. His realism, his sense of closure that creates the illusion of open-endedness, and his binaries to encapsulate the colonial encounter, have since then become staple features of Indo-Anglian writing. Writers as varied as Mulk Raj Anand, Khushwant Singh, and Kamala Markandaya have all been in some ways indebted to Forster.

In contrast, Rushdie forged an almost clear break with the Indian tradition of realism. During an interview with Jean-Pierre Durix, Rushdie makes the observation that "*Midnight's Children* was partly conceived as an opportunity to break away from the manner in which India has been written about in English" (19). The only work which anticipates *Midnight's Children* is G.V. Desani's *All About H. Hatterr*, although Desani's failure to provide a sustained corpus has prevented the novel from having a lasting impact on the Indian novel. Subversive, irreverent, self-reflexive, referential, syncretic, and encyclopedic, *Midnight's Children* is the product of an age which is essentially multiple, indeterminate, and divided. Rushdie's novel serves the function of destabilizing and questioning the ideologies perpetuated by classical realism and replaces it with a perspective that locates itself on the margins.

His insistence on the constructedness of his writing and the marriage of documentary and fiction give his work its uniquely luminous quality. Looking in from the outside, through a migrant's eyes, he achieves a perspective that is created by both remembered, empirical realities and imagined, invented worlds. Rushdie's work does not masquerade as the referential. The niche he creates for himself arises from the capacity to perceive ruptures and fissures in what is often represented as a seamless national history, and reconfigure, on the strength of fragments, an alternative vision that accommodates both the individual and the collective. Rushdie's work is by no means flawless and his ideological stance may well be faulted for various reasons, but his contribution to literary history remains important.

For those who followed him, his presence was inescapable. The influence might be openly acknowledged as in Shashi Tharoor's *The Great Indian Novel* where one whole chapter is entitled "Midnight's Parents," or it could be something more subtle as in Adam Zameenzad's *Cyrus, Cyrus* or Amitav Ghosh's *The Shadow Lines*. In some ways, as Desai points out, these writers were imitative of Rushdie in their recourse to a more demotic sensibility. As Desai claims, "Rushdie mythologized still-living people and turned events in living memory into fantastic legends. The close was made distant, the distant close" ("Indian" 211). But imitation, per se, cannot be said to distinguish this group of writers. They have absorbed the fundamental assumptions that underlie Rushdie's work and moved away, and in the process they have given Indian writing a fresh lease on life at a time when it seemed increasingly impossible to keep English writing alive.[2]

Rushdie, in his article in *The New Yorker*, talks about Indian writing in English in detail, and his attitude is mostly laudatory. Almost without exception, he has praise for everybody, and he goes on to claim—and this is where his argument begins to weaken considerably—that English has been the medium that has produced the best of Indian writing. He bases his judgment on a handful of novels and short stories in translation, not to mention that he ignores, totally, writing in several vernacular languages. For him, English is the *lingua franca* of India: "The true Indian literature of the first postcolonial half century has been made in the language the British left behind"[3] (50).

To say that vernacular literature is not strong is just not true. To make that kind of claim is to wear blinkers, to make assertions on the flimsiest of evidence. It is likely that vernacular writing is driven largely by different considerations and would require a different poetics for critical evaluation. But the idea that English has somehow replaced or upstaged other languages is hardly defensible. In a scathing attack on Rushdie's views, the editorial of the journal *Indian Literature* demonstrates, with considerable accuracy, the breadth of writing that Rushdie summarily dismisses.[4] Rushdie's generalizations are a reminder that a comparison with vernacular literatures is necessary and inevitable in any comprehensive evaluation, but it also needs to be undertaken within a much more inclusive theoretical framework. In contrast to the general euphoria about Indian writing, John Updike's review of *The God of Small Things* and *Beach Boy* in *The New Yorker*, while generally positive in its response to the novels, ends on a skeptical note about the valency of such writing. "Is there a place" asks Updike, "these novels make us wonder, for an English language literature within India, where a bristling nationalism staves off Asian neighbours and a Hindu fundamentalism arises to compete with the Islamic variety" (161). There is an awkwardness about the manner in which the question is posed, but it does point to certain dichotomies that are relevant.

In March 2000, when Amitav Ghosh was named the Eurasia regional winner for the 2001 Commonwealth Writer's Prize for his work *The Glass Palace*, he chose to decline the prize. Of the two reasons he gave, the first was political in that he objected to the memorialization of Empire implied in the term "commonwealth." Equally important was his concern that the prize "excludes the many languages that sustain the cultural and literary lives of these countries" ("Regarding"). This point has been made in the past, but Ghosh's gesture drives home the need for reassessing the institutions that function as the arbiters of quality. In fact, Paranjape extends this argument by stating that English writing "functions best as a minority or as a frontier discourse, occupying a middle ground between the West and India" (*Poetics* 93). While such a division may well lead to a further set of problems, the fact is that vernacular writing requires much more attention in postcolonial studies than it has received.

A comparative or complementary assessment of English and vernacular writing would be a necessary aspect of a larger study of contemporary South Asian writing. For the purpose of the present discussion, suffice it to reiterate the contribution of Rushdie in facilitating a new kind of writing. In an attempt to provide a broader context for placing Rushdie, Advani (having sketched the overarching influence of Rushdie in shaping a new poetics) focuses on a particular school that, literally and metaphorically, had upstaged all others to become the literary voice of Indo-Anglian writing. He locates that voice at St. Stephen's College, University of Delhi, an institution where he himself was trained, and although he concedes that other schools may have instilled among their students a similar world view, it was the St. Stephen's atmosphere that shaped the direction and provided the epistemological underpinning of new writing. Irreverent, syncretic, westernized, and upper-class—all these, according to Advani, are trademarks of this college. He is right where he recognizes that there would be some resistance to his particular slant—Shashi Tharoor in the same issue of *Seminar* objects strenuously to what he considers Advani's "myopic view." However, Advani, anticipating this kind of response, concludes by saying that "[Amitav] Ghosh & co. can say that they weren't shaped by St. Stephen's till they're blue in the face—it makes no difference to this most Seminarial reading of their writing which says they bloody well were" (18). To extend Advani's comment about St. Stephen's, one could think of such schools–often private, located in urban centres–in Sri Lanka and Pakistan, where similar attitudes and values would have been inculcated. In short, if this theory has any validity at all, it suggests that a particular group, anglicized, relatively well-to-do, upper middle-class, privileged, and located in urban centres, are the forerunners of this particular movement.

A further extension of this argument would be the kind of inevitability with which a number of authors have found their way to the West. Granting that one needs to be wary of generalizations, it is arguable that the kind of intellectual training provided in these institutions would make the West an attractive and familiar place.[5] While specific and immediate reasons for migration may well differ, it is no coincidence that a large proportion of well-known authors such as Anita Rau Badami, Michael Ondaatje, Vikram Chandra, Amitav Ghosh, Rohinton Mistry, and Chitra Divakaruni are all settled in the West.

While several South Asian writers in the last two decades have remained in South Asia and have sought local sponsors for their work, those who have acquired international reputations have often found publishers in the West. It is a curious irony that quite often novels published in the West are not available for several months in India or Sri Lanka. The spatial movement from the local scene to metropolitan capitals, such as London, Toronto, or New York, has had a significant impact on this movement itself. Bill Buford, who deconstructs the photograph of several authors seen together in *The New Yorker*, draws attention to the randomness of the group and claims that they do not form part of a movement that can be defined geographically or in relation to yet another school.[6] The authors of South Asian origin do not gravitate to a particular city, and have no real sense of being part of a collective group, but they do leave Delhi, Bombay, Karachi, and Colombo, and take up residence in London, New York, Toronto, Vancouver, San Francisco, and so forth, which then become centres of literary activity.

This shift in location means a lot more than voluntary exile. It implies readership, improvement of material conditions for writers, including writer's grants, fellowships, and events such as the harbourfront readings in Toronto. It is remarkable to note the number of South Asian writers in the West who are either full-time writers or are involved in professions that relate directly to their writing. To write from the West is not necessarily to write about it. In fact the reverse is true. The majority of writing by diasporic writers is about "home" rather than the West. But it simply means that there is a strong Western presence that determines so many aspects of writing. David Davidar speaks of a growing middle class and an extended reading public in India that takes Indian writers seriously. The numbers he documents are fairly substantial, with the average number of books sold being close to five thousand.[7] Maybe a similar scenario could be advanced for Sri Lanka as well where a relatively small but active community provides the support and intellectual atmosphere for such literary activity. But while these figures are not to be ignored, it is equally true that this kind of response is not likely to lead to the measure of self-sufficiency that a number of South Asian authors in the West are now able to enjoy.

The notion of diaspora is complex, and the more one theorizes about it the more difficult the terrain appears. Even with South Asia, diasporic activity defies any easy or monolithic definition, and it is routinely invoked as a tool to legitimize "tribal" (to use James Clifford's term) claims. As new affiliations are formed on the basis of ethnicity, religion, or race, migrancy offers itself as a way of separating (again to use Clifford's words) "root" from "route." Bapsi Sidhwa's *Cracking India* includes an anecdote about the arrival of the Parsis to India, the hostile reception given to them by the local ruler, and the reconciliation forged by the Parsis who insisted that their intention was to assimilate and enrich the local culture. That is perhaps one of the more benign evocations of diaspora. At the other end of the spectrum is the hardening of differences, leading to real and imagined identities. Writing about the rise of nationalism in Sri Lanka, Nira Wickramasinghe offers an analysis to "show

how both myths and the apparatus of the West combining to inscribe boundaries between communities and dividing them into 'migrants' and 'sons of the soil' led to the politics of exclusion and violence against the former" (154). Sri Lanka is, in fact, a classic example of the symbiotic relation between diaspora and literary activity. Writing in English received a major impetus with the political turmoil of the early 1970s, but the major thrust came with the separatist struggle and its attendant diasporic consciousness.

Sidhwa's episode refers to a particular kind of diaspora in which the idea of "return" is hardly an issue. With more recent migration to the West, "home" becomes a constitutive factor in shaping the construction and perpetuation of identities. Here again, patterns vary as waves of migration, occasioned by very different circumstances, take place and people arrive as refugees, entrepreneurs, or as high-tech professionals. Among them there are generational, class, caste, and gender differences. Given the bewildering changes that make diaspora a process rather than a product, one tends to agree with Clifford who says that "it is now widely understood that the old localizing strategies–by bounded *community*, by organic *culture*, by *region*, by *center* and *periphery*–may obscure as much as they reveal" (303).

The fact is, however, that some initial positions need to be established. Not all contemporary writers fall into the category of "diasporic." Not all local writers may be "rooted" in the traditional sense of the term. Nonetheless, the real concern is with the noticeable differences among them in literary practice. Do diasporic writers–displaced from home but who owe a part of their consciousness to the land they called "home" in the past–write differently? Is that a choice or necessity? If it's necessity, does counterrealism play an important role since a recognizable teleology is disrupted in a diasporic context? In spite of the advances in technology and communication, the idea of memory separates the exiles from the stay-at-home writers. The difference must, at some level, determine narrative mode. Paranjape makes the point that "ultimately, there is bound to be a difference in the way in which diaspora writes the

mother country and the mother country writes itself. Though there
is an umbilical relationship, there are distortions" (122). An essentialist division is likely to be no more than a generalization, but
there's a critical gap without such divisions.

Given the ambivalence of diaspora and national allegiance,
assertions are likely to be tentative.[8] But if the impulse to experiment is one manifestation of diaspora, so is the compulsion to create quest narratives. Such narratives are not exclusive to diaspora,
but the mode inherently adapts itself to the symbolic structures
often created to map the experience of exile. In a letter, Ghose
speaks of the chapter "In the Sundarbans" in Rushdie's *Midnight's
Children* which involves Saleem's "flight from the demons of the
subcontinent" and Roshan's final journey through to the Hindu
Kush in *Triple Mirror of the Self*. He adds: "in retrospect I see how
the image has repeated itself and how the buried form of that
image is that of journeying through a dark labyrinth towards a
bright valley or a bright mountain-top" (10 March 1992). Once this
motif is linked to Namjoshi's *Conversations of Cow* or Desai's *Journey
to Ithaca*, a recurrent pattern begins to emerge.

The quest narrative is one way to deal with not only the absence
of roots but also the lack of a language or a frame to recreate that
sense of cultural belonging. What remains elusive is the subtext,
made even more elusive by the language and the spatio-temporal
distance caused by the diaspora. The diasporic writer recognizes
the need to remember even while acknowledging—in some
instances—the finality of dismemberment. Experiment, then, serves
the crucial function of bridging a subjective and epistemological
gap.

A study of the post-Rushdie literary scene would, inevitably, be
an ambitious task, in scope and complexity. The very idea of Indian
writing as a single stream—a tradition which begins in the nineteenth century and works its way to the present—is now a thing of
the past as multiple streams converge to make up the South Asian
literary scene. Writing from Pakistan, Bangladesh, and Sri Lanka are
very much a part of the total corpus. More significantly, the dias-

pora has brought into the general rubric of "Indian" not only those writers who have migrated to the West but all the writers of Indian origin, regardless of national affiliations. Africa, the Caribbean, Fiji, Malaysia, and Singapore, for instance, would be part of the typology. National models are never likely to be totally displaced since the precise conditions of countries such as Sri Lanka are not replicated elsewhere. Regional models are likely to be more popular, but if critical studies feel the need to include authors such as M.G. Vassanji (who migrated to Canada from East Africa) and K.S. Maniam (who lives in Malaysia), then the typology would have to be even more inclusive.

The expectations of the West do not determine all the writing from South Asia. Rajiva Wijesinha publishes his fiction in Sri Lanka or India, as does Jean Arasanayagam. Gopal Baratham writes from Singapore and Lloyd Fernando continues to live in Malaysia. Location does not necessarily divide these writers in schematic terms but if the material conditions that enable production and distribution are constitutive, then it is hardly surprising that writers with local audiences in mind are likely to be faced with very different pressures.

Nonetheless, in countries where English as an everyday language is in decline and where vernacular literatures play a referential role that can never be matched by writing in English, the concern with the relevance of writing in English is real. And this has vexed recent writers, no less than it concerned Raja Rao and Kamala Das decades ago. Suniti Namjoshi, for instance, wonders "how to write about India in English." And she adds, "after all my Indian experience was everyday and as familiar to me as anything would be, but in English, things Indian become exotic" (*Because* 42). Upamanyu Chatterjee in his novel *English, August* has one of the characters comment about been-to figures aspiring to write: "I find these people absurd, full with one mixed-up culture and writing about another, what kind of audience are they aiming at. That's why their India is just not real, a place of fantasy, or of confused metaphysics, a sub-continent of goons" (48). What is implied here is not that the Indian experience is outside the reach of Indo-Anglian writing so much as the awareness that if Indo-Anglian writing tries to explore areas of experience that lie outside its field of vision, its achievement is likely to be dubious.

Here again, one needs to make a distinction between the pre- and post-Rushdie generation. If, for Raja Rao and those of his generation, the issue was one of moulding the language to explore a vastly different ontology and fulfil a project that is subversive and celebratory, for contemporary writers the issue is the validity of the ontology itself. Often adopting a relativistic, solipsistic, and even narcissistic perspective, the writers explore notions of reality rather than Reality itself. For example, metafictional, parodic, and entertaining, Tharoor's *Show Business* is in fact about the confusions that surround perceptions of reality in art and life. The sense of audience in these texts is complex—a fact substantiated by the simultaneous publication of books in India and abroad—the ideological stance more ambivalent and obscure, the loyalties of the authors divided, and their apprehension of reality more private than collective. The same questions are being asked, but for different reasons. If for Raja Rao the assertion of Indianness is crucial, for the contemporary writer, the probing of what it means to be Indian takes precedence. And to be Indian is a far cry from being a mirror image of the stereotype that was once created to serve the interests of colonialism.

Experiment, at least in Rushdie's sense, is not the signature of all the new writers. It could even be said that the contrary is true—a strong sense of referentiality is more typical of a number of these works. Vikram Seth's *A Suitable Boy* is probably as close as one could get to a triple-decker Victorian novel in Indian writing. So conventional, for instance, are works such as Bapsi Sidhwa's *The American Brat*, Hanif Kureishi's *The Buddha of Suburbia*, Vikram Chandra's *Love and Longing in Bombay,* or Rohinton Mistry's *A Fine Balance* that they could well be considered straightforward mimetic writing. The sense of closure in Ghosh's *The Shadow Lines* is a random instance of realism. In fact, the last lines where the narrator says, "I could tell that she was glad, and I was glad too, and grateful, for the glimpse she had given me of a final redemptive mystery" (252) recall the familiar pattern of dislocation and consolidation that pervades referential works. That this glimpse is private rather than collective and that the two are seen to establish a problematic relation to each other is perhaps an important point of departure from the pre-Rushdie novel. The marginal here asserts its provisionality without jettisoning its claim to speak for the collective as well. The joining of the marginal and the collective in the production of meaning is central to the poetics of this writing.

Faith in the values of liberal humanism hardly suffices for a novel such as *The Shadow Lines*; neither does a reassuring sense of a transcendental reality. In their place is a consciousness of separateness and its attendant fear and loneliness. As the narrator puts it:

> It is a fear that comes of the knowledge that normalcy
> is utterly contingent, that the spaces that surround one,
> the streets that one inhabits, can become, suddenly and
> without warning, as hostile as a desert in a flash flood.
> It is this that set apart the thousand million people who
> inhabit the subcontinent from the rest of the world—not
> language, not food, not music—it is that special quality of
> loneliness that grows out of the fear of the war between
> oneself and one's image in the mirror. (204)

The realism is unsettled by the questioning of boundaries that have been considered sacrosanct. As physical, spatial, cultural lines of demarcation become increasingly suspect, the insubstantiality of shadow lines replaces the ontology of traditional realism. Thus a work that preserves the illusion of realism, one that is, to use Robert Alter's term "intermittently illusionist" becomes its opposite, a self-referential one that insists on its fictionality.

Equally deceptive in its mimesis is Chatterjee's *English, August,* a novel that is ostensibly traditional in its narrative structure. The narrator, however, warns the reader up front: "But mine is not the typical Indian story. That ends with the Indian living somewhere in the First World, comfortably or uncomfortably. Or perhaps coming back to join the Indian Administrative Service, if lucky" (3). In any event, the protagonist, if that is a valid term for one who rarely initiates anything, hardly looks or behaves like one. As one of the characters tells him: "you don't look the role. You look like a porn film actor, thin and kinky….And a bureaucrat ought to be soft and clean-shaven, bespectacled, and if a Tamil Brahmin, given to rapid quoting of rules" (3). The novel is hardly experimental, but it is not entirely mimetic either. The differences in degree also make taxonomy problematic. The narrative mode is to some extent dependent on who reads a text. In any event, as Lukács maintains, "realistic detail is a precondition for the communication of a sense of absurdity" (48). That said, realism tends to draw the reader inward by evoking transparency, while experiment distances the reader and trades objectivity for the appeal of subjectivity.

The distinction between recent novels and the fiction that preceded Rushdie is a fine one. For the most part, the Indian novel has remained insular and conservative. It is this aspect that leads Paranjape to comment that Indian writing in English is "essentially a minority literature" and that its "themes and concerns are usually peripheral to the lives and experiences of the majority of Indians" (*Poetics* 215). However, one needs to distinguish between novels that masquerade as Indian and ones that destabilize this paradigm. The post-Rushdie novel remains Indian, but instead of claiming to express *the* collective experience, it focuses on one of the many experiences which constitute the collective.

The point here is that any typology for contemporary South Asian writing is going to be a complex affair. While one end of the spectrum would include referential works along the lines of Mistry and Badami, the other end would comprise experimental writers such as Rajiva Wijesinha and K.S. Maniam. In between are those whose sense of textuality enables them to fall back on an aestheticism without abandoning social concerns. Michael Ondaatje would be an example of this stance. And then there is the group of writers who work with a poetic structure without resorting to overt experiment. Roy's *The God of Small Things* would probably fall into this category.

Is it likely that for the Rushdie generation the ontological certainty that held together the fiction of previous writers no longer holds true. It is not a question of greater secularism or simply an awareness of fragmentation. Is there an awareness that the comforting pieties of cliché are no longer valid? Gieve Patel's comments in the special issue of *Daedalus* about his own experimental painting underscore this skepticism, this lack of patience with images that have sufficed in the past. Among the postcolonial elite who took spontaneously to westernization, there was also a concomitant skepticism about the ontological unity of the East. The ethos that has been paraded as normal is now seen with greater skepticism than before. As Patel puts it, "when a normality is given a canvas to itself...a breath of doubt flies at you from the caverns of your twentieth-century mind, so well-tutored to inner and outer disasters. It corrodes your momentary self-confidence" (200). Does this acceptance or flaunting of fragmentation find an audience in the West?

An aspect of writing and readership that this study does not address in any great detail is the precise composition of the target audience in the West. If the huge advance that recent writers such as Arundhati Roy have received is anything to go by, there is a substantial readership—both academic and general—that supports these novels. For the most part, the specific ethos of these works is alien to the readers. But that does not diminish their appeal. The relevance, then, must lie elsewhere—in the exoticism of the Other, the realism that is reminiscent of the literature of a bygone era, or perhaps the self-conscious artifice that is not far removed from postmodern forms of artistic expression. This is not to imply that the expectations of the West account for the formal strategies and thematic concerns of the contemporary Indo-Anglian novel. But the West is a part of Indo-Anglian writing, and that could well be both its strength and weakness.

G.N. Devy points out that "in order that a literature becomes a great literature it should develop from a language that is rooted in the soil, that grows organically from peoples' experiences piled together for generations. It will, then, have a free access to the collective unconscious of its society, its own mythological network, its own range of idiom." And then he adds that English writing has "to operate within [a] severely limited social space" (353). That this writing inhabits a limited space and that it belongs to a small, and often privileged, class can hardly be refuted. But to deny its Indianness on the basis of its class affiliation or its withdrawal from traditional structures is to be guilty of a binarism that falsifies the multiplicity of Indian life. The purpose of *The Great Indian Novel*, for instance, is to celebrate multiplicity, to destabilize the privileging of any ideology. According to Tharoor, "the novel…speaks of an India of multiple realities and of multiple interpretations of reality. It is a conscious evocation of the many truths that have helped to give shape and substance to the idea of India" (31).

Tharoor's novel does not concern itself with the immediate, but it is a perception of India seen through marginalized eyes. In fact, the traits that characterize this generation of writers are their marginalization and their consciousness of being caught between two worlds, not in the sense of a been-to who measures one culture from the perspective of another, but rather as people who do not belong, and whose desire to belong is constantly interrupted by disruptions that cannot be transcended and who must withdraw into the life of the imagination. The withdrawal is not one of cynicism or detachment; instead there is commitment, but the commitment does not entail either orientalizing India or discrediting it. Speaking about the complexity of his project in *The Great Indian Novel*, Tharoor comments that "all this demanded a style steeped in irreverence–the only viable attitude…for my appropriation of history, myth and canonical fiction, all areas overburdened in India by hagiology" ("Myth" 31).

Allan Sealy's *The Trotter-Nama* belongs to this group in chronicling the history of Anglo-Indians who are all too easily labelled, like the Burghers in Sri Lanka, as pseudo-British and dismissed as insignificant. That their story is equally valid and representative is confirmed by contemporary writing. Consciousness about the limitations of linearity coexists with the desire to record the history of those whose roles have been sidelined by political or cultural circumstance. Hence the experiment, the self-mockery, the constant punning, and wordplay. Allan Sealy's narrator defines the process in a wonderful metaphor, soon after confessing that parts of the "chronicle" are in fact purely fictive reconstructions of the past: "Anyway, the present is tricky enough, just watch your step. Potholes everywhere in this city. Now if they all join up, the road would be nice and smooth. But no, they keep patching, bit here, bit there" (*Trotter* 572). Constructs created to serve the interests of a particular ideology attain the status of truth and in that sense hardly betray their flaws, whereas his narrative would sacrifice the seamlessness in favour of a ruggedness that insists on its provisionality.

The consequent sense of indeterminacy could easily be characterized as self-indulgence, particularly in relation to vernacular literatures whose role is noticeably different. The crucial difference here is not of quality but of perspective. Vernacular literatures must, inevitably, deal with the immediate. The contradictions inherent in the process are of less significance than the pain caused by the product. For contemporary Indian writing in English, the sense of immediacy is less forceful, less than it was for Rushdie. Perhaps that is a consequence of the fate that has befallen Rushdie. But it is also a result of the urgency of the private and an investment in the public, a skepticism about nationalistic jingoism, and a desire for continuous identity that has roots in the past.

The indeterminacy, the preoccupation with the private, the syncretism, in short the unclassifiability, is often a cause for concern. Do marginalized critics empathize with marginalized writers and attempt to create a poetics to justify what is essentially ephemeral and elitist? Is one endangered species protecting another? Whether one labels Indo-Anglian writing self-indulgent or ruthlessly honest, the issues it raises go beyond Indian writing, although its manifestations in other contexts make the resemblance often difficult to detect. Indian fiction does not speak for the downtrodden, the victims of a caste or dowry system, and when it does it often fails to be convincing. One might cite *The God of Small Things*, for example, to demonstrate that the everyday is never far from the consciousness of these writers. Admittedly, Roy uses the issue of caste as the core of her novel, but the strength of her work derives from her artifice. The Indian novel is, typically, concerned with the been-to, the West, and the Westernized. But one needs to remind oneself that what parades as central has affiliations with the marginal as well. To establish a duality is to ignore the shades of grey that mark a continuum. As Allan Sealy's alienated and Anglo-Indian narrator rightly comments:

> Anyway, I was saying, not too many of us left and half
> of those waiting to leave. And we're not the only ones.
> They want to go too. You read their matrimonial
> columns. American Green Card holder preferred, only a
> doctor or engineer settled in U.S.A., Canada, Australia.
> But what to do? (*Trotter* 574)

It is curiously a kind of formalism, combined with postmodernism, that would explain the impulse behind the textuality of writing that characterizes the work of "midnight's grandchildren." But it also highlights a particular kind of reality. It is not about surfaces, but about ruptures and fissures.

Having located themselves on the cusp, counterrealist writers are often ideally placed to deal with "meta" issues that relate to history, religion, politics and, in a general sense, the construction of identity. They do not have to face the conundrum of replicating the "real" while working with a readership that is alienated from what is being portrayed and a medium that is resistant to the material. The curious paradox is that referential works such as Mistry's *A Fine Balance* and Badami's *The Hero's Walk* are immensely popular among readers. The issue, then, is whether they are acclaimed because they make a valuable contribution or because they fulfil the needs of a particular readership. Laura Moss, who claims that "non-realist writing is frequently privileged" and that "there has been a critical elevation of writing perceived to be experimental" (158) goes on to argue that "realism is a viable, perhaps indispensable form for political and social engagement in postcolonial contexts" (159). Moss's insightful defence underscores the need to study contemporary referential writing in detail. It also serves as a reminder that such a study should factor in the readers, the characters, and the language that mediates between them.

This study has tried to demonstrate that in Indo-Anglian writing, as in any other national literature, new forms of perception have been accompanied by departures from older forms. Realism and experiment have access to different worlds and they establish distinctive traditions. Experiment may not necessarily be superior to realism, but artifice certainly tests the limits of mimetic writing. For the present, suffice it to conclude by recalling the conversation between Vasco and Aurora in *The Moor's Last Sigh*. Vasco is hardly an erudite art critic, and he is certainly not the author-surrogate in the novel, but his words do offer a model for the perspective–though not the tone–of those who champion the cause of counterrealism: "Forget those damnfool realists! The real is always hidden–isn't it?–inside a miraculously burning bush! Life is fantastic! Paint that" (174).

Notes

Chapter 1

1 While it's true that rapid Westernization in India has ensured the survival of English, the language evidently no longer retains the class associations it once had. The point that Sunil Khilnani makes that the Indian prime minister H.D. Deve Gowda, who gave the Independence-Day address to the nation in 1996, could not speak English is of particular relevance to the present discussion. For more information, see *The Idea of India*, 15.

2 Anita Desai's comments appeared in the essay entitled "On the English Language in India." Kamala Das's poem has been heavily anthologized, largely because it speaks so precisely about the postcolonial author's decision to write in English. Her poem is included in C.D. Narasimhaiah's *An Anthology of Commonwealth Poetry* (47-49). A section of Raja Rao's preface is quoted in this essay. R. Parthasarathy is well known as a poet. After publishing several volumes of poetry in English, he decided to write in Tamil. For more information, see the introduction to *Ten Twentieth Century Poets*, edited by Parthasarathy.

3 For a very persuasive study of the role of education in British colonialism, see Gauri Viswanathan's *The Masks of Conquest*.

4 In his essay entitled "Domesticating the Novel: Society and Culture in the Inter-War Tamil Nadu," A.R. Venkatachalapathy offers a detailed account of the cultural nexus that provided the impetus for the growth of the novel in Tamil. As he puts it, one of the objectives of his article is to "explore how the novel was appropriated by the Tamil middle class as part of its negotiation with the West/modernity" (54). His article is a salutary reminder that easy dichotomies based on East-West binaries are likely to be more convenient than accurate.

5 Using the terms "mimesis" and "diegesis" to establish the different ways in which the realist novel deals with narrative voice, David Lodge provides a useful discussion of the implications of the decision to foreground one more than the other. See *After Bakhtin* (25-44). His discussion of *Middlemarch* is a valuable demonstration of the manner in which the realistic text achieves its purpose.

6 For an insightful analysis of the need for comparative aesthetics, read chapter 1 of *Literary India* (3-42).

Chapter 2

1 In a laudatory introduction, Graham Greene says: "I don't wait for another novel, I wait to go out of my door into those loved and shabby streets and see with excitement and a certainty of pleasure a stranger…who will greet me I know with some unexpected and revealing phrase that will open a door on to yet another existence" (viii).

2. Srinivasa Iyengar's discussion of Narayan in his *Indian Writing in English* is predicated on the "recognizably autochthonous" (359) aspect of his writing. Walsh, along similar lines, says that Narayan's "novels are regional, in that they convey an intimate sense of a given place, but not parochial. They include the intimate resonance given by village life as well as the more sophisticated tone of the impersonal city" (4).

3 In a longish and very interesting article that appeared in *The New Yorker*, Ved Mehta says: "I was drawn to Narayan because his works, though written in English…have the ring of true India in them. He had succeeded where his peers had failed, and this without relying on Anglicized Indians or British caricatures to people his novels" (51). An interesting contrast here is Anita Desai's review of *A Tiger for Malgudi*, where she says that "it could be on account of his constant peregrinations on two continents, as a reaction to physical flux, that when he takes up his pen he uses it as a compass to help his mind search out the stillness and stability of his memories of his earliest 'rooted' stage of existence" (3).

4 The description of Granny's death in part 3 of the novel is decidedly strange even in Narayan's corpus. Juxtaposed with a very referential description of the details of the funeral is the scene of Granny's "resurrection."

5 Todorov's definition goes thus: "the fantastic occupies the duration of this uncertainty. Once we choose one answer or the other, we leave the fantastic for a neighbouring genre, the uncanny or the marvellous. The fantastic is that hesitation experienced by a person who knows only the laws of nature, confronting an apparently supernatural event" (25).

6 Kiran Desai's novel entitled *Hullabaloo in the Guava Orchard* is probably the most recognizable inheritor of the Narayan mode.

7 About the novel Fakrul Alam says: "it is a narrative of identification; and it is plotted to show how the narrator-protagonist is aroused by an aggressive figure with whom he increasingly identifies until, having incorporated many features of this more instinctive, more primitive being, he can dispose of him symbolically by putting himself into a position where he can stand guard and contemplate the destruction of this other self" (150).

8 In this very comprehensive study, Eugene Irschik traces the multiple forces that shaped the social and political scene in Tamil Nadu during the first quarter of this century. Of particular interest is chapter 8 entitled "The Intellectual Background of Tamil Separatism" (275-310).

Chapter 3

1 The performative aspect of the novel, which Harrex quite rightly identifies, was evident in a recent theatrical version that was staged in Toronto. The adaptation of *Hatterr*, entitled "Damme This Is the Oriental Scene for You," directed by Rehan and Saniya Ansari, played at the Theatre Passe Muraille from 27 January to 13 February 2000. The play was modest—only sixty minutes long—and the focus was Hatterr's first encounter with the guru who also moonlights as a second-hand clothes dealer.

The play's title is interesting, mainly because it links Desani and Rushdie. Despite the four decades that separate the two, the connections are clearly there: anti-essentialism, subversion, heterogeneity, and hybridity. More significantly, the play drives home the differences between the two as well. Desani's influences are predominantly British, and the fact that the play chooses to begin with an allusion to Hamlet is both a statement about the dualities that Hatterr faces and about the need to put certain ghosts to rest. The novel is an interrogation of the premises of multiculturalism, just when India was poised to define its identity in relation to various competing claims. The very fact that Hatterr is played by Paul Lee—of Asian descent—brings home the vulnerability of the in-between position in a world dominated by assertions of homogeneity.

The play also exploits the dramatic properties of the novel. The artifice of the novel, and its conscious rejection of the premises of realism, were aspects that ensured the success of the play. The play worked well as farce but it lost a great deal of the novel's intertextuality. While the theatrical properties came across very clearly, the play also demonstrated what is lost when the counterrealism of the novel is jettisoned in favour of a linear progression. Desani's novel demands active participation by the reader while the play required a more passive response from the audience.

2 A.L. McLeod, who has written the entry on Desani in *Writers of the Indian Diaspora*, begins by saying that "inexplicably, there is little biographical material available on Govindas Vishnoodas Desani, and he does not respond to requests for information to supplement the meagre details he has seen fit to make known over the years, either in conversation or in publishers' handouts" (95). Even Molly Ramanujam, who has written a lengthy monograph on Desani, is tentative about her biographical sketch and admits that some of the dates she provides "were inferred by computing" (69). It is evident that he spent at least two decades in Britain between 1926 and 1952, during which time he was a journalist, lecturer, and public speaker. It is highly unlikely that he would have been unaware of the literary culture of Britain during the interwar years.

3 In his essay in *The New Yorker*, Rushdie makes the astute observation that "if Narayan is India's Richardson, then Desani is his Shandean other." He

then goes on to add, "My own writings, too, learned a trick or two from him" (58).

4   While Desani's novel is about a representative individual, Sealy's novel is about a whole community. But both are concerned with the predicament of Anglo-Indians, and Sealy's ambitious work is as self-conscious, parodic, and digressive as *Hatterr*.

5   A good example of Okot p'Bitek's use of oral forms is his well-known narrative poem *Song of Lawino*. Raja Rao, using the persona of a grandmother, works with the oral form in *Kanthapura*. The Trinidadian writer Sam Selvon does the same with a West Indian dialect in almost all his novels, including his popular work *The Lonely Londoners*.

6   Narayan's *My Dateless Diary: An American Journey* provides a detailed account of his experiences in the USA. While there is much that he does not approve of in America, he is unequivocal in his admiration for the West.

7   Rushdie's comment in *Imaginary Homelands* that "if literature is in part the business of finding new angles at which to enter reality, then once again our distance, our long geographical perspective, may provide us with such angles" (15) is of particular relevance here.

8   No less controversial than V.S. Naipaul's *An Area of Darkness*, Chaudhuri's *The Continent of Circe* purports to "describe the peoples of India in their natural groupings" (35), but it remains a very negative account of a "dangerous void of faith, ideas, courage, and, of course, energy" (330).

9   D.M. Burjorjee calls this novel the "most important item in Indo-Anglian literature" (191) and Ramanujam claims that it "is without question the most (perhaps the only) brilliant novel by an Indian in English" (69). Curiously enough, Miller calls the novel "a joke too long and too repetitious" and Schwartz faults it for trying to be "*too* funny, *too* witty, *too* allusive and *too* learned" (578).

10   While discussing the complex formulation of taxonomic structures in society, Bruce Lincoln says: "To hold that thought is socially determined does not mean that all thought reflects, encodes, re-presents, or helps replicate the *established structures* of society, for society is far broader and more complex than its official structures and institutions alone. Rather, such a formulation rightly implies that all the tensions, contradictions, superficial stability, and potential fluidity of any given society *as a whole* are present within the full range of thought and discourse that circulates at any given moment" (6-7).

11   In a detailed and persuasive essay entitled "Authority and Identity in India," Vaidyanathan demonstrates the many ways in which the teacher-disciple relation functions as a master paradigm in Indian society. He adds: "When the harmony and symmetry of this relationship is broken—as it increasingly is in Modern India—the guru-shishya conglomerate splits off into its component parts, precipitating the crisis of authority and identity that is rampant in India today" (148).

Chapter 4

1   Baumgartner's confusion as he explores the inner chamber, described on pages 189-90, is remarkably similar to that of Adela Quested in *A Passage to India*.

2 The reference is to Anderson's well-known work *Imagined Communities*.

3 Kiran Desai's *Hullabaloo in the Guava Orchard* is more identifiably fabulist and less associative than the work of Anita Desai.

4 The more "identifiable" forms of abuse do occur in her writing, as in the rape of Ila Das in *Fire on the Mountain*, but on the whole, such instances are relatively few.

5 Chatterjee's article is reprinted in *Recasting Women*, a collection of essays edited by Kumkum Sangari and Sudesh Vaid. Almost all the articles in this important collection provide useful information to study not only Desai but all the Indian writers who concern themselves with the marginalization of women.

6 A representative work would be Sunaina Singh's *The Novels of Margaret Atwood and Anita Desai* in which chapter 3 entitled "The 'Crazy' Ones" offers a sound analysis of the psychological approach to Desai.

Chapter 5

1 The matter-of-fact acknowledgment and reference to Márquez is in striking contrast to the ironic tone with which the note ends. After the customary note, Ghose claims that the story "was composed as a tribute to the true and 'only begetter' of literary magic."

2 Between Machado de Assis and García Márquez, Ghose's preference would be clearly for the former; lamenting academic neglect of de Assis, Ghose says: "For years I've been telling my friends among American writers that Machado de Assis is a genius who simply must be read; no one has read him, however, but several of them have read Solzhenitsyn" (*Fiction* 73). About Márquez, in a conversation with Reed Way Dasenbrock and Feroza Jussawalla, he says: "Everybody's great example of magical realistic fiction has to be *One Hundred Years of Solitude*. But if you look at it closely, you'll find that all that Márquez does is to have something extraordinary happen from time to time....It's all very delightful and carries you across the rather wide gulfs of straightforward narrative without your noticing how ordinary the narrative is, until you read the book a second time when you realize it's really a very boring book" (150-51).

3 *Hamlet, Prufrock and Language* is probably his most sustained work on the relation between language and reality. Shaped by the thought of Wittgenstein, the text demonstrates that the main concern of the writer is the status and inadequacy of language as a vehicle for the expression of reality.

4 Srinivasa Iyengar and Meenakshi Mukherjee, for instance, pay no attention to Ghose, and even more recent works such as Viney Kirpal's *The New Indian Novel in English: A Study of the 1980s* do not include critical studies of his writing. It is quite likely that he was seen to be a Pakistani writer, although such a position would be difficult to defend.

5 A case in point, perhaps, is Anita Desai, whose *Bye-Bye Blackbird*, a straightforward realistic novel, set in England, is quite unlike anything she has written, before or after.

6 The novel was republished in Pakistan in 1998 by Oxford University Press.

7 One year after the publication of the novel, Ghose wrote in a letter to Thomas Berger about an occurrence in Pakistan which bears an uncanny resemblance to the plot of *Aziz Khan*. For the full episode, see Thomas Berger's "A Selection of Letters" in *The Review of Contemporary Fiction*.

8 For an insightful discussion of the relation between realism and *mise-en-abyme*, see chapter 1 in Stonehill.

9 For a fuller discussion of this passage, see my *Structures of Negation: the Writing of Zulfikar Ghose*.

10 The fact that Ayub Shah was a thug who lived on Mohammed Ali Road may well be a coincidence, but in a much broader sense the depiction of social ritual and cultural norms establish the intertextual connection. More specifically, *Confessions of a Native-Alien*, the "fictive" autobiography, has several parallels with *Triple Mirror*.

11 Shimomura is a name given by Pons—an indication that Shimmers's identity is also altered in the process. Roshan's father deliberately uses the initials M.K.G. for his company to strengthen a Hindu connection. All these need to be seen in relation to Ghose's own name, which is Hindu rather than Muslim.

12 Having conceded that Ghose does not completely ignore the everyday world, Harris adds that "[Ghose's] response is consistent with the arousal of a voice—that seeks no profit from any fashionable alignment save to record the surplus value of memory threaded into vistas of receding horizons around the globe" (174).

Chapter 6

1 In response to a question whether she considers her audience to be exclusively lesbian, Namjoshi replies: "Absolutely. And, for a change, [let] the rest of them eavesdrop....Let them sympathize with what we consider to be our question: 'what does it mean to be a lesbian?' By which we understand: 'What does it mean to be human?' Let them exercise their imaginations and let them see the universality of the theme in this" (Brooks 15).

2 Namjoshi argues that there is really no middle ground available to the writer. The context inevitably enforces a world view, and the writer who does not write against it, by default, endorses it. In her words: "Writers are dependent on an external frame of reference, and so what is not modified by the context of the poem is reinforced by its very use. In other words, literature is always potentially revolutionary and potentially conservative" ("Poetry" 5).

3 It must be emphasized that Namjoshi's work, until the early 1980s, was less scathing in its criticism. The feminist/lesbian consciousness that informs the major part of her writing is relatively absent, causing her early critical stance to be more concerned with mythic and linguistic elements. Her analysis of the poetry of Jay Macpherson and P.K. Page appeared in *Canadian Literature*.

4 Zimmerman's very perceptive argument appears in the essay "Perverse Reading: The Lesbian Appropriation of Literature" in *Sexual Practice, Textual Theory*.

5 This fable, "Snow White and Rose Green," appears in *From the Bedside Book of Nightmares* (21).

6   Van Dyke makes the interesting observation that "for the Middle Ages, it
    was a method of exegesis operating upon a prior text or upon a 'literal'
    story within a present text. Because the prior text carries its own pre-alle-
    gorical meaning, allegory appears as the alternative (usually the superior
    alternative) to the more obvious, more common way of reading or writing"
    (16).

7   The fable entitled "Further Adventures of the One-Eyed Monkey" appears
    in *Feminist Fables* (79). The monkey as outsider, spectator, and witness
    enables a retelling of the well-known episode to reveal an entirely different
    ideology at work. Despite the evidence given by the monkey, the woman
    who is the victim is ignored and the judge (namely, Lord Vishnu) insists on
    a sacrifice that would cleanse the culprit and appease the husband. The
    fable ends with the words: "And so it came about that a horse was killed, a
    god purified, a brahmin appeased, a woman ruined, and a monkey left feel-
    ing thoroughly puzzled" (79).

8   "Every re-telling of a myth is a re-working of it. Every hearing or reading
    of a myth is a re-creation of it," says Namjoshi. "It is only when we engage
    with a myth that it resonates, that it becomes charged and re-charged with
    meaning" (*Babel* xi).

9   Along similar lines, Anne Smith observes that "*The Conversations of Cow* is a
    pleasant, pointless little work with a sixties feel to it....It's probably saying
    something about sexual roles and the nature of love, but not a lot" (30).

10 In an erudite and persuasive essay entitled "Ezra Pound and the Hex
    Hoax," Namjoshi advances the argument that "for Pound, this world is not
    a fallen world and, in consequence, evil is neither radical nor inescapable"
    (65). *Saint Suniti* is an attempt to explore many aspects of this assertion.

11 In an extraordinary and perfectly sincere note, Namjoshi tells the publisher
    about her plans: "The book is published. Then the last chapter, 'The
    Reader's Text,' goes on your Home Page on the World Wide Web with an
    invitation to Reader to contribute to the memes of Babel. Such contribu-
    tions as you accept can go on the Home Page. If there are enough, they
    can constitute an anthology, *Building Babel '97, Building Babel '98*" (xxvii).

12 While the pathos and emotional intensity of Ondaatje's poem makes the
    comparison useful, the major difference is that for Ondaatje, the compul-
    sion is to express his feelings of regret and ambivalence; for Namjoshi the
    task is to ensure the servant's agency and empower her to speak.

Chapter 7

1   Says Rushdie: "As to the claims of excessive Rushdie-itis, I can't deny that
    on occasion I've felt something of the sort myself. On the whole, however,
    it seems to be a short-lived virus, and those whom it affects soon shake it
    off and find their own, true voices" (56).

2   Desai comments: "It was Salman Rushdie again, in *Midnight's Children*, who
    finally brought the spoken language off the streets onto the printed page,
    with such energy and electricity that the Indian reader was finally won over
    and the Indian writer saw the two tongues as one. And we are back in the
    days of oral story telling, when the language employed had to be accessi-
    ble, demotic, of and for the people" ("Indian" 212).

3 As he puts it in *Imaginary Homelands*, "before *Midnight's Children*, I had one novel rejected, abandoned two others, and published one, *Grimus*, which, to put it mildly, bombed" (1).

4 He claims that, "it would be a mistake to think of Márquez's literary universe as an invented, self-referential, closed system. He is not writing about middle-earth, but about the one we all inhabit. Macondo exists. That is its magic" (*Imaginary* 302).

5 According to Slemon, "the term 'magic realism' is an oxymoron, one that suggests a binary opposition between the representational code of realism and that, roughly, of fantasy" (409).

6 Chapter 2 of Zulfikar Ghose's *The Art of Creating Fiction* includes an excellent discussion of this concept. See pages 20-32 in particular.

7 The following is the description of Ayub Khan's takeover of the state: "President Mirza formally asked the C-in-C., General Ayub, to take over political power. The general obliged and then asked the president to resign and leave the country. It was a gentlemanly affair" (62).

8 David Lodge's comment is instructive here: "Thus the realistic novel, from its beginnings in the eighteenth century, modelled its language on historical writing of various kinds, formal and informal: biography, autobiography, travelogue, letters, diaries, journalism and historiography" (25).

9 According to Ahmad, "the fictional equivalents of Bhutto and Zia are such perfect, buffoon-like characters, and the many narrative lines of the political parable are woven so much around their ineptitude…that one is in danger of forgetting that Bhutto and Zia were in reality no buffoons, but highly capable and calculating men whose cruelties were entirely methodical" (141).

10 Says Ahmad: "What this excludes–'the missing bits' to which he must 'reconcile' himself–is the dailiness of lives lived under oppression, and the human bonding–of resistance, of decency, of innumerable heroisms of both ordinary and extraordinary kinds–which makes it possible for people to look each other in the eye, without guilt, with affection and solidarity and humour, and makes life, even under oppression, endurable and frequently joyous" (139).

11 A case in point is M.D. Fletcher's article entitled "Rushdie's *Shame* as Apologue."

Chapter 8

1 Rushdie's popularity, despite all the negative publicity in the last decade, continues to be undiminished. When, for instance, he made an appearance at the University of Toronto in 1999, the audience of 1,700 people gave him a completely ecstatic welcome.

2 An anecdote of some significance is the controversy generated by Marianne Wiggins's review of Bapsi Sidhwa's *Ice-Candy Man* in which, according to Wiggins, characters and their roles "are blatantly derivative of the rambunctiousness of characters in *Midnight's Children*" (23). The charge is hardly defensible, since Sidhwa's novel is very different in texture, but the fact that the review makes the connection is in itself an indication of how readers perceived a pattern of imitation and innovation.

3 The long introduction to the anthology of Indian writing, entitled *The Vintage Book of Indian Writing in English 1947-1997* edited by Rushdie and Elizabeth West, is more emphatic and detailed in its praise of writing in English. In a sweeping and inaccurate comment, the editors say that "this new, and still burgeoning 'Indo-Anglian' literature represents perhaps the most valuable contribution India has yet made to the world of books" (x).

4 Having referred to Rushdie's "overbearing dismissive attitude," the editor K. Satchidanandan adds that Rushdie's argument "would have been further weakened had he extended his comments to poetry since Indian poetry in English has not yet gained strength enough even to dream of a Muktibodh or Faiz or Adiga let alone a Ghalib, a Kabir or Allamaprabhu or a Vyasa or Valmiki" (8).

5 An interesting example of this phenomenon is the trip undertaken by the narrator in *The Shadow Lines* and his surprise that London did not seem unfamiliar at all. In fact, he finds his way around with extreme ease.

6 Bill Buford makes the observation: "What's happening among Indian writers must be unprecedented: they work, some of them in an adopted language, and often in isolation, even thousands of miles from their homeland" (8).

7 Davidar claims that "a new generation of readers and book buyers has come of age that is postcolonial, post-Independence–people in their mid-forties downwards...and this generation doesn't necessarily carry the colonial freight which says that everything published in England is great. They're more interested in finding out what India is all about" (43).

8 Shashi Tharoor, for example, lives in New York but retains an Indian passport as a symbolic assertion of his nationality. Vikram Seth lived in the USA for many years and has now moved to India. Allan Sealy divides his time between New Zealand and India.

Bibliography

Advani, Rukun. *Beethoven Among the Cows*. London: Faber, 1994.

———. "Novelists in Residence." *Seminar* 384 (August 1991): 15-18.

Aesop: The Complete Fables. Trans. Olivia and Robert Temple. London: Penguin, 1998.

Afzal-Khan, Fawzia. *Cultural Imperialism and the Indo-English Novel: Genre and Ideology in R.K. Narayan, Anita Desai, Kamala Markandaya, and Salman Rushdie*. University Park, PA: Pennsylvania State University Press, 1993.

Ahmad, Aijaz. *In Theory: Classes, Nations, Literature*. London: Verso, 1992.

Alam, Fakrul. "Plot and Character in *The Man-Eater of Malgudi*." In *R.K. Narayan: Contemporary Critical Perspectives*, edited by Geoffrey Kain, 141-53. East Lansing: Michigan University Press, 1993.

Ali, Tariq. *Can Pakistan Survive?: The Death of a State*. London: Verso, 1983.

———. *Shadows of the Pomegranate Tree*. London: Chatto and Windus, 1992.

Anand, Mulk Raj. *Untouchable*.1935. Reprint, London: Penguin, 1986.

Anantha Murthy, U.R. *Samskara: A Rite for a Dead Man*. Trans. A.K. Ramanujam. 1976. Reprint, Delhi: Oxford University Press, 1979.

Anantha Murthy, U.R., Ramachandra Sharma, and D.R. Nagaraj, eds. *Vibhava: Modernism in Indian Writing*. Bangalore: Panther, 1992.

Anderson, Benedict. *Imagined Communities: Reflections on the Origin and Spread of Nationalism*. London: Verso, 1983.

Appiah, Kwame Anthony. "Is the Post–in Postmodernism the Post–in Postcolonial?" *Critical Inquiry* 17, no. 2 (1991): 336-57.

Ashcroft, Bill, Helen Tiffin, and Gareth Griffiths. *The Empire Writes Back*. London: Routledge, 1989.

Badami, Anita Rau. *The Hero's Walk*. Toronto: Knopf, 2000.

Ball, John Clement, and Chelva Kanaganayakam. "Interview with Anita Desai." *Toronto South Asian Review* 18, no. 2 (1992): 30-41

Belsey, Catherine. *Critical Practice.* London: Methuen, 1980.

Berger, Thomas. "A Selection of Letters." *The Review of Contemporary Fiction* 9, no. 2 (1989): 158-70.

Bhabha, Homi. "DissemiNation: Time, Narrative, and the Margins of Modern Nation." In *Nation and Narration,* edited by Homi K. Bhabha, 291-322. London: Routledge, 1990.

Brooks, Brenda. "Words Invent the World." Interview with Gillian Hanscombe and Suniti Namjoshi. *Rites* (December 1986-January 1987): 14-15.

Buford, Bill. "Declarations of Independence." *The New Yorker,* 23 and 30 June 1997, 6-8.

Burgess, Anthony. Introduction. *All About H. Hatterr.* 1948. Reprint, New York: McPherson, 1986.

Burjorjee, D.M. "The Dialogue in G.V. Desani's *All About H. Hatterr.*" *World Literature Written in English* 13, no. 2 (1974): 191-224.

Carpentier, Alejo. "Baroque and the Marvellous Real." In *Magical Realism: Theory, History, Community,* edited by Lois Parkinson Zamora and Wendy B. Faris, 89-108. Durham and London: Duke University Press, 1995.

Chandra, Vikram. *Love and Longing in Bombay.* Boston: Little, Brown, 1997.

Chatterjee, Bankim Chandra. *Rajmohan's Wife.* 1864. Reprint in *Bankim Rachnavali,* edited by J.C. Bagal, 1-88. Calcutta: Sahitya Samsad, 1969.

Chatterjee, Partha. "Colonialism, Nationalism, and Colonized Women: The Context in India." *American Ethnologist* 16, no. 4 (1989): 622-33.

———. "The Nationalist Resolution of the Women's Question." In *Recasting Women: Essays in Colonial History,* edited by Kumkum Sangari and Sudesh Vaid, 233-53. New Delhi: Kali for Women, 1989.

———. *Nationalist Thought and the Colonial World: A Derivative Discourse.* Delhi: Oxford University Press, 1986.

Chatterjee, Upamanyu. *English, August.* London: Faber, 1988.

Chaudhuri, Nirad C. *The Continent of Circe.* 1966. Reprint, Mumbai: Jaico, 1997.

Choudhuri, Indra Nath. *Comparative Indian Literature: Some Perspectives.* New Delhi: Sterling, 1992.

Clark, T.W., ed. *The Novel in India: Its Birth and Development.* Berkeley and Los Angeles: University of California Press, 1970.

Clifford, James. "Diasporas." *Cultural Anthropology* 9, no. 3 (1994): 302-38.

Coomaraswamy, Ananda K. *The Dance of Siva: Essays on Indian Art and Culture.* 1924. Reprint, New York: Dover, 1985.

Cooper, Brenda. *Magical Realism in West African Fiction: Seeing With a Third Eye.* London and New York: Routledge, 1998.

Coetzee, J.M. "What is Realism?" *Salmagundi* nos. 114-15 (1997): 60-81.

Crichton, Sara, and Laura Shapiro "An Exclusive Talk with Salman Rushdie." *Newsweek* 115, no. 7 (1990): 47-51.

Cronin, Richard. *Imagining India.* London: Macmillan, 1989.

Cunningham, Valentine. "Nosing Out the Indian Reality." Review of *Midnight's Children*. *Times Literary Supplement* (15 May 1981): 535.

Dasenbrock, Reed Way, and Feroza Jussawalla. "A Conversation with Zulfikar Ghose." *The Review of Contemporary Fiction* 9, no 2 (1989): 140-53.

Derrett, M.E. *The Modern Indian Novel in English: A Comparative Approach*. Brussels: Éditions de L'Institut de Sociologie, Université Libre de Bruxelles, 1966.

Desai, Anita. "A Secret Connivance." *Times Literary Supplement* (14-20 September 1990): 972, 976.

——. *Baumgartner's Bombay*. Toronto: Lester and Orpen Dennys, 1988.

——. *Bye-Bye Blackbird*. 1971. Reprint, Delhi: Orient, 1980.

——. *Clear Light of Day*. 1980. Reprint, London: Penguin, 1982.

——. *Cry, the Peacock*. 1963. Reprint, Delhi: Orient, 1980.

——. *Fasting, Feasting*. London: Chatto and Windus, 1999.

——. *Fire on the Mountain*. 1977. Reprint, London: Penguin, 1981.

——. *In Custody*. 1984. Reprint, London: Penguin, 1985.

——. "Indian Fiction Today." *Daedalus* 118, no 4 (1989): 207-31.

——. *Journey to Ithaca*. London: Heinemann, 1995.

——. "On the English Language in India." *The Common Wealth of Letters* 2, no. 1 (1990): 2-13.

——. "R.K. Narayan and the Grand Malgudi Circus." Review of *A Tiger for Malgudi*. *Bookworld* (4 September 1983): 3, 9.

——. "Women and Fiction in India." *The Toronto South Asian Review* 10, no. 2 (1992): 23-29.

Desai, Kiran. *Hullabaloo in the Guava Orchard*. London: Faber and Faber, 1998.

Desani, G.V. *All About H. Hatterr*. 1948. Reprint, New York: McPherson, 1986.

——. *Hali*. 1950. Reprint, New York: McPherson, 1991.

——. "India, For the Plain Hell of It." *The New Yorker* (23 and 30 June 1997): 62-68.

Devy, G.N. *After Amnesia: Tradition and Change in Indian Literary Criticism*. London: Sangam Books, 1992.

Driesen, Cynthia Van. "The Achievement of R.K. Narayan." *Literature East and West* 21, nos. 1-4 (1977): 51-64.

Durix, Jean-Pierre. Interview with Salman Rushdie. *Kunapipi* 4, no. 2 (1982): 17-26.

Dutt, Shoshee Chunder. *The Young Zemindar: His Erratic Wanderings and Eventual Return*. London: Lovell Reeve, 1885.

Eliade, Mircea. *The Sacred and the Profane: The Nature of Religion*. Trans. Willard R. Trask. New York: Harper and Row, 1961.

Fletcher, M.D. "Rushdie's *Shame* as Apologue." *Journal of Commonwealth Literature* 21, no. 1 (1986): 120-32.

Forster, E.M. *A Passage to India*. London: Arnold, 1924.

Gerow, Edwin. "The Quintessential Narayan." *Literature East and West* 10 (1966): 1-18.

Ghose, Zulfikar. *The Art of Creating Fiction*. London: Macmillan, 1991.

——. *Confessions of a Native-Alien.* London: Routledge and Kegan Paul, 1965.

——. *The Contradictions.* London: Macmillan, 1966.

——. *Crump's Terms.* London: Macmillan, 1975.

——. *The Fiction of Reality.* London: Macmillan, 1983.

——. "Going Home." *The Toronto South Asian Review* 9, no. 2 (1991): 15-22.

——. *Hamlet, Prufrock and Language.* New York: St. Martin's, 1978.

——. *Hulme's Investigations into the Bogart Script.* Austin and New York: Curbstone Press, 1981.

——. *The Loss of India.* London: Routledge and Kegan Paul, 1964.

——. *The Murder of Aziz Khan.* London: Macmillan, 1967.

——. *Statement Against Corpses.* London: Constable, 1964.

——. *The Triple Mirror of the Self.* London: Bloomsbury, 1992.

——. *Veronica and the Gongora Passion.* Toronto: TSAR. 1998.

Ghosh, Amitav. *The Glass Palace.* London: Viking, 2000.

——. "Regarding G.V. Desani." December 2000 link from home page <www.amitavghosh.com> 21 November 2001.

——. *The Shadow Lines.* London: Bloomsbury, 1988.

Grass, Günter. *The Tin Drum.* New York: Vintage, 1990.

Graubard, Stephen R. "An Interview with R.K. Narayan." *Daedalus* 118, no. 4 (1989): 233-37.

Greenfield, Sayre N. *The Ends of Allegory.* Newark: University of Delaware Press, 1998.

Harrex, S.C. *The Fire and the Offering: The English-Language Novel of India.* Vol. 1. 1935-1970. Calcutta: Writer's Workshop, 1977.

——. *The Fire and the Offering: The English-Language Novel of India.* Vol. 2. *1935-1970.* Calcutta: Writer's Workshop, 1978.

Harris, Wilson. "A Note on Zulfikar Ghose's 'Nature Strategies.'" *The Review of Contemporary Fiction* 9, no. 2 (1989): 172-78.

——. *Tradition, the Writer and Society.* London: New Beacon, 1967.

——. *The Womb of Space: The Cross-Cultural Imagination.* Westport, CT.: Greenwood, 1983.

Hogan, Patrick Holm, and Lalita Pandit, eds. *Literary India: Comparative Studies in Aesthetics, Colonialism, and Culture.* Albany: State University of New York Press, 1995.

Hospital, Janet Turner. Review of *Shame,* by Salman Rushdie. *Globe and Mail,* 1 October 1983, E8.

Hubel, Teresa. "Charting the Anger of Indian Women through Narayan's *Savitri.*" *Modern Fiction Studies* 39, no. 1 (1993): 113-30.

Hutcheon, Linda. *Narcissistic Narrative: The Metafictional Paradox.* Waterloo: Wilfrid Laurier University Press, 1980.

Irschik, Eugene F. *Politics and Social Conflict in South Asia: The Non-Brahman Movement and Tamil Separatism.* Berkeley: University of California Press, 1969.

Iyengar, K.R. Srinivasa. *Indian Writing in English.* 1962. Reprint, New Delhi: Sterling, 1964.

Jameson, Fredric. "Third-World Literature in the Era of Multinational Capitalism." *Social Text* 15 (1986): 65-88.

Kanaganayakam, Chelva. *Structures of Negation: The Writings of Zulfikar Ghose.* Toronto: University of Toronto Press, 1993.

Khilnani, Sunil. *The Idea of India.* London: Penguin, 1997.

Kirpal, Viney, ed. *The New Indian Novel in English: A Study of the 1980s.* Delhi: Allied, 1990.

———. *The Postmodern Indian Novel in English.* Bombay: Allied, 1997.

Kundera, Milan. *Testaments Betrayed: An Essay in Nine Parts.* Trans. Linda Asher. New York: HarperCollins, 1993.

Kuortti, Joel. *Fictions to Live In: Narration as an Argument for Fiction in Salman Rushdie's Novels.* Frankfurt am Main: Peter Lang, 1998.

Kureishi, Hanif. *The Buddha of Suburbia.* London: Faber and Faber, 1990.

Lahiri, Jhumpa. *Interpreter of Maladies.* Boston: Houghton Mifflin, 1999.

Lincoln, Bruce. *Discourse and the Construction of Society: Comparative Studies of Myth, Ritual, and Classification.* New York: Oxford University Press, 1989.

Lukács, Georg. *The Meaning of Contemporary Realism.* London: Merlin Press, 1963.

Lodge, David. *After Bakhtin: Essays on Fiction and Criticism.* London and New York: Routledge, 1990.

Machwe, Prabhakar. *Four Decades of Indian Literature: A Critical Evaluation.* New Delhi: Chetna, 1976.

Madan, T.N. "Religion in India." *Daedalus* 118, no. 4 (1989): 115-46.

Macpherson, Jay. *The Boatman and Other Poems.* Toronto: Oxford University Press, 1968.

Maillard, Keith. "*Middlewatch* as Magic Realism." *Canadian Literature* 92 (1982): 10-22.

Márquez, Gabriel García. *One Hundred Years of Solitude.* Trans. Gregory Rabassa, New York: Harper and Row, 1970.

McLeod, A.L. "G.V. Desani." In *Writers of the Indian Diaspora: A Bio-Bibliographical Critical Sourcebook,* edited by Emmanuel S. Nelson, 95-101. Westport, CT: Greenwood Press, 1993.

Mehta, Ved. "The Train Had Just Arrived at Malgudi Station." *The New Yorker,* 15 September 1962, 51-90.

Meigs, Mary. Review of *Feminist Fables,* by Suniti Namjoshi. *Room of One's Own* 4, no. 1 (1984): 63-68.

Merivale, Patricia. "Saleem Fathered by Oskar: Intertextual Strategies in *Midnight's Children* and *The Tin Drum.*" *ARIEL* 21 (1990): 5-21.

Miller, Nolan. Review of *All About H. Hatterr,* by G.V. Desani. *The Antioch Review* 11, no. 2 (1951): 237-41.

Mistry, Rohinton. *A Fine Balance.* Toronto: McClelland and Stewart, 1995.

———. *Such a Long Journey.* Toronto: McClelland and Stewart, 1991.

Moreiras, Alberto. "The End of Magical Realism: Jose Maria Arguedas's Passionate Signifier (*El sorro de arriba y el zorro de abajo*)." *The Journal of Narrative Technique* 27, no. 1 (1997): 84-112.

Morris, Patricia. "An Object of Desire." Review of *The Conversations of Cow*, by Suniti Namjoshi. *African Concord* (17 April 1986): 41.

Moss, Laura. "Can Rohinton Mistry's Realism Rescue the Novel?" In *Postcolonizing the Commonwealth: Studies in Literature and Culture*, edited by Rowland Smith, 157-65. Waterloo: Wilfrid Laurier University Press, 2000.

Mukherjee, Meenakshi. *Realism and Reality: The Novel and Society in India*. Delhi: Oxford University Press, 1985.

——. *The Twice-Born Fiction: Themes and Techniques of the Indian Novel in English*. New Delhi: Heinemann, 1971.

Naipaul, V.S. *An Area of Darkness*. 1964. Reprint, London: Penguin, 1987.

Namjoshi, Suniti. *Because of India*. London: Onlywomen Press, 1989.

——. *The Blue Donkey Fables*. London: Women's Press, 1988.

——. *Building Babel*. North Melbourne, Victoria: Spinifex, 1996.

——. *Conversations of Cow*. London: Women's Press, 1985.

——. *Cyclone in Pakistan*. Calcutta: Writer's Workshop, 1971.

——. "Double Landscape: A Study of the Poetry of P.K. Page." *Canadian Literature* 67 (1976): 21-30.

——. "Ezra Pound and the Hex Hoax." *Antigonish Review* 23 (Fall 1975): 65-83.

——. *Feminist Fables*. London: Sheba, 1981.

——. *From the Bedside Book of Nightmares*. New Brunswick: Fiddlehead, 1984.

——. *Goja*. North Melbourne, Victoria: Spinifex, 2000.

——. "In the Whale's Belly: Jay Macpherson's Poetry." *Canadian Literature* 79 (1979): 54-59.

——. *The Mothers of Maya Diip*. London: Women's Press, 1989.

——. "Poetry or Propaganda." *Canadian Woman Studies* 5, no. 1 (1983): 5-6.

——. Review of *A Wild Patience Has Taken Me This Far*, by Adrienne Rich. *Canadian Woman Studies* 5, no. 1 (1983): 37-38.

——. *Saint Suniti and the Dragon*. London: Virago, 1994.

——. "Snow White and Rose Green or Some Notes on Sexism, Racism, and the Craft of Writing." *Canadian Woman Studies* 4, no. 2 (1982): 11-15.

Narayan, R.K. *The Bachelor of Arts*. 1937. Reprint, London: Heinemann, 1978.

——. *The English Teacher*. 1945. Reprint, London: Eyre and Spottiswood, 1947.

——. *The Financial Expert*. 1952. Reprint, East Lansing, MI: Michigan State University Press, 1953.

——. *The Guide*. New York: Viking, 1958.

——. *A Horse and Two Goats*. New York: Viking, 1970.

——. *The Man-Eater of Malgudi*. 1961. Reprint, London: Penguin, 1988.

——. *The Sweet-Vendor*. 1954. Reprint, London: Bodley Head, 1967.

——. *A Tiger for Malgudi*. London: Heinemann, 1983.

——. *Waiting for the Mahatma*. 1955. Reprint, London: Mandarin, 1990.

Nandy, Ashis. *The Intimate Enemy: Loss and Recovery Under Colonialism*. Delhi: Oxford University Press, 1983.

Narasimhaiah, C.D. *The Swan and the Eagle: Essays on Indian English Literature*. Shimla: Indian Institute of Advanced Study, 1968.

Narasimhaiah, C.D., ed. *An Anthology of Commonwealth Poetry.* Madras: Macmillan, 1990.

Narayan, R.K. *My Dateless Diary: An American Journey.* Mysore: Indian Thought, 1964.

——. *My Days.* Mysore: Indian Thought, 1975.

——. *A Writer's Nightmare.* Delhi: Penguin, 1988.

Ngugi wa Thiong'o. *Decolonising the Mind: The Politics of Language in African Literature.* London: James Currey, 1986.

Okot p'Bitek. *Song of Lawino.* Nairobi: East African, 1966.

Ondaatje, Michael. *The English Patient.* Toronto: McClelland and Stewart, 1992.

——. *Handwriting.* Toronto: McClelland and Stewart, 1998.

Pandian, M.S.S. "Notes on the Transformation of 'Dravidian' Ideology: Tamilnadu C. 1900-1940." Working Paper no. 120. Madras Institute for Development Studies.

Paranjape, Makarand. "Journey to Ithaca: A Letter on Recent Indian English Fiction." In *The Postmodern Indian Novel in English*, edited by Viney Kirpal, 400-10. Delhi: Allied, 1997.

——. "From Absent Authority to Present Responsibility: An Agenda for Indian (English) Criticism." *ARIEL* 29, no. 1 (1998): 11-31.

——. *Towards a Poetics of the Indian English Novel.* Shimla: Indian Institute of Advanced Study, 2000.

Parmar, Pratibha. Interview with Suniti Namjoshi. *Women's Review* 1 (November 1985): 18-20.

Parthasarathy, R., ed. *Ten Twentieth Century Poets.* Delhi: Oxford University Press, 1976.

Patel, Gieve. "Contemporary Indian Painting." *Daedalus* 118, no. 4 (1989): 171-205.

Prakash, Gyan. "Writing Post-Orientalist Histories of the Third World: Perspectives for Indian Historiography." *Comparative Journal of Society and History* 32, no. 2 (April 1990): 383-408.

Prescott, Nick. "Salman Rushdie and *The Ground Beneath Her Feet.*" *Centre for Research in New Literatures in English Journal* (2000): 119-24.

Rajan, B. *The Dark Dancer.* London: Heinemann, 1958.

Rajan, Chandra. Introduction to *The Pancatantra.* New Delhi: Penguin, 1993.

Ramanujam, Molly. *G.V. Desani: Writer and Worldview.* New Delhi: Arnold-Heinemann, 1984.

Rao, Raja. *Kanthapura.* 1938. Reprint, New York: New Directions, 1967.

Rao, Subha, T.V. *Indian Writing in English: Is There Any Worth in It?* Madurai: Koodal, 1976.

Roh, Franz. "Magic Realism: Post-Expressionism." Trans. Wendy B. Faris. In *Magical Realism: Theory, History, Community*, edited by Lois Parkinson, Lois Zamora and Wendy B. Faris, 15-31. Durham and London: Duke University Press, 1995.

Ross, Robert. *The Inheritance of Animal Symbols in Modern Literature and World Culture: Essays, Notes and Lectures.* Frankfurt am Main: Peter Lang, 1988.

———. "The Murder of Aziz Khan." *The Review of Contemporary Fiction* 9, no. 2 (1989): 198-203.

Roy, Arundhati. *The God of Small Things*. Toronto: Random House, 1997.

Rushdie, Salman. "Damme, This is the Oriental Scene for You." *The New Yorker,* 23 and 30 June 1997, 50-61.

———. *Grimus*. London: Granada, 1977.

———. *The Ground Beneath Her Feet*. London: Jonathan Cape, 1999

———. *Haroun and the Sea of Stories*. London: Granta, 1990.

———. *Imaginary Homelands: Essays and Criticism, 1981-1991*. London: Granta, 1991.

———. "In Good Faith." In *Imaginary Homelands*.

———. *The Jaguar Smile: A Nicaraguan Journey*. London: Pan Books, 1987.

———. *Midnight's Children*. London: Jonathan Cape, 1981.

———. "*Midnight's Children* and *Shame*." *Kunapipi* 7, no. 1 (1985): 1-19.

———. *The Moor's Last Sigh*. London: Jonathan Cape, 1995.

———. *The Satanic Verses*. London: Penguin, 1988.

———. *Shame*. New York: Knopf, 1983.

Rushdie, Salman, and Elizabeth West, eds. *The Vintage Book of Indian Writing 1947-1997*. London: Random House, 1997.

Sangari, Kumkum, and Sudesh Vaid, eds. *Recasting Women: Essays in Colonial History*. New Delhi: Kali for Women, 1989.

Satchidanandan, K. "Moor's Last Sigh." *Indian Literature* 180 (July-August 1997): 5-8.

Scott, Philip. *Perceiving India Through the Works of Nirad Chaudhuri, R.K. Narayan and Ved Mehta*. New Delhi: Sterling, 1986.

Schwartz, Delmore. Review of *All About H. Hatterr*, by G.V. Desani. *Partisan Review* 18, no. 5 (1951): 575-81.

Sealy, Alan. *The Trotter-Nama*. London: Viking, 1988.

Selvadurai, Shyam. *Funny Boy*. Toronto: McClelland and Stewart, 1994.

Selvon, Sam. *The Lonely Londoners*. London: Wingate, 1956.

Seth, Vikram. *A Suitable Boy*. London: Phoenix House, 1993.

Shamsie, Muneeza, ed. *A Dragonfly in the Sun: An Anthology of Pakistani Writing in English*. Karachi: Oxford University Press, 1997.

Shankar, D.A. "The Absence of Caste in R.K. Narayan." In *R.K. Narayan: Contemporary Critical Perspectives*, edited by Geoffrey Kain, 49-53. East Lansing: Michigan University Press, 1993.

Sidhwa, Bapsi. *An American Brat*. Minneapolis: Milkweed, 1993.

———. *Ice-Candy Man*. London: Heinemann, 1988.

Singh, Sunaina. *The Novels of Margaret Atwood and Anita Desai: A Comparative Study in Feminist Perspectives*. New Delhi: Creative, 1994.

Slemon, Stephen. "Magic Realism as Postcolonial Discourse." In *Magical Realism: Theory, History, Community,* edited by Lois Parkinson Zamora and Wendy B. Faris, 407-26. Durham and London: Duke University Press, 1995.

Smith, Anne. Review of *Conversations of Cow* by Suniti Namjoshi. *New Statesman,* 20 September 1985, 30.

Spivak, Gayatri Chakravorty. "How to Read a 'Culturally Different' Book." In *Colonial Discourse/Postcolonial Theory*, edited by Francis Barker, Peter Hulme, and Margaret Iverson, 126-50. Manchester: Manchester University Press, 1994.

Stonehill, Brian. *The Self-Conscious Novel: Artifice in Fiction from Joyce to Pynchon.* Philadelphia: University of Pennsylvania Press, 1988.

Suleri, Sara. *The Rhetoric of English India.* Chicago: University of Chicago Press, 1992.

Tallis, Raymond. *In Defence of Realism.* 1988. Reprint, Lincoln and London: University of Nebraska Press, 1998.

Temple, Robert. Introduction to *Aesop: The Complete Fables.* Trans. Olivia and Robert Temple. London: Penguin, 1998 .

Tharoor, Shashi. *The Great Indian Novel.* New Delhi: Penguin, 1989.

———. "Myth, History and Fiction." *Seminar* 384 (August 1991): 30-31.

———. *The Show Business.* New York: Viking, 1991.

The Panchatantra. Trans. Chandra Rajan. New Delhi: Penguin, 1993.

Todorov, Tzevetan. *The Fantastic: A Structural Approach to a Literary Genre.* Trans. Richard Howard. Cleveland/London: Press Case of Western Reserve University, 1973.

Trinh T. Minh-ha. *Woman, Native, Other.* Bloomington and Indianapolis: Indiana University Press, 1989.

Updike, John. "Mother Tongues: Subduing the Language of the Colonizer." *The New Yorker,* 23 and 30 June 1997, 156-61.

Vassanji, M.G. *The Book of Secrets.* Toronto: McClelland and Stewart, 1994.

Van Driesen, Cynthia. "The Achievement of R.K. Narayan." *Literature East and West* 21, nos. 1-4 (1977): 51-64.

Vaidyanathan, T.G. "Authority and Identity in India." *Daedalus* 118, no. 4 (1989): 147-69.

Van Dyke, Carolyn. *The Fiction of Truth: Structures of Meaning in Narrative and Dramatic Allegory.* Ithaca and London: Cornell University Press, 1985.

Vellani, Sarita. Interview with David Davidar. *Seminar* 384 (August 1991): 43-44.

Venkatachalapathy, A.R. "Domesticating the Novel: Society and Culture in Inter-War Tamil Nadu." *The Indian Economic and Social History Review* 34, no. 1 (1997): 53-67.

Venkataramani, K.S. *Murugan the Tiller.* London: Simpkin, Marshall, Hamilton, Kent, 1927.

Viswanathan, Gauri. *The Masks of Conquest: Literary Study and British Rule in India.* New York: Columbia University Press, 1989.

Walsh, Richard. *Novel Arguments: Reading Innovative American Fiction.* Cambridge, MA: Cambridge University Press, 1995.

Walsh, William. *Indian Writing in English.* London: Longman, 1990.

———. *R.K. Narayan.* London: Longman, 1971.

Wickramasinghe, Nira. "Migration, Migrant Communities and Otherness in Twentieth-Century Sinhala Nationalism in Sri Lanka (up to Independence).

In *Community, Empire and Migration*, edited by Crispin Bates, 153-84. New York: Palgrave, 2001.

Wiggins, Marianne. Review of *Ice-Candy Man*, by Bapsi Sidhwa. *New Statesman* 115 (26 February 1988): 23.

Wijesinha, Rajiva. *Acts of Faith*. New Delhi: Navrang, 1985.

——. *Days of Despair*. Colombo: English Writers Cooperative, 1989.

——. *Inside Limits: Identity and Repressions in (Post)-Colonial Fiction*. N.p.: Sabaragamuwa University Press, 1998.

Williams, Hadyn. "R.K. Narayan and R. Prawer Jhabvala: Two Interpretations of Modern India." *Literature East and West* 16, no. 4 (1972): 1136-54.

Williams, Mark. *Leaving the Highway: Six Contemporary New Zealand Novelists*. Auckland: Auckland University Press, 1990.

Zameenzad, Adam. *Cyrus, Cyrus*. London: Fourth Estate, 1990.

——. *The Thirteenth House*. London: Fourth Estate, 1987.

Zamora, Lois Parkinson, and Wendy B. Faris, eds. *Magic Realism: Theory, History, Community*. Durham and London: Duke University Press, 1995.

Zimmerman, Bonnie. "Perverse Reading: The Lesbian Appropriation." In *Sexual Practice, Textual Theory: Lesbian Cultural Criticism*, edited by Susan J. Wolfe and Julia Penelope, 135-49. Oxford: Blackwell, 1993.

Index